Four Plays

FOUR PLAYS

THE WOMEN HAVE THEIR WAY
A HUNDRED YEARS OLD
FORTUNATO
THE LADY FROM ALFAQUEQUE

By
SERAFÍN *and* JOAQUÍN ÁLVAREZ QUINTERO

In English Versions by
HELEN *and* HARLEY GRANVILLE–BARKER

BOSTON
LITTLE, BROWN, AND COMPANY
1928

PQ6601
L8
A2
1928

INTRODUCTION

"A Serafín y Joaquín Álvarez Quintero, gloriosos autores dramaticos, Sevilla, su madre adoptiva, consagra este monumento en testimonio de gratitud, porque infandieron en cien comedias, gala de la scena espanola, el alma de la reina del Guadalquivir."

So runs the inscription round the charming faience fountain in the park of Seville. A tiled space, a square basin fed by running water, flowers, trees overhanging. Surrounding it a bench, and the names of chosen plays are enscrolled along the back. There are even shelves to hold the plays themselves. You may make your own choice, sit there and read. Dominating all, in painted relief, is the two-masted ship, the emblem of the authors.

Not that Serafín and Joaquín Álvarez Quintero are dead! They cannot even be called elderly, though they have — it is the fecund Spanish tradition — a hundred and fifty plays and more, long and short, to their credit; and they are still writing. But Seville has not waited to acclaim them, for they have enshrined Andalusia in drama, and in turn she does them homage. Serafín was born in 1871, Joaquín in 1873. They have always collaborated. Their first play was produced in 1888.

The four in this volume are not set forth as necessarily their best, but as representing very fairly their most characteristic work. *The Women Have Their Way*, a simple picture of life in a little Andalusian town, is the sort of thing for which they are renowned; *A Hundred Years Old*, we in England would call sentimental comedy; *Fortunato* is a picaresque farce, with a difference; *The Lady from Alfaqueque* is a comedy of the Andalusian exiled to the harsher world of Madrid.

The plays really need no prefacing. They will answer for themselves, if we bring as little sophistication to their reading as the authors have brought to the writing of them. But the English theatre (that part of it which takes itself seriously, not to say solemnly) has for a generation past been travelling paths that diverge widely from any such Arcadian dramatic country as the Quinteros inhabit. We have become, perhaps (some of us), a little artistically self-conscious, and a little apt to look down our noses at the simple thing. Not that these plays are artless in the too literal sense of the word; let us not fall into that critic's booby-trap. But as their kind is somewhat out of fashion with us we may have lost our sense of their artistic values; and simplicity was ever art's best disguise. Take *The Women Have Their Way*. A young Madrid lawyer comes to visit a little Andalusian town. His only thought is to do his business, make himself agreeable to the people he meets, and be off again. But the ladies of the town will have it that he has fallen in love with a pretty girl among them. "Nothing of the sort," he says, and the pretty girl herself most modestly scoffs at the notion. The ladies protest that it is so, they prove by chapter and verse that it is so. And they talk and talk till every tongue in the town wags to the tune; and what every one says is so, surely must be so. And in the end — much to the young man's surprise; not so much to the pretty girl's — it turns out to be so. And that, and no more, is the play! Its plotlessness might be counted to it for sophisticated righteousness. "How like Tchekov!" — one hears the chorus. But where is the mordant philosophy, the ironic character drawing, the criticism of society? Where are the epigrams — or, if epigrams are a little outmoded for the moment, where, at least, is the brilliant dialogue? Neither philosophy nor social criticism is thrust on us, and it may almost be said that not a witty or clever remark is made in the whole course of the play. Yet an idea both animates and dominates it, that is none the less an idea for being light in hand. The published play significantly is dedicated

A Don José Echegaray
insigne autor de El Gran Galeoto,

and its theme is, in fact, the tragedy of *El Gran Galeoto* turned to laughter.

The dialogue is simple, because this, it could be argued, is how people do talk. But there is a better reason. Such simplicity is attuned to the subject, to its treatment and its scope. The play is all of a piece and an artistic whole. It would be beside the point to stress the difficulties of writing such dialogue; of devising these strings of commonplaces that never sound banal, talk that is lively yet never calculated, that speeds on the action yet never seems to hurry it. For all one knows, the Quinteros may, after long practice, find this easy. If any one thinks there is "nothing in it", let him try! But it is worth remark that these simplicities are what most defeat the translator. Solid, intellectual meat can always be transposed from one language to another, and if style is lost in the process, the substance will endure. But when, as in one or two — and not the least important — scenes of this play, the dialogue resolves itself for a space into something like a series of mere musical sounds, what is to be done?

ADOLFO. Hasta después?
JUANITA. No sé si nos veremos después.
ADOLFO. Pues hasta mañana.
JUANITA. Tampoco se si no veremos mañana.
ADOLFO. Entonces . . .
JUANITA. Si; hasta que nos veamos.
ADOLFO. Hasta que nos veamos.
JUANITA. Casualmente . . .
ADOLFO. Casualmente?
JUANITA. Cosmo ahora . . . que nos hemos visto por casualidad . . .
ADOLFO. Sea como sea, yo quiero que sea pronto.

Remember that the English equivalent must be as trivial and as swift to speak if the little scene's emphasis is not to be overcharged, and that something of the happy sound of it must be reproduced if the dramatic effect is not to be missed altogether. But this introduction is not the translators' apology.

Note, however, that no less a critic than Azorin, speaking of this very play — which he calls its authors' masterpiece and thinks technically most admirable — praising the economy of its exposition, praises also this particular quality in its dialogue; a lucid simplicity, he calls it. For a Spanish verdict upon the Quinteros one need hardly look further than Azorin. He places them in the direct line of dramatic succession. From Lope de Vega, he says, the sceptre comes to Moratín. "From Moratín to Bretón, and from Bretón to the Quinteros." And, speaking of more essential qualities, he says of them that their plays show — and this is their particular gift — a finely adjusted sense of how the dramatic balance must always be held between the individual and society as a whole. In the vigour of Tamayo, and later in the impetuous force of Echegaray, a certain disequilibrium is found. The Quinteros restore the balance and hold it fairly. The "atmosphere", he insists again, for which they are so praised, is by no means the only thing of value about them; their plays are charged with emotional force.

They seem always to be asking themselves (to continue this paraphrase of Azorin's opinion): "Is right on the side of the one or of the many?" They study the social scene in all its detail, perceptively, painstakingly, bringing men and women of all sorts into their picture. But they sway to the end between those two points of view; and if their own standpoint seems to reflect a certain mild scepticism, it reflects pity and sympathy too. They seem quite unable to take one side against the other. Through all their work sounds this placid note. But now and then, by a sudden turn, comedy becomes tragedy, and we find that they have led us, all unaware, to some battle-ground of emotion. Yet however tragic the conflict we shall condemn no one wholly, hate no one very deeply. The pervading temper of the play will be so gentle, so full of compassion, that hate and anger and violence will seem to have no place there. And it may be that our own compassion, thus subdued, will be the deeper and the more enduring.

It is true. Nothing (to finish with Azorin) that the Quinteros may have to say will be pretentiously thrust on us. We may think, mistakenly, that they have nothing to say. But if we will but surrender our minds to the simple story, and let our imaginations absorb the very homely picture, we shall find life interpreted there.

The English-speaking theatre, it could be argued, broke the shackles of Sardou, a generation back, only to take on the equally alien shackles of Ibsen, and ran some risk in so doing of becoming intellectually pretentious. Ibsen, a poet and a great dramatist, was a philosopher besides and had something to say. Bernard Shaw, using drama like a flail, has much to say; and doubtless there are others. But the average man — even the average playwright — is not necessarily seething with a message for mankind whenever he opens his mouth; and of all tiresome things in the world, sham philosophy is the most tiresome. The example of the Quinteros, then, may not come amiss. Their work is evidence, at least, that great skill, taste, and judgment can be set to produce very simple effects which will yet not be artistically negligible.

It was a pity that the English theatre produced no worthy successor to T. W. Robertson, no one to enrich his technique, to bring a more catholic view of life and a robuster mind to play-writing. *A Hundred Years Old*, turn its Spanish environment to English, might be the work of a later Robertson. It is unashamedly sentimental; but is wholesome sentiment to be anathema? And see with what artistic tact the authors have placed the sentiment in the mouths of a very old man and a very young girl, have kept them briskly merry besides, and have surrounded them with vigorous comedy.

Further, one gathers that Spanish audiences must like acting for its own sake, must enjoy the interpreting of character, like to see pictured before them the comings and goings of ordinary folk, just a little heightened, coloured, clarified, made more purposeful by art. A "superior" drama, grown superior to acting, lies on its death-bed. Neo-Ibsenism in England drifted perilously towards that state. Plays grew so austerely intellectual that their performance seemed a profanation; and we saw the actors moving apologetically through their parts as if they

had been told that they were rather vulgar people with no
real right there at all. Not that acting is to be rescued from such
nihilism — as a yet later school seems to hold — by the study of
voice-production and the principles of psychology, of eurhythmics,
or by some knowledge of anatomy and of the history of costume;
excellent as these things are in their way, and good education, not
for actors only. For neither is acting the art of physical and
intellectual posing. It is concerned, first and last, with the vivid
interpretation of life. Not, again, that the Quinteros write plays
merely to provide good parts in them for actors. Their attitude
is a sounder one than that. They see the theatre very much as
our own Elizabethan dramatists saw it — and as Spanish dramatists of that day saw it. Spain, indeed, has held, in this as in other
things, to a tradition that England lost. For the Quinteros, acting,
with its airs and graces, its tricks if you will, and its simple tri-
umphs, holds not only a legitimate but a most honourable place
in the dramatic scheme. Their plays are conceived solely to be
brought to being upon the stage, and after to live a normal life
there. No unnatural burdens deform the action; nor are the
characters ever as good men struggling with the adversity of their
authors' private opinions upon this point or the other. A character has, indeed, seldom any duty to do by the Quinteros but to
abound in its own sense; consequently even the most subordinate
will be effective. On the other hand — for we all have the defects
of our qualities — they do not always discipline their work into a
very self-contained perfection. Generous in opportunity to its
actors, they rely on them now and then (yet again as our Eliza-
bethans did) to cover up a slap-dash crudity or so. The con-
struction of *The Lady from Alfaqueque* could hardly be held
up by Professor George Pierce Baker to his Yale students as a
shining example of "how to do it." The characters move in and
out all too obviously to the convenience of their authors; and —
oh, horrible! — will even fill up time, if need be, with a soliloquy.
Apparently the Quinteros' only care is to make it an amusing
soliloquy. Truly this is most incorrect. But then by what
amount of study, by what following or breaking of rules (as Pro-

fessor Baker will sigh and smile to admit) does one learn to devise such scenes of pure comedy as that in which Adoracion innocently "blows the gaff", as that last one in which Felipe is left triumphantly declaiming his poem to an audience of his victims? And it is these things and the like that make the play. In art it is sometimes paradoxically true that the strength of a chain is not that of its weakest but of its strongest link.

Now and again these authors will provide their actors with such a piece of bravura as *Fortunato*. And what actor, one asks, will not rise up and bless them for the pure histrionics of the robbing of the blind beggar, for the St. Sebastian-like immolation which ends this "tragic farce"? *Fortunato*, however, has other claims on our interest than this. It is done in the true Spanish vein; that picaresque vein which has shown its streaks of influence in European literature for these three hundred years. Here it is in a modern manifestation. Its episodic form is typically Spanish too. And, like most good farces — one might say, indeed, there could be no exception to the rule — its fun is rooted in a fundamentally serious idea. The secret of the successfully comic actor does not, for his part, lie in the fact that he is a funny man, a fellow that can make us laugh once, while at his second try we wonder what we laughed at. It lies in his power to make us fond of him. We laugh at Fortunato because he is so very lovable. Another paradox; and one that strikes deeper.

Finally, we recommend these plays to the reader — the layman in dramatic matters — as veritable pictures of Spanish life seen through the benevolently humorous eyes of their authors. They lose terribly in translation perforce; and doubtless by the shortcomings of their present translators. But we have not been at any pains to disguise and so only emphasize the loss by dressing up their phrases in what might seem Spanish fashion, or by stressing their strangeness. One must, after all, write and speak one language or another. Enough of their virtue should survive translation, if it lies — and it does — in their truth to human nature. For this does not differ much as between Spain and

England — or Patagonia, possibly. And while literary fashions change and pass, this does not change overmuch.

WE have to thank Mr. A. H. Wykeham-George for so skilfully fitting our English words to Spanish tunes, and Mr. A. E. Filmer for guidance in some details of Catholic terminology.

H. and H. G.-B.

CONTENTS

The Women Have Their Way
(Puebla de las Mujeres)

A COMEDY IN TWO ACTS

NOTES

THE "lattice" which Concha Puerto offers to Adolfo for his courting is a "reja", the iron grille to the ground-floor windows, found
everywhere in Southern Spain. The custom, too, by which the
girl sits within and the young man stands outside to woo her, is
so well known that it passes without explanation in the Spanish
text. For the sake of English hearers we have insinuated one —
we hope not too obviously.

The Spanish language provides, and Spanish custom enforces,
a great variety of greetings, more picturesque and more formal
than anything of English usage. This is a translator's difficulty,
not capable of any logical solution. We have followed no rule in
escaping it. Actors had better remember that they can hardly
err on the side of politeness. The casual "Hola" is pronounced
Ol'a, of course.

The copla (at which Juanita is so apt) is a four-line verse, something in the nature of the impromptu or epigram which the English
eighteenth century practised and admired. Sir Benjamin Back-
bite's will be remembered; though this is comic and coplas are
not, as a rule. They may be recited, or sung — usually to tradi-
tional tunes. If a Juanita can sing hers without effort, she may
as well. Below are some suggested tunes.

DIEGUILLA'S FANDANGO

There were ma-ny young men at the wed----ding..., Like you, mo-
Have I been stricken with mad---ness...? All that I

re-no, but few........ I sit a-lone of an evening, ev-en-ing,
wish is to flee...you, Yet as soon as I have my free-dom, free--dom,

Less lone-ly, thinking of you, less lone--ly, thinking of you.
I seek-for, e-ver for you, I seek for e-ver for you.

There is no brighter car--na---tion..., No sweeter rose by the
The house... where I am dwell--ing... Has walls of snow-y

foun--tain..., Than your face in its fresh-ness, fresh--ness,
white--ness..., Car-na-tions in the... win--dow, win--dow,

My girl from the moun-tain, My girl from the moun----tain.
Clear wa--ter in the well, Clear wa--ter in....the well.

JUANITA'S COPLAS

A thought to him she's ne---ver given, Nor he.......a

thought to her, But the neigh-bours tongues a' wagging May

set many thoughts a--stir..........

{ I care for whom I do not care ..... to say, }
{ Yet with-out saying I am say - - - ing it, } My

heart is .. full of joy I can-not name, Yet without

naming I am na-ming it. Ah .... me ....

Oh pass no more under my win - - - dow, For the
neigbours are e - - ver spy - - - - - - - - ing; So

pass no more un-der my win - - - dow; I ne - ver pass be

fore .. your house, Yet there am e-ver a - bi - - - - ding.

Man to a sail - - ing boat ... I li - - - - ken, Without a chart his

course he to - - - ses, And wo - - man to ... the wind ... that

blows .... him, To - wards ... what-ev - er port ... she choo - - - ses.

Concha Puerto.
Juanita la Rosa.
Santita.
Doña Belén.
Ángela.
Pilar.
Dieguilla.
A Village Girl.

Adolfo.
Don Julián.
Don Cecilio.
Pepe Lora.
Guitarra.
The Sacristan of San Antonio.

The action passes at Don Julián's; he is the priest of a small town in Andalusia.

THE WOMEN HAVE THEIR WAY

ACT I

*In the houses of many small Andalusian towns, when the visitor passes
through the wrought-iron inner door, he finds himself in a place
something like a patio (without quite being that) something like
a drawing-room (but more modest).*

*Well then, in such a cool, charming, intimate spot, in the house of our
good friend Don Julián Figueredo, the parish priest, the action
of this comedy passes. On our left, as we look at the room,
is the door of simple wrought-iron work which leads to the
square stone entry and so to the street. It always stands open.
On our right is a glass-panelled door with a fan-light over it;
and facing us another and a larger glass door, through which
can be seen a white-walled garden, with its few trees, its many
flowers, and its brick-paved walks.*

*Near the open door stands a china cupboard, with glass doors below
and above. The best plates and cups and glasses — those only
used on great occasions — are kept in it, as well as a variety of
old trumpery, more or less useless. There is not much other
furniture, and the little there is is very simple, a hat-stand,
a small table, two rocking-chairs and some old-fashioned cane-
seated chairs. Over the wrought-iron door there is an image of
the Virgin, and a dried palm branch has been nailed under it.
The ceiling of the room is built upon small pointed arches; the
floor is of red tiles. From the ceiling hangs a large lighted
lamp. It is an evening in June.*

*Don Julián and Santita are sitting together in comfort and peace.
He is studying the list of the winning numbers in the State
lottery, to see if the ones in which he has a tenth share are among
them. She is making cigarettes in a little machine. They are*

*brother and sister, both over sixty and under sixty-five. Don
Julián hears all there is to hear in the town because almost all
the women make their confessions to him.   Santita, on the
other hand, hears absolutely nothing, for she is stone deaf. Her
attitude, consequently, is one of constant watchfulness and sus-
picion.   He wears a cassock, and a little black silk cap with a
peak to it which protects his venerable head from draughts and
flies.   She wears a black dress, not unlike a nun's.*

DON JULIÁN. Lottery. Numbers drawn. Not one in the thir-
teen five hundreds. I'll never die rich at this rate. No luck!
What about my next now . . . ?

*Dieguilla is heard singing. Don Julián looks up and lis-
tens; Santita, looking up too, can see he is listening.*

There were many young men at the wedding,
Like you, moreño, but few;
I sit alone of an evening,
Less lonely, thinking of you.

SANTITA. Is that wretch of a woman singing her songs again?
DON JULIÁN. No no. . . .
SANTITA. She is! I can tell by your face. And it's her village
fandango too . . . is n't it?

*Santita's cigarettes are put down, and off she goes to put a
stop to this noise.*

DON JULIÁN. God bless my soul . . . the one person that can't
hear her singing is the one person that can't bear her singing!
Though I own . . . I must own . . . Dieguilla is a bit of a cricket.
She chirps . . . she does chirp!

*The singing comes to a sudden stop.   Santita returns, very
pleased with herself.*

SANTITA. Does the woman suppose she's still in her native pot-
house!
DON JULIÁN. Now she'll give notice . . . like the rest! They
all do!
SANTITA. What's that?
DON JULIÁN. I say . . . now she'll be giving notice, too.

SANTITA. Let her! Who cares? Is this a house for singing vulgar songs in . . . a priest's house?

She goes back to her cigarette-making, and he to his lottery list again.

DON JULIÁN. Dear me . . . dear me! I shall begin to think they print the numbers wrong. Now, if this seven were a four . . .!

A moment's silence, and there comes from the street Adolfo Adalid. He is from Madrid, a young lawyer, well turned out, alert, debonair, self-confident. Don Julián rises to welcome him.

ADOLFO. May I come in?

DON JULIÁN. You may indeed. My dear young friend . . . indeed you may.

ADOLFO. How do you do?

DON JULIÁN. Thank you . . . and how are you?

ADOLFO. You do know who I am?

DON JULIÁN. I should think so. But it's a whole week, isn't it, since the station omnibus put you down in the Plaza here? No matter, we'll make up for lost time now. Let me present you to my sister. She's deaf. But you needn't shout. She knows what we say when she sees us talking. Santita!

SANTITA. Señor.

ADOLFO. Señora.

DON JULIÁN. This is Esperanza Lucena's nephew.

SANTITA. I know that well enough. He has been past the house every day . . . three times one way and four times the other . . . so my girls tell me.

ADOLFO. Dear me! I'd not counted the times . . . but I have walked past. . . .

DON JULIÁN. And at last you've walked in. So now you're forgiven. Sit down.

ADOLFO. You're very kind.

And they sit down.

DON JULIÁN. But what . . . I ask myself . . . can the parish priest of this poor little place do for a young man from Madrid?

ADOLFO. I only fear you 'll find you can do a great deal . . . so much that I really did delay coming to trouble you. . . .

DON JULIÁN. No trouble, my son!

ADOLFO. That 's very good of you. Day after day my aunt has been telling me to come. . . .

DON JULIÁN. Well . . . we 're old friends.

ADOLFO. She thinks so highly of you. A cigarette?

DON JULIÁN. Thank you.

> *They smoke; and Santita puts an ash-tray near them. Then — with the setting back of one of the glass doors for an excuse — she walks behind them and gets a good look at the visitor. She takes a look at his hat too, examines it inside and out.*

ADOLFO. My poor uncle left his affairs in a fearful muddle.

DON JULIÁN. I know . . . I know! God has forgiven him, we trust. A bit of a muddle . . . for he was a bit of a fool. We must n't be unjust to him now he 's dead . . . but he was a bit of a rascal . . . and that 's the truth!

ADOLFO. She wrote to me in Madrid, my poor aunt, as soon as she 'd got over it a little, begging me in the name of all the saints, to come and put things straight. So of course I came . . . for I 'm very fond of her. . . .

DON JULIÁN. I know, my son, I know.

ADOLFO. And they 'll take some putting straight! She really did need some one she could trust. Well, I 'll leave her without lawsuits threatening and bad debts, at least.

DON JULIÁN. Good . . . good! Will it take you long?

ADOLFO. Six weeks . . . two months. But that 's no matter. It 's the slack time in Madrid . . . I shan't be missed.

DON JULIÁN. Well, my son . . . ! Forgive me, I talk to you as if you were one of my flock here. . . .

ADOLFO. But I hope you will.

DON JULIÁN. Well . . . whatever I can do, you know you have only to ask me.

ADOLFO. I 'm going to . . . and without more ado . . . you 'll have no cause to complain. First, then, on my aunt's behalf, a few lines to introduce me, please. . . .

DON JULIÁN. Who to?

ADOLFO. To . . . the name escapes me . . . the tenant at the Hacienda de la Colmena.

DON JULIAN. Oho . . . Pablo Lobo. Yes, he's a tough customer. A bit of a fox . . . a bit of a screw . . . a bit of a brigand!

ADOLFO. But my aunt says he is a bit afraid of you . . . and that if I take a letter from you when I go to see him . . .

DON JULIÁN. When is that?

ADOLFO. To-morrow, I hope.

DON JULIÁN. I'll write it now.

ADOLFO. No, please! I'm on my way to the Registrar's . . . he puts his shutters up early . . . I've one or two things to talk over with him. If I might call for it on my way back. . . .

DON JULIÁN. You may.

ADOLFO. Well . . . I fear you'll think my first visit has been a very selfish one.

Don Julián laughs indulgently.

DON JULIÁN. And our little town . . . how does our little town strike you? A bit dull . . . a bit behind the times?

ADOLFO. Not at all! I've had no time yet to be dull. It's not unlike other places I know in Andalusia. A little sleepier . . . a little more out of the world, it may be.

DON JULIÁN. Yes, yes! There are only two things that keep lively here . . . the church bells and the women's tongues.

ADOLFO. Ah! The bells wake me every morning. As for the tongues . . . I've not heard much of them yet.

DON JULIÁN. You will!

ADOLFO. But your flies . . . they're lively enough! Saving your presence, I do believe you have half the flies in Spain here.

DON JULIÁN. Ah, yes . . . we're famous for our flies. A bit of a pest . . . a bit of a plague! But we're not so much bothered out here. We give them the dining-room to themselves.

ADOLFO. Not many mosquitoes, though.

DON JULIÁN. Wait till July.

ADOLFO. Oh!

DON JULIÁN. They begin on the visitors in July.

ADOLFO. Do they?

DON JULIÁN. Yes. By then they 're quite used to us . . . we 're daily bread to them. But when a stranger arrives they send word round, I do believe: Here 's a new tasty dish come to town! And they eat him alive.

ADOLFO. Thank you for the warning. I 'll be on my guard.

He rises to take his departure.

DON JULIÁN. Off already?

ADOLFO. I 'll come back for the letter. I must get to the Registrar's . . . he goes to bed with the hens!

DON JULIÁN. Well . . . till your next visit, then. Forgive me if I 've not done you all the honours of a first one . . . but you 'll always be welcome. And next time I 'll show you my treasures . . . my nieces, my sister's girls. They 're not such scarecrows! We keep open house here . . . from morning till night that door 's always open. The girls' young friends run in and out . . . and my sister's friends run in and out . . . and my friends run in and out. Do you know Don Cecilio . . . the doctor? A good fellow . . . excellent company. He 's in and out all the time!

ADOLFO. Oh, I know him . . . he 's in and out at my aunt's . . . all the time!

DON JULIÁN. So whenever you 've a minute or two to spare . . . just run in. No ceremony!

ADOLFO. I will indeed.

DON JULIÁN. Though it 's whispered that you have not been wasting your time.

ADOLFO. What 's that?

DON JULIÁN. I 'm only repeating what I hear.

ADOLFO. I've no notion what you 're referring to.

DON JULIÁN. Gossip . . . women's gossip!

SANTITA. What 's that you 're saying?

DON JULIÁN. I 'm telling him what you told me they were all telling you about him.

SANTITA. Oh . . . that . . . yes! I hope all is going well. You 've shown very good taste. The pick of the basket!

ADOLFO. Honestly, Don Julián, I don't in the least know what this is all about.

DON JULIÁN. Don't you now? Oh, these chatterboxes! Why, they've all made up their minds that there is a certain young lady . . . who runs in and out here a good deal . . . has made very short work of you.

ADOLFO. Of me? But I hardly know a soul in the place. And I haven't said two words to any girl here since I came.

SANTITA. What's that? Won't her aunt hear of it? Take no notice of her. It's all airs . . . the silly woman!

DON JULIÁN. No, not her aunt! He says he doesn't even know her.

SANTITA. Don't you believe it.

DON JULIÁN. You see . . . I'm not to believe it.

ADOLFO. Well, how can I convince you? Good-bye for now.

DON JULIÁN. For the moment.

ADOLFO. Good-bye, Señora.

SANTITA. Good-bye to you, Señor.

Adolfo departs.

DON JULIÁN. That's a very nice fellow.

SANTITA. Not so bad. She's too good for him. But they always are.

She picks up the ash-tray and with a grimace calls out "Die-guilla! Dieguilla!"

DON JULIÁN. What is it?

SANTITA. She must take this away! Pf . . . it smells! Ah, if only the good God had made my ears a little sharper . . . and my nose not quite so sharp! Ouf! !

Dieguilla appears, drying her hands on her apron.

DIEGUILLA. The Señorita called?

SANTITA. I did. Take away this object . . . and clean it.

DIEGUILLA. Yes, Señorita.

SANTITA. And bring it back at once.

DIEGUILLA. Yes, Señorita. Don Julián . . . have you smoked two . . . or have you had a gentleman to see you?

DON JULIÁN. Be off with you . . . be off!

Dieguilla, quite unintimidated, departs as she came, singing the forbidden fandango. And, though she sings it softly enough, Santita can tell.

SANTITA.   A nice obedient girl, is n't she!

Concha Puerto comes from the street followed by her man-servant, Guitarra. A playwright given to symbolism would say that Concha Puerto was the very genius of this little town. But we, who are not, will be content with calling her a handsome, meddling, and officious lady, who knows every-thing about everybody.

CONCHA.   Good evening to you both.

GUITARRA.   Evening all.

DON JULIÁN.   How are you, Concha?

CONCHA [*loudly.*]   Good evening, Santita.

SANTITA.   Bless you!

CONCHA.   Guitarra . . . be off to the kitchen. I 'll call you when I 'm ready to go.

GUITARRA.   Very good, Señorita.

He goes through the garden and away to the left.

CONCHA.   I brought Guitarra . . . for if I stay late every lamp in the street is out . . . it 's as black as pitch . . . and one of these nights I shall get a bad scare. Has he just gone?

She seats herself.

DON JULIÁN.   What 's that?

CONCHA.   Has n't he just gone?

DON JULIÁN.   Who?

CONCHA.   I made sure he 'd just gone.

DON JULIÁN.   But who?

CONCHA.   Why, the young man from Madrid . . . whoever else? Esperanza Lucena's nephew.

DON JULIÁN.   Oh, to be sure . . . yes, he 's just gone. He came in to pay his respects to me.

CONCHA.   Did he? Then he chose the wrong time. She 's never here till later.

DON JULIÁN.   Now what is all this?

CONCHA.   A nice young man, is n't he?

DON JULIÁN. A charming young man . . . a most superior young man.

CONCHA. And a most eligible young man. He has a future . . . any one can see that. A full-fledged lawyer at his age . . . and something besides.

DON JULIÁN. What besides?

CONCHA. I forget. My husband told me. Quite to his credit. But I forget. Anyhow, Juanita's in luck. He's worth two of her. [*To Santita.*] Where are your girls? [*Then, as this does not penetrate, fortissimo.*] Where are the girls?

SANTITA. In the garden.

CONCHA. I'll call them. We must have a talk about this. [*She calls from the doorway to the garden.*] Girls! Ángela! Pilar! I've come.

DON JULIÁN. How is your husband?

CONCHA. Bobadilla? He's got his toothache as usual.

DON JULIÁN. Heavens above us! However he endures it! Why does n't he have it out?

CONCHA. You know Bobadilla. The dentist and the Day of Judgment are one to him. Holy Mother Mary . . . he's a coward about it! But the noise he was making when I left . . .! Are the lottery lists out?

> *Dieguilla comes back with the clean ash-tray, which she leaves on the table, departing without a word. But coming and going her face is one stare.*

DON JULIÁN. They are. Do you want a number?

CONCHA. I do. See if 14525 is there.

DON JULIÁN. 145 . . . no, it is n't.

CONCHA. I'm sorry. Martinez, the little curate, has got that. What about 7304?

DON JULIÁN. 7304. No . . . nothing at all in the seven threes. Did you ever?

CONCHA. They had that at the chemist's.

DON JULIÁN. What about yours?

CONCHA. I've none. But I always remember other people's numbers. I like to know what's going on.

*At which Don Julián laughs. Ángela and Pilar, fresh
pretty girls of 15 and 20, Santita's daughters, come from
the garden.*

PILAR. Hola!

ÁNGELA. Hola!

CONCHA. Hola. Have you heard the news?

PILAR. We know.

ÁNGELA. We know.

DON JULIÁN. What news?

CONCHA. What news! That the young man from Madrid is
head over ears in love with Juanita La Rosa.

DON JULIÁN. Nonsense.

CONCHA. Nonsense indeed! It's a fact. Juanita hasn't
slept a wink since she saw him.   Love at first sight!

DON JULIÁN. I know where you'll go for a tatler. And you
won't lack company there, either. [*He wags his head at his nieces.*]
Will you listen to me?   The young man from Madrid has just left.

ÁNGELA. Oh . . . has he been to call?

PILAR. What . . . he has been to call!

DON JULIÁN. Yes, children, he has been to call.

CONCHA. He came, if you please, to pay his respects to your
uncle!

DON JULIÁN. And why shouldn't the poor young man pay his
respects to me?

CONCHA. Oh . . . fiddle-de-dee!

DON JULIÁN. And I told him quite casually of the talk in the
town . . . and he told me very candidly that he hardly knew
Juanita.

Concha Puerto and the girls burst into laughter.

CONCHA. Show me a plaster saint on a pedestal that's as inno-
cent as you are!

PILAR. Uncle, how can you be such a baby?

ÁNGELA. Hardly knows her! Everybody knows he's crazy
about her.

CONCHA. If he doesn't know her . . . why did he come here
to look for her?

ÁNGELA. Is n't he coming back?

DON JULIÁN. Yes, he 's coming back. What of it?

CONCHA. Simpleton!

Santita has been growing most impatient to get a finger in the pie.

SANTITA. What 's all this . . . what is all this gibberish?

CONCHA. Don Julián wants us to believe that Esperanza Lucena's nephew from Madrid does n't even know Juanita La Rosa.

SANTITA. And the moon 's made of green cheese, I believe.

CONCHA. There . . . I told you!

PILAR. Why, of course!

SANTITA. As if I could n't tell he came here on the track of her!

CONCHA. You see!

DON JULIÁN. I see . . . that you 're all as bad as each other.

ÁNGELA. Uncle! You don't believe it yet?

DON JULIÁN. My child, when the person who after all has most right to know, tells me himself that he is n't even acquainted with the young lady. . . .

CONCHA. Well . . . *I* tell you that he is acquainted with her . . . and he 's in love with her . . . and he is writing her a declaration.

DON JULIÁN. Pooh!

CONCHA. Oh . . . a lot you know about it! If he is n't in love with her why has he walked down the street she lives in three times this very day?

DON JULIÁN. But it 's the main street of the town. Must a man climb over the roofs?

CONCHA. And if he 's not going to write to her why did he buy a stamp at the tobacconist's this morning . . . a local, penny stamp?

PILAR. Did he buy a stamp?

ÁNGELA. Think of that!

DON JULIÁN. However did you know that?

CONCHA. How do I know that? Why, everybody in the place knows it. How often does the tobacconist sell a local, penny

stamp? When you can carry a letter half round the town quicker
. . . and cheaper! Well, then . . . when a man walks in and
asks for a local, penny stamp . . .! Oh, you can't be such a
simpleton as not to see. . . .!

ÁNGELA. Such a baby, Uncle, such a baby!

DON JULIÁN. Tsch! Somebody's coming.

*Concha seems to divine almost by instinct who the newcomer
is. And she makes a portent of the event.*

CONCHA. Ah! Pepe Lora!

PILAR. Pepe Lora?

CONCHA. Pepe Lora.

ÁNGELA. Pepe Lora!

PILAR [*to her uncle*]. Pepe Lora!

*And indeed it is Pepe Lora that comes in from the street. A
gloomy suspicious young man and slow of speech. He wears
the short jacket and broad-brimmed Andalusian hat.*

PEPE. Good evening, Don Julián . . . and everybody.

DON JULIÁN. Good evening, Pepillo.

The others respond to his greeting with "good evenings."

PEPE. Have you got the Diario . . . by any chance?

DON JULIÁN. The newspaper . . . yes. Children . . . where's
the Diario?

PILAR. The Diario! It was here half-an-hour ago.

ÁNGELA. I think Piña sent round for it.

CONCHA. It's not at Piña's. I've just left there. She has
given it to some one.

PEPE. Mother's reading the serial. She wants to get on
with it.

ÁNGELA. Victoria has it I expect.

PILAR. Yes . . . she's reading the serial.

CONCHA. And if she hasn't it, it's opposite . . . or if it isn't
opposite, I may have it at home by now.

DON JULIÁN. Then that's the scent you've to follow.

PEPE. Thank you. I'll ask opposite first.

DON JULIÁN. And when your mother has quite finished with
it you'll send it back here, won't you?

PEPE. Have n't you read it yet?

DON JULIÁN. Yes, but I always post it on to my brother . . . to my brother Ramon. He 's so out of the world, poor fellow, in that wretched little village of his.

PEPE. Right. Don't worry. I 'll bring it back. Thank you. Good-bye.

DON JULIÁN. God bless you.

CONCHA. Good-bye.

Pepe departs and he is hardly out of hearing before we learn why he really came.

ÁNGELA. Ah! It was n't the Diario he was after.

DON JULIÁN. Eh?

CONCHA. The Diario, indeed! He wanted to find out if she was here.

DON JULIÁN. Who?

CONCHA. Juanita, of course.

PILAR. Well, of course!

DON JULIÁN. But what should he want with Juanita . . . now?

PILAR. Was n't he in love with her?

DON JULIÁN. But she would n't have him.

ÁNGELA. But he takes that very badly. And he has sworn an oath . . . yes, a real oath . . . that she shan't marry any one if she does n't marry him.

PILAR. And he has kept it. He scared off Manolo Corrales.

CONCHA. I 'll just see which way he has gone now.

DON JULIÁN. Well . . . the good Lord knows whether I 'm only fit for an asylum . . . or whether these chatterboxes are!

Don Julián goes into the garden. Concha, who had slipped out to the front door, hurries back.

CONCHA. Pepe Lora has gone up the street. And he's muttering to himself.

ÁNGELA. Is he?

CONCHA. And what else do you think I saw?

PILAR. What?

CONCHA. Innocencio Parra . . . opposite . . . on his balcony . . . whistling to his parrot . . . and wearing white trousers!

ÁNGELA.   Wearing white trousers?

CONCHA.   White trousers. And his wife only dead three
months!

ÁNGELA.   Mother of God!

PILAR.   It 's incredible!

ÁNGELA.   He can't be.

She dashes out to the door and comes back horror-stricken.

CONCHA.   Well . . . you see! Oh, no one thinks of mourn-
ing for any one now. People do exactly what they like. He 's
shameless.

ÁNGELA.   But how shocking . . . how shocking! Pilar, go
and look. Don't miss it.

Pilar dashes out and back.

PILAR.   White trousers!

ÁNGELA.   And your cousin, who was only her sister-in-law,
still wearing a black veil . . . as long as that!

CONCHA.   And were my doors open to a soul . . . for a whole
week after she was in her grave?

PILAR.   I 'd never have believed it. Do you think the man 's
right in his head?

Santita can contain her curiosity no longer.

SANTITA.   What 's all this running in and out for, children?

CONCHA.   Señora, you will never believe it. Innocencio Parra
is sitting on his balcony . . . playing with his parrot . . . and
with white trousers on.

SANTITA.   Glory be to God . . . no, it can't be true!

And she goes out to see.

ÁNGELA.   That 's a bit of a scandal, as Uncle would say!

CONCHA.   It 's more than a bit of a scandal. My husband will
take it very seriously. Why, he still wears a black hat-band for
his first wife . . . and I honour him for it.

Santita returns crossing herself.

SANTITA.   It 's impious! And here we are . . . the country dry
as a bone . . . praying for rain. Does he think God 's to be trifled
with like that? Still . . . if he 'd been the one to die she 'd
have been out on the balcony in a pink dressing-gown before now!

CONCHA. Yes, the man has that much excuse.

SANTITA. I saw Juanita La Rosa.

ÁNGELA. Juanita La Rosa?

PILAR. Coming here?

CONCHA. With her aunt?

SANTITA. With her aunt.

ÁNGELA. Listen now! Let 's pretend we know nothing about anything.

PILAR. Yes, let 's! Her aunt 's getting simply intolerable.

ÁNGELA. And I know she thinks we 're jealous of Juanita. So we know nothing at all. Mum!

CONCHA. Well, I don't find it so easy to be mum.

SANTITA. What 's all this?

ÁNGELA. We 're going to pretend to Doña Belén and Juanita that we know nothing at all about the young man from Madrid.

SANTITA. I quite agree. Let them talk about it if they want to. *They all settle themselves with a most indifferent air and wait for the heroine of the play to arrive. And after a moment Doña Belén Zurita and her beautiful niece Juanita La Rosa arrive. Doña Belén is a suave and circumspect lady, somewhat conscious of her gentility. She speaks most correctly, though she hardly opens her mouth to do so. At the end of any important sentence she draws in her breath again with a slight hiss as if to make it still more important. And she smiles patronizingly as she speaks. Juanita speaks prettily and softly; for she is Andalusian. And the young man from Madrid may well find her very attractive when he does meet her — if it 's true that he has n't met her yet. As they come in Doña Belén is saying quietly to Juanita . . .*

DOÑA BELÉN. Now remember . . . not a word . . . from either of us.

JUANITA. I 'll remember.

DOÑA BELÉN. Good evening.

JUANITA. Good evening.

CONCHA. Good evening.

ÁNGELA. Hola, Juanita.

JUANITA. Hola, Pilar.

PILAR. You look very pretty to-night, my dear.

DOÑA BELÉN. And how is Santita?

SANTITA. Quite well, thank you.

DOÑA BELÉN. And your Bobadilla, Concha?

CONCHA. At home with his tooth.

DOÑA BELÉN. That tiresome tooth!

CONCHA. And how 's José?

DOÑA BELÉN. Who?

CONCHA. Your husband, to be sure.

DOÑA BELÉN. Oh . . . my husband! Thank you, my husband is very well. He 's in the country.

> *They sit down. A silence falls. They look at each other and smile.*

CONCHA. Is n't that the frock you were keeping for Assumption Sunday?

JUANITA. Yes . . . but I thought I 'd put it on to-day.

DOÑA BELÉN. Does it signify when?

CONCHA. Not a bit.

ÁNGELA. It is smart though, is n't it?

PILAR. It 's very pretty.

JUANITA. It 's nothing. I made it myself.

DOÑA BELÉN. And the best educated young woman is the better educated, in my opinion, with a little knowledge of sewing.

> *It is after such a beautiful sentence as this that we hear her breath hiss back again.*

CONCHA. Well . . . that 's no news, is it?

DOÑA BELÉN. And what might your remark imply?

CONCHA. Nothing.

> *Silence falls again. Then Juanita finds a conversational opening; the usual one.*

JUANITA. It 's a little cooler to-day, I think.

CONCHA. Not a bit.

> *Concha indeed is very flushed and fans herself impatiently. Santita at this moment blows loudly into her cigarette-making machine, and everybody smiles at that.*

SANTITA. It's always getting choked.

DOÑA BELÉN. Choked! Fancy that!

And now Dieguilla in her kitchen bursts into song.

ÁNGELA. Doesn't Dieguilla sing well?

PILAR. That's the fandango they all sing in her village.

JUANITA. She puts so much expression into it.

They sit listening, and Santita can guess from their faces the dreadful thing that is happening. Up she springs and off she goes.

SANTITA. Well, she's made up her mind that I'm to show her the door . . .!

ÁNGELA. Now Mama's off again!

JUANITA. Why, what's the matter?

ÁNGELA. She will not have the servants sing. Yesterday she dismissed Catherine for it.

DOÑA BELÉN. She is perfectly right. I entirely approve.

CONCHA. But she's the only one in the house that can't hear them . . . that's the joke of it!

They laugh politely. But their thoughts are elsewhere. Santita comes back to her cigarettes; and silence — as of the tomb — falls yet again.

JUANITA. Ay . . . ay . . . ay!

ÁNGELA. What are you sighing for?

JUANITA. I wasn't. But no one was talking . . .!

PILAR. In this town whatever there is to talk about always has been talked about.

DOÑA BELÉN. And there never is much to talk about.

ÁNGELA. No!

Another pause, though not such a long one.

CONCHA. To-day's Thursday, is it?

JUANITA. Thursday.

DOÑA BELÉN. Yes . . . to-day's Thursday. Yesterday was Wednesday.

CONCHA. Then it must be Thursday.

Upon such altitudes silence is almost tragic.

SANTITA. What are you all talking about?

CONCHA. Nothing.

The rest silently corroborate her.

SANTITA. Still nothing?

DOÑA BELÉN. We are unusually silent.

CONCHA. To all appearances.

DOÑA BELÉN. Whatever do you mean by that?

CONCHA. But I'd like to know what we're thinking about . . . some of us.

Her glance falls on Juanita.

JUANITA. Nothing I could n't talk about, I'm sure . . . if I wanted to.

Silence yet again; though Ángela does start to hum Dieguilla's fandango.

CONCHA. I can't stand it one second longer. It's against nature!

DOÑA BELÉN. I beg your pardon.

JUANITA. What's the matter?

CONCHA. What's the matter . . . what's the matter! How you can keep this up I don't know. Six women . . . all panting to be talking about one single thing . . . and all sitting talking about nothing at all. Well, if you can, I can't . . . so there! Has he written to you?

And now every one laughs.

SANTITA. Ah! I knew the kettle would boil over soon!

DOÑA BELÉN. There! I said they'd start making fun of you . . . I knew we'd better have stayed at home.

CONCHA. Come on . . . let's have good friendly talk about it.

ÁNGELA. Has he written to you?

JUANITA. Saints in Glory! . . . what should he be writing to me about?

PILAR. Then he has n't written to you?

JUANITA. No.

CONCHA. But then what can he have done with the stamp?

JUANITA. You really must n't take it all so seriously . . . please. I can't imagine how this hubbub began. We've not so much as spoken to one another. We've only seen each other once.

PILAR. Oh, come!

JUANITA. It 's the sacred truth. As far as I know he has only seen me once . . . the day after the day he came.

CONCHA. That was the 18th.

JUANITA. It was the 19th, then. He was going into the club with the Registrar . . . and I was coming out of the Silva's house. He passed me . . . and then he half-turned to look at me . . . and I did think I heard him say: "What a pretty girl!" That 's all that has happened . . . no more nor less. And I 've not seen him since . . . and he has not seen me . . . and as far as I know he has not given me one single thought.

CONCHA. Well, if you suppose we 're going to believe that!

PILAR. Of course not.

ÁNGELA. We may be fools . . . but we 're not such fools.

CONCHA. How could the whole town be agog with it if there was no more in it than that?

DOÑA BELÉN. Please let me assure you, Concha, upon the word of a gentleman . . . or rather a lady . . . that Juanita has told you the simple truth. And if it 's true . . . as I hear from everybody . . . that this young man from Madrid did walk past my house in the hope of another look at her . . . he had none . . . for she was n't even at the window to see him pass. Not one single thing has Juanita done to add . . . if I may so express it . . . fuel to his flame. Her mother . . . as I think you know . . . was a lady of distinction and refinement . . . her father was the same. And we . . . her uncle and aunt . . . in giving her a home and an upbringing have set ourselves to make her a pattern of what a young lady should be.

After this she hisses quite loudly.

CONCHA. Still there 'd be nothing unrefined in her marrying a young man who was a pattern of what a husband should be . . . would there?

They all laugh at this sally of Concha's.

DOÑA BELÉN. Our dear Concha . . . always so full of wit! Juanita.

JUANITA. Yes, Aunt.

DOÑA BELÉN. Recite us the little verses . . . the copla you made up this morning.

JUANITA. Oh, no, Aunt . . . I could n't . . . please!

ÁNGELA. Yes, do . . . do! I love your coplas.

PILAR. Let 's hear it.

CONCHA. Do!

JUANITA. Very well. But I don't like repeating my coplas. Girls, in a place like this, are n't supposed to write coplas.

ÁNGELA. Never mind . . . there 's no one here but us.

JUANITA. But, after all, there 's no great harm in a copla.
So she hums it through for them.

> A thought to him she has never given,
>   Nor he a thought to her.
> But the neighbours' tongues a' wagging
>   May set many thoughts astir.

DOÑA BELÉN. I don't call that bad.

JUANITA. It 's nothing.

ÁNGELA. It 's a wonderful copla, my dear.

PILAR. I call it marvellous.

CONCHA. And it 's to the point.

SANTITA. What 's this . . . what 's this?

ÁNGELA. A quite delicious copla!
Thinks Santita: It 's Dieguilla again. And she springs up determined to turn her out of the house without more ado.

SANTITA. Oh! So she means to defy me, does she? Then out she goes this minute . . . after that other tartar of a woman! Yes . . . if I have to wash the saucepans myself!
She starts towards the kitchen.

ÁNGELA. Mama . . . where are you going?

SANTITA. To turn that hussy out of doors.

ÁNGELA. But it was n't Dieguilla. It was Juanita reciting her new copla.

SANTITA. Oh! You . . . was it? Well . . . I knew there was impudence about somewhere!

At which they all burst into laughter, Santita included. And into the midst of the fun Don Julián comes back from the garden.

DON JULIÁN.   Hola! Hola! We 're all very merry to-day!

DOÑA BELÉN.   A very good evening to you, Don Julián.

DON JULIÁN.   God bless you, my daughter! And how is the pearl of the village?

JUANITA.   Oh . . . quite well, thank you, Father.

DON JULIÁN.   Why don't you all go into the garden . . . or sit out by the door? It 's a beautiful evening.

ÁNGELA.   Yes . . . let 's go and sit by the door.

JUANITA.   Yes.

DOÑA BELÉN.   Why, if you wish.

CONCHA.   I 'll come when I 've told Guitarra to run across and see how Bobadilla and his tooth are getting on. I 'll have to go and change the poultice, I expect.

Concha goes out towards the kitchen.

SANTITA.   Where 's Concha gone?

ÁNGELA.   To see after Bobadilla's tooth.

SANTITA.   Poor man . . . he has enough to put up with . . . his tooth and his wife besides.

At this most inopportune moment, disconcerting every one, Pepe Lora returns. He has brought back the Diario. Juanita's face falls at the sight of him.

PEPE.   Good evening.

DOÑA BELÉN.   Good evening.

PEPE.   Don Julián . . . your Diario.

DON JULIÁN.   Thank you, my dear boy. But has your mother read the serial already?

PEPE.   She has. And I 've found what I was looking for too. Good evening.

DON JULIÁN.   Good-night.

DOÑA BELÉN.   Good evening.

Pepe Lora departs as he came, giving a meaning glance at Juanita, who does not meet his eye.

ÁNGELA.   Now the fat 's in the fire.

DON JULIÁN. He's a bit of a fool, that boy . . . just a bit of a fool.

JUANITA. A bit of a fool, Father! He's a great big brute. And if he thinks that because there was once upon a time some childish nonsense between us I 'm never going to look at another man as long as I live . . . well, he 's more than half wrong.

PILAR. I should think so.

ÁNGELA. He 'll have to be taught a lesson.

DOÑA BELÉN. He will be. My husband intends to take steps!

SANTITA. Tut! . . . a storm in a teacup!

ÁNGELA. Come along.

JUANITA. Oh . . . the air 's good! So cool. . . .

Juanita and Ángela vanish into the porch, taking their chairs with them. Pilar leaves hers behind.

PILAR. Never mind . . . I can sit on the bench.

Santita has gathered her things together and put them away in the cupboard. And now she follows the girls, carrying her chair, too.

SANTITA. Are n't you coming, Belén?

DOÑA BELÉN. In one moment. Don Julián . . . a word with you, if you please.

DON JULIÁN. What 's the trouble, my daughter?

DOÑA BELÉN. You cannot imagine what a shock Pepe Lora's coming here gave me.

DON JULIÁN [*sympathetically*]. Yes . . . we all felt the same.

DOÑA BELÉN. I thought he was going to say, then and there, that never . . . cost what it might . . . should Juanita be another's. Don't you think you could talk seriously to the misguided boy?

DON JULIÁN. I will . . . yes, I will. But is n't it still a little . . . premature?

DOÑA BELÉN. Premature? Ah, Father, you 've never been one and twenty. . . .

DON JULIÁN. What do you mean?

DOÑA BELÉN. You 've never been in love.

DON JULIÁN. Well . . . now I 'm sixty and more! And I tell you I 'd better say nothing to Pepe Lora yet . . . till it 's quite clear that this young man from Madrid has set his heart on Juanita. For half-an-hour ago on this very spot he swore to me he did n't even know her by sight. . . .

DOÑA BELÉN. Ah . . . that is not precisely so. Know her by sight . . . oh yes, he knows her by sight. . . .

DON JULIÁN. Sh! here he is.

DOÑA BELÉN. Fancy! What a coincidence!

*Through the garden come Adolfo and Don Cecilio, the doctor;
a discreet, capable, perceptive man; past middle age.*

DON JULIÁN. I say . . . I say! With a house with two doors to it . . . I need a watch dog!

DON CECILIO. Yes . . . we came in by the garden gate to steal your oranges. I wish you a very good evening, Doña Belén.

DOÑA BELÉN. And to you, Doctor.

ADOLFO. I 'm here again, Don Julián, you see. Señora!

Don Julián formally presents him.

DON JULIÁN. Doña Belén Zurita.

DOÑA BELÉN. No, Father . . . no, no, no!

DON JULIÁN. To be sure! . . . Zurita de Gómez Valdivieso.

ADOLFO. Your most humble servant.

DON JULIÁN. Don Adolfo Adalid.

DOÑA BELÉN. Delighted. I know your dear aunt so well. So glad you are making a stay. Our little town is honoured indeed.

ADOLFO. Señora . . . the honour is mine . . . of such a welcome!

DOÑA BELÉN. You are too good.

ADOLFO. You are most kind.

DOÑA BELÉN. Au revoir, Martínez.

DON CECILIO. Good-bye, Señora.

*Doña Belén turns away from them graciously smiling, and
departs.*

DON JULIÁN [*to Adolfo*]. That 's the Aunt.

ADOLFO. What aunt?

DON JULIÁN. Her aunt.

ADOLFO. Whose aunt?

DON JULIÁN. And she 's out there too.

ADOLFO. Who is?

DON JULIÁN. She. What a piece of luck!

ADOLFO. Really? But why?

DON JULIÁN. Come, now, come! My nieces have told me all about it. You 're taking the plunge, then.

ADOLFO. I assure you there 's not one word of truth in this.

DON JULIÁN. Well . . . I only tell you what 's told me, my young friend.

ADOLFO. Certainly, when I said just now I had never even seen her . . . I was mistaken, it appears.

DON JULIÁN. Aha!

ADOLFO. I admit that. They began talking about her just now at the Registrar's! And his wife reminded me that I did see the young lady in the street the other day . . . I was with some other men . . . and that I thought her very pretty.

DON JULIÁN. So she is. And a good girl. And a clever girl. I 'll go and write that letter for you.

ADOLFO. Oh, it 's troubling you for nothing, I 'm afraid. But to please my aunt . . .!

DON JULIÁN. Tut, tut!

Don Julián departs.

DON CECILIO. My dear young friend . . . we are alone. I have a piece of advice for you. Don't get married.

ADOLFO. What do you mean?

DON CECILIO. Don't . . . get . . . married.

ADOLFO. I 'm not going to get married.

DON CECILIO. Take a friend's counsel . . . who knows what he 's talking about . . . and knows this town, what 's more. Don't you get married.

ADOLFO. You need not worry. I repeat: I have no intention of getting married. It 's not at all what brought me here.

DON CECILIO. Then keep your wits about you.

ADOLFO. But what perfect nonsense . . .!

Guitarra crosses from the garden to the street door muttering as he goes.

GUITARRA. . . . singing away there to ourselves and all so cosy . . . and now I 'm to go and see if the master's tooth still aches. And I wish you a very good evening.

DON CECILIO. Good evening.

ADOLFO. Good evening. Who on earth 's that?

DON CECILIO. Concha Puerto's servant. You know Concha Puerto.

ADOLFO. I 've met her two or three times. A most officious lady. And what a chatterbox!

DON CECILIO. Ah . . . if that were the worst of it!

ADOLFO. Why . . .?

DON CECILIO. Why . . . if Concha Puerto has made up her mind you 're to get married . . . you 'll get married.

ADOLFO. Are you joking?

DON CECILIO. Far from it. Her mother, who was just such another, took me in hand. It was far from a joke.

ADOLFO. Well . . . you must allow me to think it one.

DON CECILIO. She made up her mind that I should get married . . . and I got married.

ADOLFO. Will you forgive me for saying that you seem to have marriage on the brain?

DON CECILIO. My dear young friend . . . I know what I 'm talking about, believe me. When I think of all the little things I 've done in my life . . . though heaven knows that 's not a little thing . . . only because this town had made up its mind I should do them! For here, let me tell you, the women have their way . . . and what they want done is done.

ADOLFO. That may be because there are no such things as men here.

DON CECILIO. There 's something in that. But how is one to circumvent such plottings and plannings. No . . . what men there are here don't amount to much, that 's a fact. They 've hardly grown to be men before they 've dawdled and debauched away whatever brains they 've got. So of course the women have the best of it. They 've the sense and the pluck. And as they never stop talking what chance has any one against them?

ADOLFO. Well . . . I 've heard the same thing said about other towns in Spain.

DON CECILIO. Do you know the nickname we rejoice in? Petticoat-town! And we deserve it. So keep your wits about you. I 've given you fair warning.

ADOLFO. And all this because I own to seeing a girl in the street and thinking she was pretty.

DON CECILIO. That 's how I began.

ADOLFO. What?

DON CECILIO. Thirty-five years back . . . I 'd been here three days . . . just three days . . . when the little tricks began. "What, doctor, already? My dear doctor . . . so soon! Well, you show very good taste, I must say." "I do?" "Yes, you do. You can't take us in. You 've your eye on so and so . . . " "But I don't know the lady." "Don't know her? Nonsense." "No, I assure you." "Fancy that! He does n't even know her! Really, who 'd have thought it!" Till after a bit I found, you know, that I rather wanted to know her.

ADOLFO. I see.

DON CECILIO. And so will you.

ADOLFO. Why, yes . . . I admit that I feel already . . .

DON CECILIO. Aha!

ADOLFO. . . . a certain curiosity.

DON CECILIO. Oh . . . you 're on the brink! One step and in you go . . . and you 're a lost man! You 'll find there 's no difficulty in getting to know her. Then you 'll find yourself at a party with her. Then at a dance where you 'll come to know her a little better. Then there 'll be the lattice window . . . Concha Puerto's probably . . . that she 'll sit in while you stand outside and talk to her. Then they fix the date of the wedding. That 's the programme.

Adolfo roars with laughter.

DON CECILIO. You may laugh . . . as loud as you like. But

once they get seriously to work you 'll find that you 're going the
way you 're meant to go. So why waste time arguing about it?

ADOLFO. Now, my dear doctor. . . .

DON CECILIO. Now, my dear young lawyer . . . have a good
look at me. Would you take me for a bull-fighter, by chance?

ADOLFO. No.

DON CECILIO. Well . . . I turned bull-fighter for an afternoon
here once. The ladies thought they 'd like to see me fight a bull.
So I fought a bull. It was for a fund for poor widows, or a new
cloak for their pet Madonna, or to sell the peasants cheap seeds
after a drought . . . I forget. They got up an amateur bull
fight . . . with three nice young bulls . . . and I had to fight them.

ADOLFO. Will it come to that with me, d' you think?

DON CECILIO. Probably not. They have other plans for you.
Now you don't suppose I wanted to play at bull-fighting, do you?
I was never so terrified in my life. You can't think how big the
smallest bull grows as he gets near to you.

ADOLFO. I 'd better start practising with that mastiff at my
aunt's.

DON CECILIO. Ah, it 's a joke to you now . . . !

*Santita comes from the front door followed by a young peasant
girl.*

SANTITA. Yes, here 's the doctor. [*As she sees Adolfo.*] Hola!
We came in by the garden door, did we?

ADOLFO. Yes, Señora.

SANTITA. Then you missed seeing something at the front door.

ADOLFO. Did I!

SANTITA. This young woman wants you, doctor.

She disappears into the garden.

DON CECILIO. What 's the matter, my child?

THE GIRL. Sister 's bad.

DON CECILIO. Bless me! And who 's Sister?

THE GIRL. José's her father.

DON CECILIO. And who 's José?

THE GIRL. He 's my father, too.

DON CECILIO [*to Adolfo, who is smiling*]. Phew! Now, we

know just who Sister is . . . and soon we'll know who Father is as well.

THE GIRL.   Father's the knife-grinder.   Who else could he be?

DON CECILIO.   Why, of course . . . who else could Father be but the knife-grinder!   Good.   Now, what's the matter with Sister?

THE GIRL.   She's been insulted.   She had a fight with her young man . . . and he insulted her . . . hard.

DON CECILIO.   I suppose they were insulting each other.

THE GIRL.   No, Señor.   Sister's not that sort.   But he was drunk, he was.   He'd had four glasses extra, he had.   And she told him to be off.   And he gave her such an insult!   So Mother said: "Go for the doctor."   So I went.   Then they said you were at Doña Magdalena's . . . and at Doña Magdalena's they said you were here.   So I came.

DON CECILIO.   Well, I'll come presently.   Don't worry about Sister.   Where do you all live?

THE GIRL.   You turn down the street by the corner where the pump is.

DON CECILIO.   But there are two streets where the pump is.

THE GIRL.   You turn down by the house with a marble door-step.

DON CECILIO.   Good.   What number?

THE GIRL.   It's the house with the lamp on it.

DON CECILIO.   But what number?

THE GIRL.   The number's come off.

DON CECILIO.   My child, you'd better take me there . . . or we shall never get that insult mended.   Good-bye, Adolfo.   We meet to-morrow.   At the club?

ADOLFO.   To-morrow.

DON CECILIO.   Come along.

THE GIRL [to Adolfo].   I wish you good evening.

ADOLFO.   I am very much obliged to you.   And good luck to the patient.

THE GIRL.   Thank you, Señorito.

Don Cecilio departs and the girl follows him.

ADOLFO. Funny old fellow! Marriage on the brain! And in such terror of Concha Puerto!

He is laughing to himself at this when Concha Puerto comes from the garden on her way to the porch again. Seeing him, she stops, surprised and very pleased.

CONCHA. What! Good evening. I did n't know you were here. Well . . . and how are you?

ADOLFO [*a little nonplussed*]. Thank you. How are you?

CONCHA. Very well. Why are you all alone?

ADOLFO. Don Cecilio has just left me.

CONCHA. Does Don Julián know you are here?

ADOLFO. He does.

CONCHA. And Santita?

ADOLFO. She also.

CONCHA. And the others . . . out there?

ADOLFO. That I cannot say. I have n't seen them. I did n't come in by the front door this time.

CONCHA. Shall I introduce you?

ADOLFO. You are too kind.

CONCHA. Does that mean Yes or No?

ADOLFO. It can mean either, can't it?

CONCHA. By the way, though, you must think my poor Bobadilla has no manners at all.

ADOLFO. Bobadilla?

CONCHA. My husband.

ADOLFO. God forbid, Señora, that I should think any such thing.

CONCHA. He ought to have left a card on you. But he has been having such a time of it, poor fellow, that he 's just good for nothing.

ADOLFO. Dear me! What has been the matter?

CONCHA. It 's the same tooth.

ADOLFO. The same tooth?

CONCHA. Ah! . . . here I am talking to you as if you were one of us already. But when people are so sympathetic . . . don't you feel as if you 'd known them all your life?

ADOLFO. You flatter me.

CONCHA.   Well . . . my husband has had a toothache for these three months.   Why not have it out?   That 's what every one says.   I assure you I 've taken him to Huelva . . . I 've taken him to Seville . . . I 've taken him to Cadiz . . . and each time he 's brought that tooth back with him again.   He no sooner sets eyes on the dentist than he starts shaking all over!   Would you believe it?   Breaks out in a cold sweat and shivers . . . you 'd think he was going to die.   So we just have to come home.   And it 's been going on like this for three months.   There he sits with his face tied up . . . calling on his Creator . . . and he can't make up his mind to have it out.   But don't think he 's a coward. Far from it . . . he 's very much a man.   He 's been to sea . . . fought three duels . . . he was all through the war . . . and he has been married twice.   But when he sees the dentist and the forceps he just goes down on his knees and begs for mercy.

ADOLFO.   Most extraordinary!   A man with such a record . . . and such spirit!

Guitarra returns.

GUITARRA.   Señorita. . . .

CONCHA.   You 're back, are you?   Well, how 's the Señorito?

GUITARRA.   Jumping round the room with it.

CONCHA.   My poor dear!

GUITARRA.   Never seen him so bad.   He says if you don't go and change the poultice he 'll shoot himself.

CONCHA.   My poor dear!   Fancy that.   Of course, I 'll go. You do see, don't you, why he has n't left a card on you?

ADOLFO.   Señora, I think only of his sufferings.   Please tell him not to trouble himself about me for one single moment.

CONCHA.   How good you are!

ADOLFO.   Don't mention it.

CONCHA.   Till we meet again . . . and very soon!

ADOLFO.   Good-bye, Señora.

Concha, on the point of leaving him, turns back.

CONCHA.   But if you want me to introduce you to her . . . it will only take a minute.   And it 's such an opportunity.

ADOLFO.   To . . . her?

CONCHA. To Juanita La Rosa . . . as you 're so struck with her.

ADOLFO. But that 's all a legend.

CONCHA. Señor Adalid . . . believe me, there are no secrets here. We know about that stamp. We know all about everything.

ADOLFO. I assure you there is nothing to know.

CONCHA. Now . . . now . . . now!

ADOLFO. And for that very reason, if I let myself be introduced. . . .

CONCHA. I understand. You 'd prefer it . . . just to happen . . . as if by chance!

ADOLFO. Señora . . . if nothing I say will convince you that this is all the purest fiction . . . ! Well, you must believe what you want to believe.

GUITARRA. Señorita!

CONCHA. What is it?

GUITARRA. You don't mind my saying that if you stay here much longer you may n't find the Señorito alive when you get back. He was about off his head when I left.

CONCHA. My poor dear! We 'll start in a moment. Really I 'm a martyr to Bobadilla and his sufferings. But I won't go without telling you this: Concha Puerto is your friend . . . a true friend . . . and no nonsense about it. A friend in need and a friend indeed.

ADOLFO. I am most grateful to you.

CONCHA. You 've only to say the word . . . and we 'll have a little dance at the club . . . or a party.

ADOLFO. No!

CONCHA. But it 's quite the thing to do here.

ADOLFO. I 'm well aware of it.

CONCHA. That 's settled then. Are you ready, Guitarra?

GUITARRA. And waiting, Señorita.

CONCHA. Oh . . . one moment!

GUITARRA [to himself]. He 'll have blown his poor brains out before we get there.

CONCHA.   And we keep up the old courting customs here, you know. The window with its iron lattice . . . she sits behind it . . . and you stand outside to woo her. The Piñas are going to offer you their lattice window. Don't take it. There's a lamp-post not ten yards off. How can you make love under a lamp-post?

ADOLFO.   But Señora . . .!

CONCHA.   No . . . you shall have mine. It's dark there and most romantic. Every one says so that's tried it. It has been a very lucky lattice.

ADOLFO.   No doubt!

CONCHA.   Close to the garden, too. You can smell the magnolia and the jasmine . . . you can hear the fountain. Half way to Heaven! I'll see you again soon.

ADOLFO.   Good-bye, Señora. Good-bye, good-bye!

CONCHA.   Be off, Guitarra. [*Turning back yet again.*] Firm friends, remember. Till to morrow . . . at latest!

She departs and Guitarra follows her.

ADOLFO.   God save us . . . what a whirlwind of a woman! And the impertinence! Is she off her head? A good thing I didn't let her introduce me. It would have made it pretty awkward!

But Concha whirls back yet again, followed by Juanita, Ángela, Pilar . . . by Guitarra bringing up the rear.

CONCHA.   How perfectly senseless! A young man all alone here . . . and three pretty girls . . . like three roses growing on the wall! Let me introduce you. The Señoritas Ángela and Pilar, Doña Santita's daughters, Don Julián's nieces.

ADOLFO.   Most happy . . .

ÁNGELA.   Delighted . . .

PILAR.   So pleased to meet you.

CONCHA.   And Señorita Juanita La Rosa. There now!

ADOLFO.   Señorita.

Juanita smiles and blushes very prettily.

CONCHA.   And you all know who he is.

GUITARRA [*to himself*].   Well, if she's going on enjoying herself . . . so will I.

Concha catches sight of Guitarra on his way . . . where?

CONCHA. Where are you off to, Guitarra?

GUITARRA. Back to the kitchen.

CONCHA. What . . . with your master calling out for us in
agony. Heartless fellow!

GUITARRA. No, I'm not . . . no more than others.

CONCHA. Impertinent creature! Hold your tongue. Pilar,
your mother's calling you. She's in the garden.

PILAR. Is she? Forgive me.

ADOLFO. Don't mention it.

With a smile for Adolfo she vanishes.

CONCHA. Ángela . . . come to the door with me.

ÁNGELA. I . . .! Forgive me.

ADOLFO. Don't mention it . . . please.

CONCHA. Come along now, Guitarra.

GUITARRA. Come along . . . I should think so!

*Concha Puerto and Ángela go off chattering together. Gui-
tarra follows and almost before they know it the two are left
alone.*

JUANITA. Concha is really. . . .

*The sentence dies away into a rather embarrassed silence.
Don Julián arrives with the letter he has written. But, seeing
the pair before they are aware of him, he crosses himself and
prudently retires into the garden. They smile at each other
and search for some phrase to begin their talk. Juanita finds
one at last, for she asks the young man from Madrid very
simply and frankly . . .*

JUANITA. And you've just arrived . . . by the afternoon
train?

ACT II

It is the same scene, ten days later, about three in the afternoon. The windows on the garden are wide open, but their light linen curtains are half drawn. On one chair is a fly-flapper; on another Ángela sits sewing, and in a rocking chair is Santita, fast asleep.

ÁNGELA. Holy St. Barbara . . . but it's hot! And the flies! This might be a sweet shop!

Mechanically she begins to hum and then sing under her breath the fandango which Dieguilla so affects. It seems to have taken root in the house.

> There is no brighter carnation,
> No sweeter rose by the fountain,
> Than your face in its freshness,
> Oh, young girl from the mountain.

And from the kitchen Dieguilla's voice echoes her.

> Have I been stricken with madness?
> All that I wish is to flee you,
> Yet as soon as I have my freedom,
> I seek for ever to see you.

ÁNGELA. Now she's begun!

And from somewhere in the house Pilar can be heard.

> The house where I am dwelling
> Has walls of snowy whiteness,
> Carnations in the window
> And, in the well, clear water.

ÁNGELA. Pilar even . . . with her cold in her head! The fandango's all the rage! And as Mama's asleep . . . sound as the seven sleepers . . . and can't see us sing . . .

And, as if by accord, they all three begin together, each setting her own words to the one tune. Into the midst of this comes Don Julián from the street. He wears his soutane and his hat, but has no cloak on.

DON JULIÁN. Here's a hullaballoo!

ÁNGELA. Uncle!

She stops and bursts out laughing. Don Julián sees the sleeping Santita.

DON JULIÁN. Aha! That explains it.

ÁNGELA. And where have you been? Over the way?

DON JULIÁN. Having a little chat. But they all looked as if they longed for their siesta . . . so I left. [*He gives her his hat.*] Bring me my little cap . . . it's in my room . . . will you?

ÁNGELA. I will!

DON JULIÁN. How's Pilar?

ÁNGELA. You heard her. There's not much wrong with her voice, anyhow.

DON JULIÁN. Did the doctor come?

ÁNGELA. Yes.

DON JULIÁN. What does he say it is?

ÁNGELA. Nothing at all. A summer cold.

DON JULIÁN. But she's to keep her room?

ÁNGELA. Yes, she mustn't go out.

DON JULIÁN. Well, get me my cap . . . or I shall catch cold too . . . for I'm sweating like a . . .!

ÁNGELA. In a twinkling!

She vanishes and Santita wakes.

SANTITA. Hola! You're back already. What's the time then?

DON JULIÁN. The church clock has just struck three.

SANTITA. Three! Time for the Rosary.

Santita gets up and takes the fly-flapper, which she wields vigorously.

SANTITA. Little brutes! They're like leeches to-day.

The fly-flapper catches Don Julián a slap.

DON JULIÁN. God reward you, sister!

Ángela comes back with her uncle's cap.

DON JULIÁN. And God reward you, my child.

SANTITA. Rosary, my dear. It 's past three.

She puts down her fly-flapper and departs.

ÁNGELA. We shall all fall asleep in the middle.

DON JULIÁN. Behave yourself, flibbertigibbet!

ÁNGELA. Uncle, I 've something to ask you.

DON JULIÁN. Ask away.

ÁNGELA. Did the young man from Madrid come to see you in the Sacristy?

DON JULIÁN. Now what business is that of yours?

ÁNGELA. Then he did? What for?

DON JULIÁN. If I tell you, you 'll know as much as I do.

ÁNGELA. That 's why I want you to tell me.

DON JULIÁN. You go with your mother and say your Rosary.

ÁNGELA. Yes . . . as soon as I 've told Pilar that he did come to see you in the Sacristy.

And off she flies.

DON JULIÁN. They 're all agog about him! [*He chuckles to himself.*] Let 's have a look at the Diario. Now where is it? Where have they . . .? Tut, tut . . . a needle in a haystack! [*He flaps at the flies with his handkerchief.*] Yes, they are a bit of a plague, I must say.

Adolfo comes from the street.

ADOLFO. Good afternoon, Don Julián.

DON JULIÁN. Aha . . . welcome, Señor Adolfo. I did n't expect you so soon. But I 'm glad.

ADOLFO. Why?

DON JULIÁN. Sit down. My sister and the girls have just started their beads. So we 'll have all the time we want . . . and quite to ourselves.

ADOLFO. Good. For it 's a perfect curse here in this little hole of a town . . .! I beg your pardon.

DON JULIÁN. Don't apologise. It is a hole . . . a bit of a hole.

ADOLFO. Must every step I take and every word I say be

marked down and talked over and improved upon? How does it get about? Things I do with the doors closed and the blinds down! One might as well live in a shop-window at once.

DON JULIÁN. It 's true . . . it 's true. These dear ladies . . . they have eyes like gimlets and ears like . . . I don't know what. And Concha Puerto beats them all.

ADOLFO. That woman! She 'll drive me mad. She 'll be the death of me. I 'm sorry . . . but these last few days my nerves have been all on edge.

DON JULIÁN. I thought this morning that you seemed upset.

ADOLFO. And I 've cause to be.

DON JULIÁN. What is it now?

ADOLFO. Don Julián . . . ten days ago I was introduced here to Juanita La Rosa.

DON JULIÁN. Oh . . . it 's about Juanita La Rosa, is it?

ADOLFO. Who else should it be about? Have I heard another name spoken since I set foot in this place?

DON JULIÁN. Well . . . what about her?

ADOLFO. Just this . . . that I 've been manœuvred into an outrageous and intolerable situation with regard to her. And it must be set right.

DON JULIÁN. So!

ADOLFO. And without delay.

Adolfo jumps from his chair and begins to pace up and down.

DON JULIÁN. But keep cool, my dear fellow, keep cool!

ADOLFO. While I 'm staying here I have to get to know people . . . it would be odd if I did n't. With business on my hands . . . I can't well help it. And I 'm not a savage. I like to be civil and to go to people's houses if I 'm asked. Good! But can I enter a single one, Don Julián, without finding that girl there? Very well, then! I meet her . . . I greet her . . . as coldly as I can. It makes no odds. The rest of the company start to look at each other . . . and there 's a chair next to her . . . heaven knows how it gets there . . . in which no one else will sit . . . you 'd think it would bite them . . . and so I must. Well . . . when I 'm sitting near her I can't be so rude as not to speak to her. But

I 've only to open my mouth . . . and they all begin to talk among themselves . . . leaving the two of us as much alone as if we were on our honeymoon! What 's a man to do?

DON JULIÁN [*laughing*]. Come, come, come . . . don't make a mountain out of a molehill.

ADOLFO. Don Julián, I assure you . . . if you could see the looks . . . and the little smiles . . . and the nudges! If I take no notice of her, they say: "Why is he pretending not to notice her?" If I talk to her, then it' s: "There they are again . . . oh, it 's no use pretending!" If I walk down the street she lives in: "Poor fellow, he can't keep away from her." If I don't walk down it: "See . . . he knows when she 's not at home." And if I say one word to another woman it 's: "Now who 'll be jealous?" And the never ceasing flow of: "She has so much a year from her vineyards . . . and her uncle may do more for her." Every day and all day . . . from early morning till I go to bed at night! And let me tell you quite plainly that I can't stand it any longer.

DON JULIÁN. Well, there 's only one remedy I can see. You 'd better bolt. Women to men here . . . it 's five to one. What can we do? I could easier keep the fields dry under my umbrella than I could stop their tongues. But what does it all matter? Don't think about it.

ADOLFO. But something else has happened . . . far more serious.

DON JULIÁN. Oh! Well . . . out with it!

ADOLFO. Now whether this started in the club . . . or at the tobacconist's . . . or at that place where you sit round and talk while you have your boots blacked, I don't know. But somebody, it 's evident, has accused me of saying something offensive about her.

DON JULIÁN. Dear me, dear me . . . that is serious . . . that 's a bit serious. What is it they say you 've said?

ADOLFO. I don't know. But whatever it is . . . it 's not true. I 'm really ashamed to be troubling you about this.

DON JULIÁN. Better that I should hear of it than that she should.

ADOLFO. Ah . . . but she has heard of it. And she believes it of me. That's the worst.

DON JULIÁN. Are you sure?

ADOLFO. Well . . . three nights ago I met Señorita Juanita and her aunt at the Romeros'. When I walked into the room they got up as if they'd been moved by clockwork and walked away without a look at me. The next night at Concha Puerto's . . . the same thing happened. Yesterday, after Mass, they cut me dead. Well . . . whether I care a button for the girl or not I can't have her supposing I've said something about her which no gentleman would say. So I sat down and wrote her a few lines . . . in simple self-defence . . . assuring her that I am quite incapable of such a thing. She has never had them.

DON JULIÁN. How do you know?

ADOLFO. A note came this morning . . . not signed by any one . . . saying so.

DON JULIÁN. An anonymous letter! Come, you're not going to take any notice of that.

ADOLFO. But if she neither answers me nor stops cutting me I must notice it. The aunt, it appears, intercepted my letter. Forgive me . . . but that woman's a dreadful goose!

DON JULIÁN. A bit of a . . . yes, you might perhaps call her a bit of a goose.

ADOLFO. So here I am, my dear Don Julián, to beg you to do me a service . . . and to forgive me for asking it of you.

DON JULIÁN. I should n't forgive you if you did n't.

ADOLFO. Will you say what I've been prevented saying . . . and see that justice is done me?

DON JULIÁN. This very day.

ADOLFO. I'm deeply grateful. For if *I* can't have five minutes alone with her. . . .

DON JULIÁN. Oh . . . you'd prefer that?

ADOLFO. Why . . . if it could be managed with nobody about but you . . . why, yes.

DON JULIÁN. Good, my son, good. Very good!

He gets up and goes first to one door, then to the other.

ADOLFO. What's the matter?

DON JULIÁN. I thought Dieguilla might be listening. Well . . . you're in luck.

ADOLFO. How?

DON JULIÁN. You'll have your chat with Juanita . . . and with no one the wiser . . . with no one about but this old priest!

ADOLFO. Really?

DON JULIÁN. Yes. My little niece Pilar has been ill in bed this last day or two.

ADOLFO. I'm so sorry . . . I hadn't heard. . . .

DON JULIÁN. Oh, it's nothing . . . a cold in the head. But she's great friends with Juanita . . . who came yesterday and the day before to keep her company . . . came by herself. And if she comes to-day as well . . . and you happen to be here . . . why, there you are!

ADOLFO. D' you think she will?

DON JULIÁN. I feel sure she will. And if it's at the same time as yesterday . . . why, there you are again! For Santita and the girls are at their Rosary . . . or taking their siesta . . . or both. Well . . . in this heat one must relax a little. So what a chance!

ADOLFO. True. I hope it'll turn out as you say.

DON JULIÁN. Stay where you are. I'm going to put on my alpaca jacket . . . it's cooler. And I'll be back in a minute . . . half a minute.

ADOLFO. Very well. I'm deeply grateful to you.

DON JULIÁN. But my dear fellow, do you know . . .

ADOLFO. What?

DON JULIÁN. I believe you're not quite so indifferent as you were.

ADOLFO. Every bit . . . I assure you.

DON JULIÁN. Ah . . . you think an old priest knows nothing about such things. Not quite so indifferent, I think . . . not quite!

He goes out, leaving Adolfo to wait rather restlessly; though he tries to hide it even from himself. He paces the room. Then he looks at his watch.

ADOLFO. Past three . . . I 'm due at the Registrar's.

But he sits down and glances idly at the things on the table, at some photographs; and one of them, from his expression, might be hers. And at this moment Juanita — all in white, carrying her sunshade and fan, a charming figure — comes in. Naturally she never expects to find him there. Before he sees her she sees how he is occupied; and from her expression we are quite sure that the photograph is hers.

JUANITA. Oh!

At the sound Adolfo jumps up.

ADOLFO. Señorita.

JUANITA. Señor.

ADOLFO. This is great luck. How . . . how are you?

JUANITA. Thank you, I 'm very well. How are you?

ADOLFO. I was waiting to see you.

JUANITA. How did you know I was coming?

ADOLFO. I get to know all sorts of things.

JUANITA [*glancing at the photograph in his hand*]. With nothing better to do while you waited! Photographers always try to flatter me . . . and the result is it 's not a bit like. D' you think?

Quite fairly she lets him take a good look at her.

ADOLFO. Not one bit.

JUANITA. Whoever would have thought of your being here? I 'm on my way to ask after Pilar.

ADOLFO. No . . . one moment.

JUANITA. What?

ADOLFO. Please give me a moment first. I 've something to say to you.

JUANITA. Something so important?

ADOLFO. Yes, it is.

JUANITA. Then I 'll call Señora Santita or Don Julián. Because . . . well, we 're all alone here. But I really must go. Suppose some one came in.

ADOLFO. No one will come . . . they 're taking their siesta. Besides . . . really I 'm capable of behaving myself . . . for all the lies they 've been telling you about me! I do beg you to listen to me one instant. No, no one is coming. Listen . . . and I won't keep you long.

JUANITA. Well, I 'm listening . . . I 'm listening. I won't say " No " to the very first thing you ask me. To a stranger . . . it would n't be quite courteous, would it?

ADOLFO. Won't you sit down, then?

JUANITA. Oh . . . I don't think I ought to sit down. Is that really necessary?

ADOLFO. Even if it is n't . . . please sit down.

JUANITA. Very well. I was so surprised to see you here . . .!
So they both sit down, and he chooses a chair very near her.

ADOLFO. Señorita . . . your kindness to me now . . . after the way you 've been avoiding me lately . . . is, I do assure you, Señorita, a very great relief to me. I . . .
It 's the way things happen in this world. The sentence which our good friend Adolfo is beginning with such an air is cut short — and will be lost to us for ever — by the sudden arrival of Concha Puerto. There she stands in the doorway. She is carrying three or four parcels of things she has bought at the pastry-cook's. The sight of the pair so delights her that she bursts out laughing. Adolfo gives a violent start as if awakening from a dream; and even Juanita is more than a little upset.

ADOLFO. What 's that?

JUANITA. Concha Puerto!
Another outbreak from Concha Puerto.

ADOLFO. May I ask what this burst of merriment is meant to convey to us, Señora?

CONCHA. You may. It is meant to convey to you that I 'm quite delighted . . . that I always expected it . . . and that everything 's as it should be. That 's what it 's meant to convey. So don't let me disturb you.

ADOLFO. Señora, you will please allow me to explain.

JUANITA. Oh . . . please don't misunderstand.

CONCHA. I don't . . . and there 's nothing to explain . . . and I won't interrupt you one moment longer. I came to dip some sponge-cakes in wine for poor Pilar. They say it's a cure for a cold. It is n't . . . but what does that matter? It's very tasty. So I'm going straight to the kitchen. . . .

ADOLFO. Señora!

CONCHA. Not a word . . . not a word! I won't disturb you . . . I won't disturb you. . . .

She vanishes.

ADOLFO. That's done it. We shan't hear the last of this in a hurry. We shall be the laughing-stock of the whole place.

Juanita is fanning herself. If she is as agitated as her fan is . . .!

JUANITA. Yes . . . it looks like it.

ADOLFO. Of all the officious impertinent women . . .! What does she come poking her nose in here for? Why can't she dip her sponge-cakes in her own wine in her own kitchen? Why can't she stay indoors as every one else does at this time of day? Is n't it hot enough for her? Why need she come and find us here? Heaven knows now what she thinks . . . and Heaven only knows what she'll say!

JUANITA. I told you I did n't mean to stop a minute . . . and I ought n't to have stopped a single minute. It was most wrong of me. And I'm going now . . . this very minute.

ADOLFO. But what's the use of that? The mischief's done. Please don't go till you've answered my question. Did you get the letter I wrote you?

JUANITA. Not till this morning. I thought you'd guess that. My aunt never gave it to me till this morning.

ADOLFO. Do you believe what I said in it?

JUANITA. You had no need to say it. And by the look of things now . . . you'll have more right, I'm afraid, to complain of me than I of you.

ADOLFO. Not at all . . . not at all! But you've been turning your back on me when we met. . . .

JUANITA. But with things like this I've hardly known what to do. And my aunt's so unaccountable . . . and she magnifies everything so. . . .

ADOLFO. Well . . . as long as you did n't for one moment believe . . .

JUANITA. No . . . never for one moment.

ADOLFO. I hoped you would n't . . . I felt sure you could n't! But I wanted to make sure and to hear you say so. You can understand that, can't you?

Pilar's cold is a perfect magnet. The visitors it brings, and at such unlikely moments! Now it is Don Cecilio who comes suddenly through the porch, and can't repress an exclamation when he finds these two together.

DON CECILIO. Ye gods and little fishes!

Adolfo leaps to his feet.

ADOLFO. Now what is it?

DON CECILIO. It 's only I! No need to be alarmed!

ADOLFO. Well!! Well . . . how are things with you, my dear doctor?

DON CECILIO. How are they with you, my dear friend? No need to ask! Oh . . . an old fellow must n't complain! And how is this young lady? As pretty as ever! Well . . . I won't interrupt your little *tête-à-tête.*

JUANITA. But it is n't!

DON CECILIO. Is n't it? My mistake! [*To Adolfo under his breath.*] I told you so!

ADOLFO. What did you tell me?

DON CECILIO. You 've forgotten already.

ADOLFO. Oh, my very dear sir . . . you told me such a lot of things . . .

DON CECILIO. Come now . . . what did I tell you?

ADOLFO. Just at this moment, I really don't remember.

DON CECILIO. No . . . you would n't! But you will! My little patient 's waiting. Oh . . . the devil! History repeats itself . . . and there 's no help for it.

This last to himself as he goes off to his patient.

JUANITA. Our dear doctor . . . such a reputation for wit that he must keep it up at all costs! A very poor joke, I 'm sure!

ADOLFO. Very.

JUANITA. Still . . . I ought not to be here . . . and now you 've asked me what you wanted to ask me and I 've told you what you wanted to know. . . .

ADOLFO. Thank you . . . yes.

JUANITA. Then . . .

ADOLFO. No . . . I must n't keep you. Till we meet again.

JUANITA. Not for some time, I think.

ADOLFO. Till to-morrow?

JUANITA. Oh, not to-morrow!

ADOLFO. Then . . .

JUANITA. Until we do.

ADOLFO. Until we do.

JUANITA. Accidents will happen!

ADOLFO. For instance?

JUANITA. Our meeting now.

ADOLFO. Why, of course! Then I 'll hope for another.

Nor do they seem now to be in any great hurry to separate. And at this moment the sacristan of San Antonio appears in the doorway. He is an affected, sugary-voiced personage, and he carries a contraption, the top part of which is not a very flattering portrait of the saint; the lower half an alms box.

THE SACRISTAN. In the name of the blessed St. Anthony!

ADOLFO. What?

JUANITA. Oh . . . what 's this?

THE SACRISTAN. Place yourselves under the protection of the blessed St. Anthony!

JUANITA. He 's the sacristan. What 's to be done now?

ADOLFO [*searching his pockets.*] Here . . . for I 'm sure we need it. Here, my friend. . . .

He fetches out two pesetas; and at the sight of them, the sacristan's eyes round till they are like another two, and as bright and shining.

THE SACRISTAN. May the blessed St. Anthony shower blessings upon you . . . and upon your young lady too! Long life to you both . . . and happiness . . . and all your hearts desire!

He departs, ecstatic; and Adolfo and Juanita can only burst out laughing.

JUANITA.   How much did you give him?

ADOLFO.   Only two pesetas.

JUANITA.   Then we're lost! Two pesetas to St. Anthony! Every single soul in the town will hear of it.

Don Julián appears. He has put on his alpaca coat and is comfortable.

ADOLFO.   Don Julián. . . .

DON JULIÁN.   Hola! So the little lady did turn up!

JUANITA.   Oh, dear Don Julián!

DON JULIÁN.   Just this minute come? [*Guilelessly.*] When did she come?

ADOLFO.   You'd been gone just one minute when she came.

DON JULIÁN.   Good! And by the look of it you've had your talk . . . a bit of a talk . . . the sort of a talk you wanted.

ADOLFO.   Quite.

DON JULIÁN.   With nobody by . . . did n't I promise you? . . . not a soul the wiser!

ADOLFO.   Oh . . . nobody!

JUANITA.   Not a single soul!

And they both burst out laughing.

DON JULIÁN.   What's this? What are you laughing at? You don't mean to say . . . did anybody come?

JUANITA.   Concha Puerto dropped in. . . .

DON JULIÁN.   Holy Queen of Heaven!

JUANITA.   To dip some sponge-cakes in wine for Pilar.

DON JULIÁN.   Dear me now . . . and she told me last night she meant to. However did I come to forget that?

ADOLFO.   And Don Cecilio came in. . . .

DON JULIÁN.   Did he? Yes, of course . . . to see his patient. God bless my soul!

JUANITA.   And, for a finish, the sacristan of San Antonio dropped in too.

DON JULIÁN.   Holy St. Barbara . . . you don't say so! Why

. . . he 's the town crier. I 'm a duffer . . . I fear I 'm a bit
of a duffer. But it really looks as if it were the will of God.

ADOLFO. I expect it is!

Don Julián's eye travels towards the front door.

DON JULIÁN. But that 's all a trifle, though, to what 's coming
now.

JUANITA. Why . . . whatever 's coming now?

DON JULIÁN. Her Majesty, your aunt.

JUANITA. My aunt! [*Then she really rounds on Adolfo.*] This
is the last straw! How dare you get me into this mess?

ADOLFO. I . . . get you into . . . ?

JUANITA. Yes . . . you!

*Doña Belén arrives; she has quite lost her benevolent smile,
though.*

DOÑA BELÉN. Good afternoon.

DON JULIÁN. And to you, my daughter.

ADOLFO. Señora.

Doña Belén bows to him in frigid silence.

DON JULIÁN. So you 've dropped in to see our poor little Pilar.
No?

DOÑA BELÉN. Yes. But I 'd first like a few words with you,
Father. . . . (*she turns from the chair he offers her*) in private.

DON JULIÁN. By all means. Come into the drawing-room.

ADOLFO. I 'll be off.

DON JULIÁN. No, no . . . no, no!

ADOLFO. I really must be . . . I 've an appointment . . . I
shall be late for it.

DON JULIÁN. Very well, then.

JUANITA. We 've been having such a pleasant talk . . . all
three of us.

DOÑA BELÉN. So the sacristan of San Antonio has just informed
me.

*It is doubtless a hot afternoon, but with this, the temperature
seems to drop five degrees.*

JUANITA. Oh, yes . . . the sacristan did drop in, did n't
he?

DOÑA BELÉN. Silence, Juanita, if you please. And as for **you**, Señor . . . may I say two words to you before you go?

ADOLFO. By all means.

DOÑA BELÉN. When a gentleman . . .

JUANITA. Aunt!

DOÑA BELÉN. When a gentleman . . .

DON JULIÁN. Now, my dear Doña Belén . . .

DOÑA BELÉN. When a gentleman, I repeat, wishes to have a talk with a young lady . . . whether he is very particularly interested in that young lady or no . . . let us, for the moment, ignore mere gossip! . . . then, as I take it, the first thing a gentleman will do is to ask permission of the person or persons who exercise paternal or maternal authority over the young lady. Am I wrong?

ADOLFO. May I, in my turn, say two words to you, Señora?

DOÑA BELÉN. Nothing prevents you.

ADOLFO. When a gentleman finds that his credit with a young lady needs restoring because those who are exercising paternal or maternal authority over her have . . inadvertently no doubt . . . permitted and encouraged the spread of slanders about his conduct towards her . . . what is he to do? He will go, I think, to his kindest and wisest friend for advice. And if, by good luck . . . by the very happiest of chances . . . he finds her there, he will take that opportunity of telling her the truth and of righting himself in her eyes. He owes that much to his self-respect and to his respect for her. Nor in this house, I suggest, need he be suspected of having failed in either. I have the honour to wish you, Señora, a very good day. Till we meet again, Don Julián. Señorita.

> *And with a bow to Juanita he is gone. Doña Belén stands there hissing as if it were she that had just finished making the speech . . . such a speech!*

JUANITA. There . . . you see, Aunt . . . you see! That's the sort of snub you get.

DOÑA BELÉN. Snub! Snub!! Simply and solely out of consideration for Don Julián I did not answer that young man as he deserved. Oh yes, they're glib enough . . . these briefless

barristers! But they don't hoodwink me! And as to you . . .
go and see Pilar . . . since that's what brought you here . . .
so you tell me!

JUANITA. Yes . . . that is what brought me here.

*She goes, with just a glance at Don Julián as if she hoped
that he at least would take her part. But, once she has gone,
behold, Doña Belén's smile returns.*

DOÑA BELÉN. Well . . . come now! Tell me all about it.

DON JULIÁN. My dear lady . . . you seem to have heard all
about it. The young man comes to see me. I go to put on my
jacket. Your young woman arrives . . . by chance, quite by
chance. They pass the time of day. He's an excellent young
man.

DOÑA BELÉN. No doubt. But now you'd better tell me exactly
in what his excellencies consist . . . for when young women for
whom I'm responsible take to passing the time of day with young
men, I like to know . . . well, exactly what o'clock it is.

DON JULIÁN. You're right . . . you're right. . . .

*Concha Puerto, a cooking apron on, her sleeves turned up,
dashes in from the kitchen in a great state of mind.*

CONCHA. What has happened? What's gone wrong? Why is
Don Adolfo dashing down the garden like a lunatic?

*The words are n't out of her mouth when Santita and Ángela
appear too . . . also in a great state of mind.*

ÁNGELA. What is it . . . what has happened? How do
you do?

SANTITA. What has happened? How are you, Belén? What
has happened?

DOÑA BELÉN. Nothing has happened . . . and good afternoon
to you both. Nothing has happened, as I think, Father.

DON JULIÁN. Nothing at all. Though I must own I consider
this good lady is a bit severe . . . just a bit too rigorous with
our Juanita. We're not still in the dark ages, you know.

SANTITA. Eh? What's that?

CONCHA. He thinks Doña Belén is being a bit hard on
Juanita.

SANTITA.   Does he?   Would you like to know what I think? She knows more ways of catching a fish than whistling to it.

And at this everybody laughs.   Even Doña Belén does not lose her smile, though she crosses herself with an " Ay, ay, ay !"

SANTITA.   Well, I 'd say it behind your back and I say it to your face . . . and I 'm going to tell Juanita so, what 's more . . . to stop her crying.

Santita departs.

DOÑA BELÉN.   Dear Santita!   There 's no one like her.   You never know what she 'll say next.   Come along, Father . . . let 's have a look at the little patient.   And we 'll finish our talk besides.

DON JULIÁN.   Yes, yes . . . yes, yes!

DOÑA BELÉN.   Dear Santita . . . no one like her!

DON JULIÁN.   Nobody like her . . . for putting things plump and plain.

They depart together laughing over " Dear Santita."

CONCHA.   Yes . . . your mother hit that nail on the head.

ÁNGELA.   Did n't she?   I 'll go and tell Pilar.

CONCHA.   Oh, that Belén.   She 's a deep one!   Oh, she 's a slyboots.   And Adolfo . . . dashing down the garden . . . in such a state!   She 's right . . . he 'll be dashing back again before you can say knife.

Pepe Lora now appears in the porch . . . surlier than ever.

ÁNGELA.   Concha!

CONCHA.   What is it?

ÁNGELA.   Look . . . Pepe Lora!

CONCHA [*with bland surprise*].   Why, Pepe Lora . . . is that you?

PEPE.   Don't you know me when you see me?   Good day, Angelita.

ÁNGELA.   Good day, Pepe Lora.   Well, what 's the news?

PEPE.   Yesterday 's past and to-morrow 's coming.

CONCHA.   Is it indeed?   Fancy that.   But what has brought you here, is what Ángela would like to know.

PEPE.   My feet.

ÁNGELA.   How subtle we 're getting!

PEPE. Well . . . is the evening paper about?

CONCHA. Yes, that's a good safe opening. Oh, don't stand shuffling there. What bee is in your bonnet now?

PEPE. Bee . . . I should say so! When he's buzzing round . . . yes, that sacristan is . . . telling every one how he found that fellow from Madrid here making love to Juanita. I want to know if it's true.

ÁNGELA. But you see it is n't. They're not here . . . either of them.

PEPE. Then I'll go back and break that sacristan's head for him. That's what I'll do!

CONCHA. Well, I would n't exactly break it. They're not here now . . . but they were!

PEPE. Oh, they were . . . were they?

CONCHA. Having a very happy time together. And I daresay they did n't miss you.

PEPE. So that's how it is! Dress like a dandy and talk a lot of soft romantic nonsense . . . and all the women go mad about you!

ÁNGELA. What soft romantic nonsense?

PEPE. Out of books . . . poetry and such! She's always at it too. Verses! I'll put a full stop to their verses, so I will.

CONCHA. What's this . . . what's this?

PEPE. I'll go now and break that Madrid fellow's head for him. That's what I'll do!

ÁNGELA. Heavens above us . . . that's two broken heads to begin with.

PEPE. Well . . . you know the sort of man I am.

CONCHA. I know the sort of man you think you are.

PEPE. Oh, no, Señora . . . I don't think. I went courting Juanita . . . did n't I! And first she would and then she would n't . . . would she? Was that fair? Am I to let her make a fool of me like that? No . . . you'll see if I will.

ÁNGELA. But Heavens above us! Suppose you don't attract her any longer?

PEPE. Attract her! Sentimental rubbish!

ÁNGELA.   Pepe, she was never meant for you.

PEPE.   Rubbish!

ÁNGELA.   And there's a girl in the town now just breaking her heart about you.

PEPE.   No, you don't take me in with any romantic rubbish!

CONCHA.   Don't waste time talking to him, Ángela.   Whatever does n't mean his breaking some one's head is silly romantic rubbish.

ÁNGELA.   Yes, it's a waste of time talking to you.

PEPE.   If you'd both had the letter I had yesterday morning . . .!

ÁNGELA.   Who from?

PEPE.   An anonymous letter.

CONCHA.   Dear me . . . has some one sent you an anonymous letter?   Well, I never!

PEPE.   Yes, they have.   And you never saw such a letter! It made me see red, I tell you!   I'd meant to take no notice of those two . . . so I had.   But after that letter . . .!

CONCHA.   That letter did the trick!

PEPE.   If I can find out who wrote it, Señora . . . I'll break his head.

CONCHA.   Mother of Mercy, we'd better be on our good behaviour . . . or we may have all our beauty spoilt!

ÁNGELA.   But what was in the letter?

PEPE.   I'll tell you.

CONCHA.   Oh . . . you've brought it with you?

PEPE.   Yes . . . I have brought it with me.

He takes the letter from his pocket.

PEPE.   "Good morning, Pepe Lora."   What a way to begin! And how dare he wish me good morning?

ÁNGELA.   It came by the first post, I suppose.

PEPE.   "Who said that Juanita La Rosa should never never never have another sweetheart?   Well, she has got one."

ÁNGELA.   To think that there are people who'll write things like this!

PEPE.   You wait!   "But your bark is worse than your bite, it seems." Is it? "If you don't mind being laughed at of course it does n't matter. But if you mean to sit down under this what can people think but that you 're a perfect pol . . . pol . . . pol. . . ."

CONCHA. Poltroon.

PEPE. How do you know?

CONCHA. "Poltroon" . . . it 's quite plain.

Concha has taken the letter from him — to make sure of the word apparently. Ángela catches her eye though, and they smile at each other meaningly and mischievously.

PEPE. What 's a poltroon?

CONCHA. It 's a kind of coward, I think.

PEPE. A coward, am I? Well . . . why does n't the man who wrote that show his face?

CONCHA. Why should he . . . if you mean to spoil it for him?

ÁNGELA. I should n't be a little bit surprised, Pepe Lora, if the person who wrote that letter just wanted you to make yourself unpleasant to this fine gentleman from Madrid . . . and thought that 'd only make him fall more in love with Juanita than ever.

CONCHA. Do you think it would? Well, of course it might.

PEPE. What 's that romantic nonsense? Well . . . whatever they wanted, the next time I do meet that fine gentleman I 'll knock the romance out of him and all his like, so I will . . . with just one knock and a half. I 'll let him see if I 'm a pol . . . pol . . . whatever it was . . . or not! And my bark 's worse than my bite, is it? Is it?

At this moment Adolfo — most opportunely — returns.

ADOLFO. Good afternoon to you.

ÁNGELA. My gracious!

PEPE. Good afternoon.

CONCHA. Back again, Don Adolfo?

ADOLFO. Yes . . . though I left such a turmoil that I was n't sure I 'd better . . .! Why . . . what 's the matter now?

PEPE. Very shortly. . . .

ADOLFO. I beg your pardon?

PEPE. . . . we shall see . . . what we shall see.

ADOLFO. Might I ask who you are?

PEPE. You may have heard of me. I am Pepe Lora.

ADOLFO. That, I feel sure, explains everything. You are Pepe Lora.

CONCHA. Yes . . . he is Pepe Lora.

ÁNGELA. Pepe Lora.

ADOLFO. Well . . . my name 's Adolfo Adalid.

PEPE. I want one word with you.

ADOLFO. You 've already had several.

PEPE. There are too many people present.

ADOLFO. If you think so . . . suppose you make them fewer.

CONCHA. Don Adolfo . . . please . . . please!

PEPE. Yes . . . I will make them fewer. I want a word with you alone.

ADOLFO. Wherever you please.

PEPE. And with no interruptions.

ADOLFO. For as long as you like.

PEPE. There 's a reading-room at the Club . . . no one 's ever there.

ADOLFO. Excellent!

PEPE. And then we can settle . . . on another place to meet.

ADOLFO. Capital.

PEPE. I 'll be there in five minutes.

ADOLFO. I 'll be there in six.

PEPE. Good afternoon.

CONCHA. Good afternoon.

PEPE. Romantic rubbish! I 'll show 'em!

Pepe departs.

ÁNGELA. I must tell Pilar . . . I must tell Pilar . . . I must tell Pilar at once!

She runs away to do so.

ADOLFO. Now what harm have I done to him . . . the sulky booby!

CONCHA. He can't be jealous of you by any chance? It can't be anything to do with Juanita?

ADOLFO. Jealous of me! Why in heaven's name should he be? The man's a lunatic. He should n't be left at large.

CONCHA. Don Adolfo . . . what ever is happening to you? You're not yourself at all.

ADOLFO. Oh, dear me! He's not your nephew or your cousin or anything like that, is he?

CONCHA. Pepe Lora! God forbid!

ADOLFO. Quite so! I'd say the same. I'm sorry. But everybody seems to be somebody's cousin or nephew in this town! *Don Cecilio, on his way out, comes from the left.*

DON CECILIO. Hola! Hola! So you're still here!

ADOLFO. No, Señor.

DON CECILIO. I beg your pardon . . . you are still here.

ADOLFO. I am not still here. I've been away . . . I'm back.

DON CECILIO. Oh . . . worse and worse!

ADOLFO. What do you mean by "worse and worse"?

DON CECILIO. What should I mean?

ADOLFO. Who knows if you don't?

DON CECILIO. Showing temper besides! That's worst of all.

ADOLFO. Why should n't I come back, may I ask . . . to see Don Julián?

DON CECILIO. To see Don Julián?

ADOLFO. Yes . . . to see Don Julián!

DON CECILIO. Prevarication too! That's a sure sign. Poor wretch, you're lost . . . you're lost! A fly caught in the web . . . a lamb led to the slaughter! The women have their way!

CONCHA. And luckier for him they do than if you had yours.

ADOLFO. Because you were a fly and a lamb and the rest of it, you've made up your mind that I'm going to be! Have n't *I* a mind to make up? I'm a rational being, I suppose.

DON CECILIO. We all like to suppose that. All right, Concha . . . all right! I'm off. I leave him to your tender mercies. I've a patient who's very ill indeed . . . there's to be a consultation. Well . . . between us we may just be able to save the poor fellow. But you're past praying for, even. I leave him to you, Concha. Good afternoon.

CONCHA.   Good afternoon.

ADOLFO.   Good luck!

DON CECILIO [*to himself, as he goes*].   He'll be bull-fighting for them next, I dare say!

Don Cecilio disappears, laughing rather grimly.

CONCHA.   What turns that gentleman sour is that his home is a perfect freak show.   His wife's as ugly as sin and his daughters are frumps.   D'you know what we call them?   The bargain counters!   We're very good at nicknames here.

ADOLFO.   Please . . . please . . . tell me no more of this town's tittle-tattle!   There's just one thing I want to ask. . . .

CONCHA.   Well . . . then now's your time, I think.   Yes . . . now's your time!   Oh . . . my wine will be boiling . . . if I don't go.   But I'll be back.   I'll be back.

She has glanced through the glass door; some one is coming. She vanishes . . . and as she vanishes Juanita appears.

ADOLFO.   Juanita!

JUANITA.   Oh . . . Angelita told me Concha Puerto wanted me.

ADOLFO.   I am much obliged to her for her very kind mistake!

JUANITA.   Are you?   Then I'm not.   Will you please be off this very minute . . . if you don't want my aunt to find us and start scolding me again!

ADOLFO.   I'll be off . . . this very minute!   Don't be afraid.

JUANITA.   Then go . . . go . . . go!   There's the door.   Once we start talking we shall go on talking . . . as we did before.

ADOLFO.   Did you mind that?

JUANITA.   I've been made to mind!   My aunt is very, very cross with me.

ADOLFO.   But you're not sorry for anything you said to me, are you?

JUANITA.   I shall be sorry I ever saw you if you don't go away.

ADOLFO.   No . . . don't say that!   I'm going.   You tell me to go . . . I go!

JUANITA.   But you don't go!

ADOLFO.   Well . . . the fact is . . . now I see you again . . .

there 's something else I want to know.   I went off before without
asking you . . . so let me ask you now.

JUANITA.   Something you want to know?

ADOLFO.   Very much.

JUANITA.   About me?

ADOLFO.   Of course.

JUANITA.   Well, ask away . . . if that 's the quickest way of
getting rid of you.

ADOLFO.   Do you write coplas?   Is it true you do?

JUANITA.   Really . . . really . . . really! You could have
asked that without making so much fuss about it, I should think!

ADOLFO.   Well, do you?

JUANITA.   What business is it of yours?

ADOLFO.   But it 's so charming of you to write coplas!

JUANITA.   Indeed!

ADOLFO.   I did n't know girls did write coplas.

JUANITA.   Well . . . I happen to know a good many coplas.
And at times . . . when I 'm feeling very happy . . . or when
I 'm not feeling very happy . . . and at other times . . . well,
I may write a copla.   Just to please myself.   They come to me.

ADOLFO.   Say one over to me.

JUANITA.   Certainly not.

ADOLFO.   Why not?

JUANITA.   They 're very silly.

ADOLFO.   I 'm quite sure they 're not.

JUANITA.   And I 'm quite sure they are.   How can you tell?
Besides . . . I don't remember any now.

ADOLFO.   Try.

JUANITA.   You make me feel such a fool.

>   I care — for whom I do not care to say,
>   Yet without saying I am saying it;
>   My heart is full of joy I cannot name,
>   Yet without naming I am naming it.

ADOLFO [*apprehensive, but not altogether unpleasantly*].   That 's
a charming copla.

JUANITA.   You like it?

ADOLFO. Yes, indeed!

JUANITA. It is n't mine. It 's a real copla.

ADOLFO. Now for one of yours, then . . . please!

JUANITA. When I 've said a real one I don 't feel quite so shy. Can I think of one of mine, now, that 's not so bad as it might be?

ADOLFO. Try! Try!

JUANITA. Pass no more under my window,
        For the neighbours are always spying.
        I never pass before your house,
        Yet there I am ever abiding.

ADOLFO. [apprehensions forgotten]. Far better than the real one.

JUANITA. I 'm greatly obliged. But I fear I knew you 'd say so.

ADOLFO. Really?

JUANITA. It 's only polite to say so. And who is politer than you?

ADOLFO. I 'm not being polite.

JUANITA. No? No! Oh . . . if you won't be off . . . I will! Good-bye . . . good-bye!

ADOLFO. Just one second more!

JUANITA. With a thousand regrets, Señor . . . I have no more seconds to spare!

ADOLFO. When did you write that copla?

JUANITA. When? What a catechism! One can see you 're a lawyer.

ADOLFO. How?

JUANITA. And is n't that what is called a leading question?

ADOLFO. Won't you please answer it?

JUANITA. No, I won't. But . . . for the last time . . . will you please go away?

ADOLFO. I 'm going . . . I 'm going . . . I 've said a dozen times that I 'm going. I don't want to go. Here we are together . . . at last . . . the two of us . . . and no one to disturb us. That 's as it should be. I can really look at you at last . . . and talk to you. I 've been longing for a look at you . . . a real look. I suppose that surprises you . . . or does n't it? But of course . . . no! . . . it does n't. Well, I can't help it! I can't help myself . . . that's the truth! They've got their way. It has turned out as they said it would. But please understand . . . please do believe I don't feel about you . . . as I do feel . . . just because they said I should. We won't give them their way . . . because it's their way. I don't know how this has happened or when it began. But I do know that I don't want to go away . . . to go away from you. And I won't, what's more! I won't.

JUANITA. Oh . . . Adolfo . . . please . . . !

ADOLFO. Have n't you . . . anything at all . . . of the same sort of feeling for me? When did you write that copla? Before ever you saw me?

JUANITA. I can't tell you. That is . . . I'd very much rather not tell you.

ADOLFO. But I want to know! And I've a great many other things to ask you . . . which I can't ask you here . . . with heaven knows how many people getting ready to drop in. Is n't there a single place in this town where we can have a really quiet talk?

Concha Puerto has come back just in time to overhear.

CONCHA. Yes . . . there's my lattice window! My dear young man . . . I've been offering you that window ever since you came here.

ADOLFO. Your lattice window?

CONCHA. You might have the grace to remember that the very first thing I did was to offer you that lattice window.

ADOLFO. But of course I remember! It has a moon shining down on it . . . and there's a fountain somewhere near . . . and there's the smell of the jasmine! I remember perfectly. But what has Juanita to say to it?

JUANITA. Juanita has nothing to say. I sit in the window . . . and you stand outside . . . and we talk. That's the custom. And it's quite . . . without prejudice! Is n't that how a lawyer puts it? I shall ask my aunt, of course.

ADOLFO. When will you be in that window?

CONCHA. You be outside that window at ten o'clock to-night . . . and ask no more questions.

ADOLFO.   Juanita?

JUANITA.   I think we might leave it to Concha to settle.   She 's so kind.

ADOLFO.   Till to-night.

CONCHA.   Any complaints of me now?

ADOLFO.   Not one!   Ten o'clock.

CONCHA.   Ten o'clock.

JUANITA.   About ten.

Adolfo goes off, ready for that appointment with Pepe Lora, or for anything else.

CONCHA.   I should so liked to have asked him if he 's been in love with you from the beginning . . . or if we did drive him into it.   But one must be tactful.

Ángela returns.

ÁNGELA.   Pilar thought that most amusing.   Has the young man from Madrid departed?

CONCHA.   Yes, he has departed.   But look what he 's left behind him . . . look at her!

ÁNGELA.   What has happened . . . what has happened?

JUANITA.   Nothing whatever has happened.   But if my aunt approves. . . .

CONCHA.   She 'll approve!

JUANITA.   I may sit for a little in Concha's window this evening . . . and he may come there for a talk.

ÁNGELA.   Bless you . . . oh, bless you!   I 'm so glad . . . I 'm so glad . . . I 'm so glad!   And I 'll go and tell Pilar this very minute . . . and she 'll be so glad.   For whatever people say of us . . . they can't say we 're jealous.   And after all . . . there is only one of him!

JUANITA.   Thank you, dear Angela . . . thank you for being glad.

She walks up and down.   And she looks prettier than ever. Ángela whispers to Concha Puerto.

ÁNGELA.   Concha Puerto.

CONCHA.   What is it?

ÁNGELA.   That letter to Pepe Lora . . . did you write it?

CONCHA. Of course I did. A young man from Madrid walking about with his cold-blooded nose in the air . . . he had to have some sort of a pin stuck in him. But nothing 'll come of that. They 're probably hobnobbing by now over a glass of wine. You know what men are!

ÁNGELA. I must tell Pilar.

CONCHA. But what 's the matter with her?

For Juanita is still pacing up and down, deeply cogitating, apparently.

ÁNGELA. Juanita.

JUANITA. Sh!

CONCHA. What is it?

JUANITA. Sh, please! I 've thought of a copla.

ÁNGELA. Let 's hear.

JUANITA. Wait a minute . . . I have n't quite got it.

They wait a minute.

JUANITA. Now I 've got it.

ÁNGELA. Say it then.

CONCHA. Say it.

JUANITA. Man to a sailing-boat I liken,
Without a chart his course he loses,
And woman, like the wind, then blows him
Towards whatever port she chooses.

A Hundred Years Old

(El Centenario)

(1909)

ACT II

EULALIA.

Even as the birds in spring--time Sing of the sor-rows of lo----ving

So I this jo-ta am sing--ing To comfort me in my sad---ness.

ANTOÑÓN.

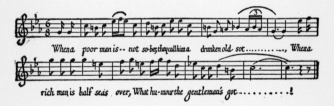

When a poor man is-- not so-ber, they call him a drunken old sot..........., When a

rich man is half seas over, What hu--mour the gentleman's got..........!

PAPÁ JUAN.

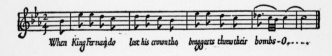

When King Fernando lost his crown, the braggarts threw their bombs - O,.....

ACT III

THE SONGS HEARD IN THE GARDEN

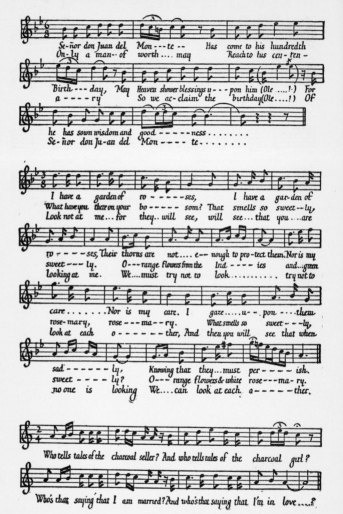

Se-ñor don Juan del Mon---te -- Has come to his hundredth
On-ly a man of worth.... may Reach to his cen--ten-

Birth---day, May Heaven shower blessings u---pon him (Ole....!) For
a----ry So we ac-claim the birthday(Ole....!) Of

he has sown wisdom and good------ness........
Se-ñor don Ju-an del Mon---- te........

I have a garden of ro------ses, I have a gar-den of
What have you there on your bo------som? That smells so sweet--ly,
Look not at me...for they.. will see, will see... that you....are

ro------ses, Their thorns are not.... e--nough to pro-tect them. Nor is my
sweet---ly. O---range flowers from the Ind----ies and...green
looking at me. We....must try not to look........... try not to

care........Nor is my care. I gaze.....u--pon....them
rose-mary, rose--ma--ry. What smells so sweet---ly,
look at each o------ther, And then you will see that when

sad------ly, Knowing that they...must per----ish.
sweet----ly? O---range flowers & white rose---ma--ry.
no one is looking We....can look at each a-----ther.

Who tells tales of the charcoal seller? And who tells tales of the charcoal girl?

Who's that saying that I am married? And who's that saying that I'm in love.....?

The little wi-dow little wi - - - dow..... The little wi—
I do not love the Count de Cab - - ra..... The Count de Cab —

— dow they want to... wed To the Count de Cab- m Count de Cab - - ra
— ra ah......poor me! I... do not love the Count de Cab - - ra

To the Count de Cab - - - ra she'll be led..........
The Count de Cab - - - ra but on - - - ly thee..........

A - - ve ma-ris stella......, De-i Ma — ter al ma,

At-que semper Vir-go......., Fe-lix cae-li por-- ta.

THE PEOPLE IN THE PLAY

CURRITA.
DOÑA MARCIALA.
DOÑA FILOMENA.
EULALIA.
CARMEN CAMPOS.
ROSA.

PAPÁ JUAN.
TRINO.
DON EVARISTO.
ANTOÑÓN.
ALONSO.
MANUEL.

A HUNDRED YEARS OLD

ACT I

*The action passes in the small Andalusian town of Arenales del Río
and in a room of Papá Juan's house there. At the back three
arches resting on marble columns lead into a gay flowering
garden. Across each of them can be drawn a light transparent
curtain. There is a door on the right and another on the left.
The furniture is more or less modern, and it is very well cared
for. Everything in the room seems to have its place and to be
in it. The floor is of polished mosaic. The walls are half-
tiled and a few good pictures hang on them.*

It is a morning in May.

*From the garden come Manuel and Carmen Campos. He is one of
the men servants; the coachman among other things. When
she was younger she was in service here too.*

MANUEL. Wait here, Carmen Campos, and I'll tell the Señora.

CARMEN. But say I'm in no hurry.

MANUEL. What's that?

CARMEN. Say I'm in no hurry.

MANUEL. Oh!

*With this grunt he goes out to the left. Carmen Campos, left
alone, looks around open-mouthed.*

CARMEN. Why . . . if you could n't eat off the floor! As neat
as a new pin she'd always have everything . . . would Doña
Marciala.

Manuel returns.

MANUEL. The Señora's coming.

CARMEN. But really I'm in no hurry.

MANUEL. God be with you, Carmen Campos.

CARMEN. And with you, Manuel Paez.

After which exchange of compliments Manuel goes out through the garden. A moment later Doña Marciala comes from the left, a lady of sixty-five, well preserved, benevolent, calm.

DOÑA MARCIALA. Well . . . and how are you, Carmen Campos?

CARMEN. God's blessing on you, Doña Marciala. Are you well?

DOÑA MARCIALA. Very well . . . thank God!

CARMEN. And the old master . . . and the young master?

DOÑA MARCIALA. Both well, thank you.

Her eye falls upon a dead leaf lying on the floor. She picks it up and throws it out of the window.

DOÑA MARCIALA. And Pepilla's this moment told me she's done the room. And look here!

CARMEN. The wind will blow them in, Señora.

DOÑA MARCIALA. I know that wind! These maids grow more slovenly every day. Ah . . . things were different in your time. Sit down.

CARMEN. Thank you, Señora. You're very kind, Señora.

DOÑA MARCIALA. Well . . . can you guess what I want you for?

CARMEN. Why . . . I don't say I can't, Señora. For every one's talking about it in Arenales.

DOÑA MARCIALA. They would be! Still . . . it's no secret.

CARMEN. About the old master's birthday.

DOÑA MARCIALA. That's it. And we'll have to turn the whole house topsy-turvy in honour of it. Next Thursday week will be his hundredth birthday . . . and he means to make a day of it indeed.

CARMEN. Only fancy . . . his hundredth! Why, that's a century, isn't it?

DOÑA MARCIALA. Yes . . . a whole century!

CARMEN. Who'd ever think it . . . to see him walking about the streets as he does!

DOÑA MARCIALA. You should see him at home here. He's livelier than I am . . . and far livelier than the young master!

CARMEN. They say his brother's coming from Madrid . . . though he must be very old.

DOÑA MARCIALA. Yes, he 's pretty old. But he means to come. My sister is coming from Granada . . . with her children . . . and her grandchildren. The Señora Carolina 's coming . . . you remember her . . . and her two daughters . . . they 're both married. There 'll be the old master's three cousins . . . with their families. And I don't know how many more. So from now till it 's over we shan't know where we are.

CARMEN. What a din there 'll be! You 'll be driven mad, Señora.

DOÑA MARCIALA. It won't worry me. But the Señor . . . the young master . . . he wants things to go like clock work . . . and he 's getting so fussed! Only this morning, my father gets up and gets dressed and because the Señorita Currita is n't here and ready to go out with him . . . at this hour! . . . he wants to go over and fetch her.

CARMEN. That 's his granddaughter?

DOÑA MARCIALA. No . . . she 's his great-granddaughter . . . Señor Joaquín's daughter. He 's forty and more now, you know.

CARMEN. Glory be to God . . . and I still think of him playing at bull-fights!

DOÑA MARCIALA. And those two . . . for Currita 's up to any mischief and he 's like a child about this birthday of his . . . are getting themselves into such a tangle of invitations and letters and telegrams! He thinks of some one who 's been left out . . . and Currita must come along and write the letter for him . . . and you hear them laughing over it . . . just like a couple of children. The other day he remembered he 'd a cousin in South America and he wanted to cable to him to come. . . .

CARMEN [crossing herself]. Think of that now!

DOÑA MARCIALA. Where are we to put them all, I 'd like to know . . . though you 'd think this house was large enough. Some can go to my brother's . . . and Joaquín can take a few. . . .

CARMEN. Only think!

DOÑA MARCIALA. The question is . . . can you and your girls come and help us out here?

CARMEN. But of course we can, Señora . . . if you want us.

. . . under my very eyes. And look at me. I'm as strong as a horse.

Doña Marciala returns with the brush.

DOÑA MARCIALA. Here you are . . . here's your whisk brush. Tyrant!

DON EVARISTO. Tyrant! When if I so much as open my mouth . . .!

DOÑA MARCIALA. If little things like this are going to fuss you what'll you do when the time comes?

CARMEN. And the real turmoil begins?

DON EVARISTO. I know . . . don't talk of it! Not a single soul has turned up yet . . . and look!

DOÑA MARCIALA. Now what's wrong?

DON EVARISTO. Well . . . look!

CARMEN. But what's the matter, Señor?

DON EVARISTO. Look at my shoes, Marciala! They've not been cleaned since Saturday . . . and this is Monday! What's wrong? You may well ask! Did you ever in your life, Carmen Campos, see me with shoes like this? And where's that leaf from my calendar?

DOÑA MARCIALA. On the bookcase by the window.

DON EVARISTO. Well, I'm sure I hope it is. Good-bye, Carmen Campos.

CARMEN. God be with you, Señor don Evaristo.

Don Evaristo returns whence he came.

DOÑA MARCIALA. You see! And every day he finds something fresh to worry about. Well . . . the older we get the more crotchety we grow! And he's an old man now.

CARMEN. But he always was a little fussy.

DOÑA MARCIALA. How d' you find him? When did you see him last?

CARMEN. He seems very well.

DOÑA MARCIALA. I know . . . he seems so. But when I lie awake at night and listen to his coughing. . . .!

CARMEN. But all gentlemen at his age have their little coughs and such, Señora.

DOÑA MARCIALA. I 'm not happy about him. One must face the inevitable, of course. The odd thing is he thinks I 'm the one that is failing. And as it happens I 'm very well . . . twice the woman I was ten years ago.

CARMEN. You don't need to tell me, Señora. I 'd never guess your age. You 'll keep your hundredth birthday too . . . like the old master.

DOÑA MARCIALA. I think not, Carmen . . . and I rather hope not. Here he is, though . . . with his hundred years on his back.

CARMEN. He 's a sight for sore eyes.

It is indeed Don Juan del Campo (Papá Juan as his family call him), who comes in from the right. He has his hat in his hand and he carries a stout stick, though he hardly needs, it seems, to lean on it. He moves with energy, as if his feet gripped the ground he trod. His clothes are formal and plain and they hang loose on him, for the body within them is shrunken. But even yet the embers of the fires of his youth glow in his eyes.

PAPÁ JUAN. Has n't Currita come yet?

DOÑA MARCIALA. Not yet.

PAPÁ JUAN. Snoring still, I 'll be bound! Never knew such a little lazy bones.

CARMEN. God be with you, Señor don Juan.

PAPÁ JUAN. And with you, Carmen Campos. Hey! [*This stands for a little chuckle that he gives from time to time.*] He has been with me for a pretty long spell, has n't he? And what are you doing here? Are your girls coming to lend us a hand?

CARMEN. We 're all coming, Señor don Juan. Señora Marciala never forgets us.

PAPÁ JUAN. That 's right . . . you 'll be wanted! Look here, Marciala. [*He fetches a letter from his pocket.*] Raphael 's got leave from his chief . . . so he 'll be here with his little flock.

DOÑA MARCIALA. Little flock? Little swarm!

PAPÁ JUAN. No . . . only a dozen of them. Carmen Campos . . . you won't know the place. Grandchildren and great-grand-children alone . . . we could sit down forty-five! And from thirty months old to thirty! There'll be one granddaughter missing . . . and I'm very vexed about it.

CARMEN.   Which of them is it, Señor?

PAPÁ JUAN.   Josefina . . . and she's my godchild as well. And they won't let her leave her convent for a single day. It's only four years since she professed . . . silly child, what did she do it for? . . . and now they won't let her out . . . not for one day.

DOÑA MARCIALA.   Why, of course they won't, Papá! What ideas you have!

PAPÁ JUAN.   But not for one single day? She'll never have another chance . . . and so I wrote to the little goose. For though I mean to live to be two hundred . . . by that time the rest of you will all be dead. Hey! So I must have my family party while I can.

At which they all three laugh.

PAPÁ JUAN.   Well . . . I mustn't stop dawdling here. If Currita's not out of bed yet she'll get a touch of my stick.

DOÑA MARCIALA.   Won't you let Evaristo go with you?

PAPÁ JUAN.   No, I won't. I want no decrepit old men hanging round me. Hey!

And off he goes through the garden, laughing still.

DOÑA MARCIALA.   Well . . . it's only across the street.

CARMEN.   Isn't he a wonder?

DOÑA MARCIALA.   Yes . . . but I wish this birthday were over. The excitement's very bad for him . . . and he thinks of nothing else. His garden . . . his birds . . . he's forgotten their existence. And from morning till night he's on the go. Is he back again?

She has heard steps in the garden.   Carmen Campos goes to see.

CARMEN.   No, Señora. It's Señora Filomena.

DOÑA MARCIALA.   My sister-in-law?

CARMEN.   And her eldest with her.

DOÑA MARCIALA.   She'll be the death of me!

CARMEN.   When shall I send the girls, Señora?

DOÑA MARCIALA.   As soon as you like.

CARMEN. That 'll be my Carmen . . . and my Andrea. What a treat for them! It was good of you to think of it, Señora.

DOÑA MARCIALA. That 's settled, then. Go out the kitchen way and have something to eat with the rest. They won't have finished breakfast yet.

CARMEN. Thank you, Señora . . . and thank you again, Señora.

Carmen goes out to the left as Doña Filomena and her daughter Eulalia come from the garden. Doña Filomena is a peevish, thin-skinned lady; and Eulalia, the readiest victim of her mother's ill-temper, lives in constant apprehension of its outbursts. To pay this morning call they have both merely thrown shawls round their shoulders. But before she comes in Doña Filomena stops to ask, in her most acrid tones. . . .

DOÑA FILOMENA. Did Papá Juan go out on purpose to avoid me?

DOÑA MARCIALA. No, of course not. He did n't see you. Currita 's not here yet . . . he has gone to fetch her.

DOÑA FILOMENA. His little favourite!

DOÑA MARCIALA. Yes . . . she is. Won't you come in?

DOÑA FILOMENA. I suppose I must. Three months ago, Marciala, I vowed never to set foot in this house again . . . nor to let my daughters set foot in it . . . since our rags disgrace you, it seems. . . .

DOÑA MARCIALA. Grant me patience!

DOÑA FILOMENA. But . . . as usual . . . I give way.

DOÑA MARCIALA. As usual, is it? Come and kiss me, child. I can't argue with your mother.

EULALIA. You 're quite well, Aunt?

DOÑA MARCIALA. Well enough. You get prettier every time I see you . . . and rosier.

EULALIA. Thank you for the tonic. It did me lots of good.

DOÑA MARCIALA. That 's right.

DOÑA FILOMENA. And is Evaristo at home?

DOÑA MARCIALA. I think so.

DOÑA FILOMENA. How fortunate! Still, I have known him

. . . when I called . . . to be both at home and not at home . . . strange as that may appear!

DOÑA MARCIALA. Have you something to say to him?

DOÑA FILOMENA. I have. And to you as well.

DOÑA MARCIALA. I 'll see if I can find him.

Doña Marciala goes out to the right.

DOÑA FILOMENA. See if she can find him! We know what that means.

EULALIA. Oh, please, Mamma!

DOÑA FILOMENA. Eulalia . . . I have told you already that I have not come here to make myself pleasant. I mean to speak my mind . . . and they shall know what I think of them.

EULALIA. But, Mamma, you 're always speaking your mind.

DOÑA FILOMENA. And I shall speak it very clearly to-day. No, indeed, I am not here to make myself pleasant. I have been trampled on long enough.

EULALIA. Mamma . . . can't you see what the end of all this will be? They 'll get tired of it at last . . . and of us . . . and there 'll be an end to the help they give us. Then what shall we do . . . what shall we have to live on?

DOÑA FILOMENA. But it 's their duty to help us. And does a wretched little monthly allowance, may I ask, give them the right to insult us? If your poor dear father could look up out of his grave . . .! Your aunt . . . fixing that eye of hers upon you! Did n't you notice?

EULALIA. No, Mamma, I did n't.

DOÑA FILOMENA. What do you notice? Why did she call you to come and kiss her? She wanted to see if your blouse was silk, or not. A smooth-tongued serpent! An artful smooth-tongued serpent! And as for Evaristo . . . he 's the worst of the lot.

EULALIA. Uncle Evaristo!

DOÑA FILOMENA. My poor child . . . you think every one 's a saint . . . except your mother! The life I 'm led . . .!

Doña Marciala comes back with Don Evaristo.

DON EVARISTO. Glad to see you, Filomena.

DOÑA FILOMENA. Why tell me that when it 's not true?

DON EVARISTO.   Now look here, Filomena, if you 've come here in your usual frame of mind I shall be glad if you 'll go away again. For I 've just had my morning chocolate and I don't want it to disagree with me.

DOÑA FILOMENA.   I have come quite in my usual frame of mind.

DON EVARISTO.   And how are you, little girl?

EULALIA.   Pretty well, thank you, Uncle.   How are you?

DON EVARISTO.   I keep alive.

EULALIA.   Very much alive.

DON EVARISTO.   You 're amazing smart.   All in your Sunday best.

Doña Filomena coughs exultingly.

DOÑA FILOMENA.   Ahem!

DOÑA MARCIALA.   Yes . . . such a pretty blouse!

DOÑA FILOMENA.   Ahem . . . ahem!

EULALIA.   Oh . . . d 'you think so?

DOÑA FILOMENA.   From Paris . . . needless to say!

DOÑA MARCIALA.   Quite needless, Filomena . . . as I know the child makes every stitch she wears.   So why try that sarcasm on me?

DON EVARISTO.   Or any other.   Nothing so detestable!   Say what you 've got to say and be as agreeable as you can about it.

DOÑA FILOMENA.   Since whatever I 've got to say will in any case be disagreeable!

DON EVARISTO.   Have it your own way!

DOÑA MARCIALA.   But we may as well all sit down, may n't we?

DOÑA FILOMENA.   Thank you.   I 've been wondering when you 'd ask me to sit down.   Did you think if you did n't, I might go?   Thank you . . . for what 's likely to be my last visit here, I will sit down.

EULALIA.   Oh . . . Mamma!

For Eulalia could bear it no longer.   But, thankful for the chance, Doña Filomena rounds on her.

DOÑA FILOMENA.   Oh, Mamma . . . oh, Mamma!   And what, may I ask, does "Oh, Mamma" mean?   What have I done to deserve such a daughter!   Pray to God, child, that your mother-

in-law . . . if ever you have one . . . may be just half as good to
you as your poor mother has been. Not that you 're ever likely
to have one! Where 's your dowry to come from . . . since
you 've not found favour here . . . as others have!

> *Eulalia sighs resignedly. Her aunt sighs, her uncle sighs in
> sympathy. Then they all sit down.*

DOÑA MARCIALA. But was this what you wanted to say to us?

DOÑA FILOMENA. No, it was not. I am coming to that. One
thing at a time. Am I . . . may I ask . . . a recognised member
of this family . . . or am I not?

DOÑA MARCIALA. Why, of course! You married my brother —
did n't you?

DON EVARISTO. May he rest in peace!

> *While the sisters-in-law talk Don Evaristo sits twisting his
> fingers into every imaginable contortion. Eulalia listens
> distressedly; but what can she do?*

DOÑA FILOMENA. One would hardly suppose so.

DOÑA MARCIALA. Why?

DOÑA FILOMENA. When every other soul in Arenales seems to
know of this family celebration you are planning here.

DON EVARISTO. But you seem to know of it, Filomena.

DOÑA FILOMENA. How can I possibly know of it?

DOÑA MARCIALA. Papá Juan has been twice to see you to tell
you all about it . . . and each time you 've been out.

EULALIA. We told you he 'd been, Mamma.

DOÑA FILOMENA. Will you kindly hold your tongue? And the
fact that he came . . . twice . . . when I happened to be out
. . . that was a mere coincidence, I suppose.

DOÑA MARCIALA. Well, what did you expect me to do about it,
Filomena?

DOÑA FILOMENA. Are there no pens and ink in this house?

DOÑA MARCIALA. Oh, if a formal invitation will make you
happy, you shall have it.

EULALIA. There, Mamma!

DOÑA FILOMENA. Will you be silent while your elders are
talking?

*Don Evaristo here gives poor Eulalia a consolatory wink.
Doña Filomena turns like a flash on him.*

DOÑA FILOMENA. Ah! I saw you wink. These things don't
escape me. I overlook them . . . and God knows I 've enough
to overlook. Well . . . now for the next thing. What . . .
precisely . . . is this family festival?

DOÑA MARCIALA. My dear . . . you don't need to be told that.
We 're all going to celebrate Papá Juan's hundredth birthday . . .
and the dear old man can think of nothing else.

DOÑA FILOMENA. All?

DOÑA MARCIALA. As far as may be.

DOÑA FILOMENA. We are all to assemble?

DOÑA MARCIALA. I 've just said so.

DOÑA FILOMENA. Very well. I should naturally be sorry to
disturb the harmony of such an occasion. But if Guadaloupe is
to come . . . then, if you please, my daughters and I will stay at
home. We will eat our bread and cheese . . . at home.

DON EVARISTO. This is outrageous! And I knew it . . . I
knew it! My chocolate 's disagreeing with me. I never heard
anything so outrageous.

DOÑA FILOMENA. Outrageous! When you know perfectly well
that Guadaloupe and I are like this!

*"Like this" is a most eloquent crossed-swords gesture of the
fingers.*

DOÑA MARCIALA. Well . . . even if you are, surely you can
forget your feuds on such an occasion.

EULALIA. Oh, yes, Mamma. . . .

DOÑA FILOMENA. Eulalia, I have already told you to be silent.
And this latest insult Guadaloupe has heaped on me . . . I 'm
to forget that, am I?

DOÑA MARCIALA. Filomena, you 'd try the patience of a saint.
I know nothing of the latest insult . . . but I know what the first
was. When your husband died Guadaloupe made you a present
of the house you live in.

DOÑA FILOMENA. And a fine house it is, too! I spend more
on stopping the leaks in the roof than the place is worth.

Why could n't he give me something watertight while he was about it?

DON EVARISTO. Really, Filomena . . . this is all most ridiculous.

EULALIA. Oh, don't be vexed, Uncle . . .!

DON EVARISTO. My dear child . . . who would n't be vexed?
Doña Filomena suddenly rises.

DOÑA FILOMENA. No, indeed . . . why be vexed? Keep calm, Marciala.

DOÑA MARCIALA. Thank you. I 'm perfectly calm.

DOÑA FILOMENA. You have gained your end. By one means or another I was to be kept out of this family gathering. I quite understand. My poverty shames you. I am a fly in the ointment. Let us go, Eulalia.

DOÑA MARCIALA. Filomena!

DOÑA FILOMENA. Eulalia . . . let us go.

DOÑA MARCIALA. This will upset Papá Juan very much.

DOÑA FILOMENA. I also am upset! Eulalia . . . let us go.

DOÑA MARCIALA. Can't she stop for the rest of the day . . . now she 's here?

EULALIA. Oh, yes . . .

DOÑA MARCIALA. After lunch there 'll be so much she could help me with.

EULALIA. Yes, I 'm sure I could.

DOÑA FILOMENA. While her mother lives my daughter shall not wash dishes.

EULALIA. Oh, Mamma . . .!

DOÑA MARCIALA. If I did n't know you so well, Filomena, I should get angry with you. I shan't be washing dishes nor wiping them . . . nor will she be. However . . . take her away. She must n't do anything you don't want her to.
Poor Eulalia struggles with her tears.

DOÑA FILOMENA. And now of course we 're going to have a scene! Very well, child . . . stay . . . if you mean to cry about it. You 'd sooner be anywhere than in your own home . . . I know that!

DON EVARISTO.   And it might have been molten lead I drank instead of chocolate . . . I know that.

DOÑA FILOMENA.   But why not say outright that it's *I* that am not wanted here?   You'd not have to say it a second time, I assure you!   Good-bye, Marciala.

DOÑA MARCIALA.   Good-bye Filomena.

DOÑA FILOMENA.   Good-bye, Evaristo.

DON EVARISTO.   Good-bye, Filomena!

DOÑA FILOMENA.   I leave you, Eulalia, to the humiliations of this abode of wealth . . . since that's your preference.   I return to my hovel with my head held high.   Mother of God . . . the lessons life teaches one!

Filomena, stiff as a poker, goes the way she came.

DOÑA MARCIALA.   But . . . heavens above us . . . what's wrong with her?

DON EVARISTO.   I know what's wrong with me!

DOÑA MARCIALA.   What have we done?

EULALIA.   Dear Aunt . . . it's not you . . . it's the same with every one.   And her tantrums get worse every day.   I hate saying it . . . I ought n't to . . . for she is my mother.   But, really, it's almost impossible to live with her.

DON EVARISTO.   Quite, I should think!

EULALIA.   She makes us all so ashamed!   And if I put on a pound one week, thanks to your tonic, I lose it the next, I'm sure, when I've to go through some scene like this.   The only happy moments I have are when I'm away from her.   It's wicked of me to say so . . . but it's true.   And she is just like this with Guadaloupe.

She repeats her mother's gesture.

DOÑA MARCIALA.   But what has he done?

EULALIA.   Nothing at all.   It's her nature . . . and I suppose she can't help it.   It's the same with Papá Juan as with you and with Uncle.   It's the same with Currita . . . and with any one who comes here.   Oh . . . I can't bear it any more Aunt Marciala . . . I can't . . . I simply can't.   Why does n't somebody come along and ask me to marry him?

Manuel comes from the garden.

MANUEL. Beg pardon, Señora.

DOÑA MARCIALA. What is it, Manuel?

MANUEL. There's a man at the gate wants me to hand you this.

"This" is a piece of paper with something written on it.

DON EVARISTO. Marciala . . . if you go on giving to every beggar that asks we shall all be ruined.

DOÑA MARCIALA. No doubt. Read it, child . . . I've not got my glasses.

EULALIA. Yes.

She reads the paper, which she and her uncle and aunt find most surprising.

EULALIA. "To the lord of this stately dwelling: Most noble sir . . ."

DON EVARISTO. What's all that?

DOÑA MARCIALA. Sh!

EULALIA. "A minstrel from far off lands, in whose poor talent the great ones of the earth find pastime, hears, by a happy chance, that Heaven has preserved for a hundred years, no less, the life of this most illustrious family's illustrious head. And he begs your hospitality for an hour while he sings to you the songs he has made to celebrate the auspicious occasion."

DON EVARISTO. Why . . . the fellow must be wrong in his head.

DOÑA MARCIALA. Evaristo . . . what had we better do?

DON EVARISTO. What sort of a fish is he, Manuel?

The laughter Manuel has been choking with breaks out at last.

DOÑA MARCIALA. What are you laughing for?

DON EVARISTO. What's the matter with you, man?

And in from the garden comes Trino, laughing too. He is one of Papá Juan's grandsons. He is thirty and — so his family think — a rolling stone.

DOÑA MARCIALA. Trino!

EULALIA. Trino!

DON EVARISTO. Trino . . . of course!

DOÑA MARCIALA.   I might have guessed it was Trino.

TRINO.   Dear Aunt Marciala! Well, Uncle Evaristo?

DOÑA MARCIALA.   But why all this mystery?

DON EVARISTO.   Why did n't you tell us you were coming?

TRINO.   What . . . a minstrel from afar telegraph you the time his train 's due! And how is Eulalia?

EULALIA.   Very well. And you?

TRINO.   Never better. Was that your mother I met going out?

EULALIA.   Yes . . . that was Mother.

TRINO.   Then why did she pass me without a word? I spoke to her.

EULALIA.   Did she? Oh, dear!

TRINO.   Manuel says Papá Juan's over the road.

DON EVARISTO.   He won't be long. He will be glad to see you.

DOÑA MARCIALA.   But you 've some luggage, I suppose?

TRINO.   Besides my harp? Yes. I 've a portmanteau.

DOÑA MARCIALA.   Manuel . . . see the things are taken upstairs. Then I 'll arrange. . . .

MANUEL.   Very good, Señorita.

Manuel departs.

DON EVARISTO.   Well, well, well . . . that was a good joke! A minstrel from afar!

DOÑA MARCIALA.   You always drop out of the skies.

TRINO.   Is n't that the best way? It saves me a lot of trouble . . . and you 're twice as pleased to see me.

DON EVARISTO.   Are your father and mother coming?

TRINO.   But of course they 're coming.

DOÑA MARCIALA.   That 's right! What a time since I 've seen your father! Is he looking much older?

TRINO.   Not a bit.

EULALIA.   And is Pepe coming?

TRINO.   Pepe's coming.

EULALIA.   And Rorri.

TRINO.   Rorri 's coming. All my sisters are coming. Pilar will bring her husband and her three children. Anita will bring her husband and her two children. Rosita will bring her husband

and her baby. And Rorri will bring the young man that 's going to be her husband. Yes . . . the whole Noah's Ark full is floating towards Mount Ararat. And I am the dove!

DON EVARISTO. Merciful Father . . . what is to become of us all in this house I do not know!

TRINO. Poor Uncle Evaristo! I 've been thinking of you! Farewell the tranquil mind . . . the punctual meal . . . the well-brushed coat . . . the boot-trees in the boots!

DON EVARISTO [laughs]. Ah . . . it 's all very fine for you to joke!

DOÑA MARCIALA. And now you 're here, Trino, will you stay a little?

TRINO. No, dear Aunt Marciala . . . I fear I can't.

DOÑA MARCIALA. A miracle if you could!

EULALIA. You always come and go like a streak of lightning, Cousin Trino.

TRINO. I try to come and go like a streak of lightning.

DOÑA MARCIALA. Well . . . you succeed!

DON EVARISTO. A clap of thunder, I call him!

TRINO. As soon as Papá Juan's hundredth birthday party 's over . . . I 'm off to Paris!

EULALIA. Paris, if you please!

DOÑA MARCIALA. Why Paris?

TRINO. I 'm going to be married.

EULALIA. You 've a sweetheart in Paris?

DOÑA MARCIALA. Now, now . . . don't ask us to believe that.

EULALIA. But some one . . . in Paris . . . you 're engaged to?

TRINO. No . . . neither.

DON EVARISTO. But, my dear boy . . . something of the sort you must have!

EULALIA. Or how can you be going to get married? Fibber!

TRINO. I saw an advertisement in a French paper . . . a quite respectable French paper: "Wanted, a husband. Lady of unexceptionable character, young, rich, beautiful, romantic disposition, wishes to meet with a gentleman of such and such qualifications, Spanish preferred." And I believe I shall suit. I have written her a most fervent letter. I have sent her two photographs . . . one in my best bathing suit, one as you see me . . . to show her what a bargain she 'll be getting. And as soon as her answer comes, I take the Paris train.

DOÑA MARCIALA. I don't believe one single word of it.

EULALIA. How can you tell us such lies?

DON EVARISTO. But they 're not. Why should they be? He 's capable of it. Ever since he wanted to become a naturalised Japanese . . . I 'll believe anything of him.

DOÑA MARCIALA. Well, Trino, when your French lady jilts you . . . and I 'll ask God in my prayers that she may . . . come to us for a month and let us console you. A promise?

TRINO. It is. There 's nothing I like better than quiet family life.

DOÑA MARCIALA. Really! You manage to dissemble it very well.

TRINO. I beg your pardon! Who is the first to arrive for this family festivity? I am. You wait and you 'll see! This bird of passage is at heart the most domestic fowl of the lot of you. I adore my family . . . and I 'm going to give you all a proof of it. I have an idea for a . . .

DOÑA MARCIALA. You 've never wanted for ideas!

TRINO. I repeat . . . I have an idea for a book, which will be the most diverting . . . the most extraordinary book ever written.

EULALIA. It will be, I 'm sure, if you write it.

DON EVARISTO. Don't be afraid! He may turn Japanese . . . but, trust me, he 'll never write a book. It takes a little time to write a book . . . and a little trouble.

TRINO. I shall have the honour of reading you that book before it goes to the printer's. And I 've settled on the title: My Progenitors.

DON EVARISTO. Magnificent!

TRINO. There 's nothing to laugh at.

DON EVARISTO. What do you know, may I ask, about your progenitors?

TRINO. Aha! Far more than you do with all your pedigrees

and parchments. I have been making a most private and particular study of them. I know just the sort of men they were and the sort of lives they lived . . . for they are living them all over again at this very moment in me!

DOÑA MARCIALA. Ave María Puríssima!

TRINO. It 's a fact. You need n't laugh, Eulalia. We 've had heroes and martyrs and poets and saints and rogues and adventurers for ancestors . . . and I 've something of all of them in me. Did n't Papá Juan's grandfather go out to the Indies to preach the Gospel there?

DOÑA MARCIALA. Yes, indeed he did.

TRINO. Many 's the time I 've longed to rouse this torpid world to some faith in what 's beautiful and true. I mean it! Then there 's that Mayor of Arenales who burnt his own house sooner than see it taken by French invaders. I accommodate some of him too. And once I bought myself a violin . . . I did indeed . . . and sat alone hour after hour playing it . . . as Uncle Gustavo used to . . . to see if music could tell me the sort of man I was at heart. The sailor great-grandfather in me wants to go round the world. And often and often I want to sit here in peace with you. Now the choppings and changings don't matter. You can be a mystic one month and a pirate the next . . . and no great harm done. But I tell you . . . when your various ancestors begin tugging you all ways at once . . . !

DOÑA MARCIALA. Saints above!

TRINO. D 'you know what I do then? I go to bed for a fortnight . . . till it 's over. For no man in such a state of internal anarchy should be allowed out in the streets.

The other three are laughing heartily.

EULALIA. Trino . . . was there, by any chance, a lunatic among your ancestors?

TRINO. Not that I know of.

EULALIA. Your descendants won't be able to say that, I 'm afraid!

DOÑA MARCIALA. One to little Eulalia!

TRINO. I daresay I sound mad. But anything 's better than

going through life like a machine. I 've no use for people that are
born good and go on being good because they can't think of anything else to be . . . or for people who are born bad and stay bad.
What we want in this world is variety!

DOÑA MARCIALA. Don't you think, Trino, that you 've talked
about enough nonsense for once? Go up to your room now and
get yourself tidy.

TRINO. I go! Observe that for the moment I am under the
sole and absolute influence of this pearl of an aunt!

DOÑA MARCIALA. Am I to be in your book?

TRINO. Need you ask? I shall praise you to the skies. And I
shall particularly mention that you make the best honey cakes in
the world.

DOÑA MARCIALA. You shall have some. Come along, Eulalia,
. . . we must choose a room for this minstrel from far away who
is starving for honey cakes.

EULALIA. I hope there is lots for me to do.

DOÑA MARCIALA. Lots! Trino, wait here a minute or two.

TRINO. At your orders, Doña Marciala.

DOÑA MARCIALA [to Eulalia as they go]. When we 've settled
him we 'll go upstairs and make a start with the table-linen. Oh
. . . there 's plenty to do!

TRINO. You don't deceive me, Aunt Marciala. You just love
it. You 're in the seventh heaven.

Doña Marciala and Eulalia have gone.

DON EVARISTO. Yes . . . but at her age! Anno Domini . . .
Anno Domini! Though what does that mean to you? How
d 'you think she 's looking?

TRINO. Splendid! Much younger than my father. Much
younger and much handsomer than when I saw her last.

DON EVARISTO. Yes, yes . . . oh, no doubt! But appearances
are deceitful.

TRINO. Why . . . what 's wrong?

DON EVARISTO. Poor darling . . . she 's an inward wreck.
Any day . . . any day, I feel, she may break down.

TRINO. Surely you 're exaggerating.

DON EVARISTO. Not at all! I face the facts. The amazing thing is that I 'm as well as ever I was in my life. Better!

Doña Marciala comes back.

DOÑA MARCIALA. Trino.

TRINO. Aunt Marciala.

DOÑA MARCIALA. Come along. The bird of passage had better choose his perch.

TRINO. Anywhere will do for me. I can sleep on the hard side of a paving stone.

DON EVARISTO. Come to my study when you 're ready. I want to show you the library. We 've made changes. I think they 'll astonish you.

TRINO. What have you done?

DON EVARISTO. I 've had all the books bound the same size.

TRINO. However have you managed that?

DON EVARISTO. Quite simply. The large ones are bound as usual, and the small ones are bound to look like the large. I know! When you open some of them it seems rather queer . . . there 's too much binding and too little book. But you can't tell from the outside. And I never read any of them now . . . and the whole effect 's magnificent! Well . . . I 'll wait for you.

Don Evaristo departs.

TRINO. What an odd notion!

DOÑA MARCIALA. I know! Poor dear! It 's very sad. But he 's been failing for some time, Trino. How do you find him?

TRINO. He seems all right.

DOÑA MARCIALA. Yes . . . he seems so. But he 's shaky . . . very shaky. The end 's in sight.

TRINO. Mercy on us!

DOÑA MARCIALA. I do all I can for him. And I often thank God so much health and strength has been spared me to devote to him.

TRINO. Well . . . there is that to be thankful for.

Manuel appears and is going out again towards the right.

DOÑA MARCIALA. What is it, Manuel?

MANUEL. This letter for Don Evaristo.

DOÑA MARCIALA. Was that all the post?

MANUEL. There's this for Don Juan. He told me to leave his here.

DOÑA MARCIALA. Give it me. Ah! [*As she looks at it.*] I knew this would happen!

TRINO. What?

DOÑA MARCIALA. I'll tell you in a minute. Quite right, Manuel . . . take the Señorito his . . . and then I shall want you upstairs.

MANUEL. Very good, Señorita.

DOÑA MARCIALA. And . . . Manuel . . . you need n't tell Don Juan there was a letter for him.

MANUEL. Just so, Señorita.

Manuel goes on his way.

DOÑA MARCIALA. Papá Juan is simply impossible!

TRINO. Why, Aunt?

DOÑA MARCIALA. D' you know who this letter's from?

TRINO. Who?

DOÑA MARCIALA. Gabriela.

TRINO. Gabriela!

DOÑA MARCIALA. Think of it. He has taken it into his head to ask her too. You know all the scandal there was about her in Seville. Well . . . the man left her and she's living with the other. And she has a baby. And, once for all, Trino, we cannot have her here.

TRINO. And Papá Juan means to have her here?

DOÑA MARCIALA. Oh, my dear boy . . . if we had a cousin or so in gaol . . . he'd ask them!

TRINO. Bravo, Papá Juan!

DOÑA MARCIALA. Nonsense! Come along.

TRINO. Well . . . I think he must have his own way, you know.

They go out to the left. Then Manuel passes across at the back muttering and chuckling. . . .

MANUEL. . . . and as pleased as Punch he is . . . when he finds that the letter's for Doña Marciala . . . and addressed to him. He's a caution.

*After a moment Papá Juan and Currita come in from the
garden. Currita is a beautiful girl, imaginative, sensitive,
alive to her finger-tips. And her eyes are so bright that they
seem to light up what they rest on.*

*If Trino should write a book upon Papá Juan's posterity
he ought certainly to give a chapter to his eldest great granddaughter. She is very simply dressed, and has a light scarf
thrown round her shoulders.*

PAPÁ JUAN. Now, it won't do, Currita, it won't do! If you
can't get up in the morning I must find another secretary. Why,
half the day 's gone before we know where we are! And I know
what does it. It 's those novels you read lying in bed of a night.

CURRITA. Yes . . . that 's what does it. When I 've finished
reading and put the light out I lie awake imagining all sorts of
nonsense. And then in the morning I 'm so sound asleep that it 's
like being down at the bottom of a well. But I 'm going to reform
. . . from now on. To morrow I shall call the cock in time for
him to crow.

PAPÁ JUAN. Fine words butter no parsnips!

CURRITA. Well . . . what do we do now?

PAPÁ JUAN. We wait for the postman.

CURRITA. But he has been. I saw him going down the street.

PAPÁ JUAN. The devil he has! Then again there 's no answer
from Gabriela.

CURRITA. No . . . Manuel would have left it here.

PAPÁ JUAN. Ay . . . ay . . . ay . . . ay! Why . . . she 's
never going to be so unkind to me as this!

CURRITA. Well . . . shall we go to call on Antoñón? Last
night you said you meant to.

PAPÁ JUAN. Yes, we will. Poor Antoñón . . . he will be
astonished! But he 's one of the family. So why can't he come
to dinner with us . . . market gardener or no?

CURRITA. Papá Juan . . . you are good.

PAPÁ JUAN. Think so?

CURRITA. As good as bread.

PAPÁ JUAN. Yes . . . I am good! If I had n't been good I

should n't have lived so long. Now . . . how do we explain that?

CURRITA [*repeating her lesson*]. Because the wicked go around snarling and snapping . . . till their bad temper poisons their blood and they die young.

PAPÁ JUAN. Quite right. But goodness alone won't do it. The wicked man 's miserable too, is n't he? And if you can't be happy . . . why, you 'll never live to be a hundred.

CURRITA. Well . . . I want to be the best woman in the world and live to be the oldest woman in the world. So tell me, Papá Juan, please, exactly how it 's done.

PAPÁ JUAN. I 'll tell you. Live your life as if there were a God in Heaven. We can't be sure there is, you know. Nor you nor I nor any one can be quite sure. But live as if there were.

CURRITA. I 'm sure there is. When I see the stars at night and the sunrise in the morning . . . I 'm quite sure.

PAPÁ JUAN. And when did you ever see the sunrise in the morning, may I ask? Dormouse!

CURRITA. I shall see it to-morrow morning. But I often try to count the stars. And there 's one star I call mine. It 's mine and nobody else's.

PAPÁ JUAN. I 'm glad you look at the stars.

CURRITA. You taught me to. And there 's that saying you 're so fond of . . . I always think of it when I look at them.

PAPÁ JUAN. The one about the Devil?

CURRITA. No . . . not the one about the Devil! Quite another kind. Whenever you see a thing . . . any sort of thing . . . that 's so beautiful or so wonderful there seems nothing to be said about it . . . don 't you know you always say: "Well . . . if this is n't God's work it 's good enough to be!"

PAPÁ JUAN. Do I? Yes, I do.

CURRITA. So I always say that when I see my star. And there 's another thing I say that you taught me . . . though this feels as if I 'd thought of it myself . . . about the little light.

PAPÁ JUAN. What 's that about a little light?

CURRITA. In the fairy tales . . . don't you remember? . . .

there 's almost always a tired traveller on a dark night. And all he can ever see is a little light . . . far off . . . that guides him and gives him hope. So he goes on and on . . . though it never seems to come nearer. But as long as he sees it he can go on and on . . . and hope. Life 's like that, you once said. Who 'd ever go on if it were n't for some little light ahead!

PAPÁ JUAN. I think you 're a very good pupil. Yes, I remember saying that . . . but I wanted to hear you say it. Yes . . . one can't get far without the little light. I 've always seen one, I can see one still.

CURRITA. Still, Papá Juan?

PAPÁ JUAN. Why, of course I can! When I was sixty-seven I built this house. And every one in the place laughed at me. They made jokes about me . . . they wrote rhymes about me.

> Old Juan del Monte
> Is slightly at fault,
> When he builds him a villa
> Instead of a vault.

What d 'you think of that? Well, I 've been living here thirty years in spite of them. And the man who wrote that . . . he 's in another place now . . . and writing rhymes, I daresay, about the Devil.

CURRITA. Building the house had been your little light?

PAPÁ JUAN. Yes . . . for a bit. In these last years this day that is coming close now has been the light . . . when I 'm to see around me my children and their children and their children . . . in whom I live and shall go on living. Ah . . . but that 's not all! I begin to see another little light now . . . further off still. Another chance for that good gentleman to make rhymes about me . . . if he were here to take it.

CURRITA. What can you be hoping for now, Papá Juan?

PAPÁ JUAN. You 're opening those eyes of yours very wide. You 'll be writing rhymes about me next, I suppose. Well . . . I 'll tell you. I 've seen my children . . . and my grandchildren . . . and great-grandchildren. Now I want a great-great-grandchild.

CURRITA. A great-great . . .!

PAPÁ JUAN. Yes. I've not got one. But there's no reason I should n't have one . . . is there?

CURRITA. No . . . I suppose not.

PAPÁ JUAN. Very well then! See to it.

CURRITA. I don't call that work for a secretary.

PAPÁ JUAN. But all you 've to do is to find the right young man and marry him.

Currita bursts out laughing.

CURRITA. Well, Papá Juan . . . anything to please you!

PAPÁ JUAN. You must hurry up, though . . . you must hurry up. For if you don't do it for me nobody else can. The other great-grandchildren are all still children themselves. So set about it. What young man is there in Arenales that you fancy? Point him out. I 'll get his range and bring him down . . . bang!

CURRITA. I 'm afraid there 's no one in Arenales.

PAPÁ JUAN. Then we must look further.

CURRITA [*with little sigh*]. I 'm afraid it 's waste of time looking further.

PAPÁ JUAN. But if he 's not in Arenales. . . .!

CURRITA. Papá Juan . . . I am in love. You 're not to look for him. Here 's where he lives. [*She taps her forehead just between the eyes.*] Loving him is my little light.

PAPÁ JUAN. Now, now . . . I want no romancing about this! Girls of your age are always in love with some wonderful being . . . who only exists there. [*He taps her forehead in his turn.*] But when a man of real flesh and blood comes along . . .!

CURRITA. Oh . . . he 's flesh and blood too!

PAPÁ JUAN. The devil he is!

CURRITA. Very much so.

PAPÁ JUAN. Then I 'd like to know, please, who he is.

CURRITA. He 's not to be found in Arenales.

PAPÁ JUAN. But who is he?

CURRITA. It 's Trino.

Papá Juan is amazed.

PAPÁ JUAN. Trino?

CURRITA. Yes . . . it 's Trino.

PAPÁ JUAN. My grandson Trino?

CURRITA. Unless it 's his ghost.

PAPÁ JUAN. But this is n't a little light . . . this is a house on fire. How did you get to know Trino?

CURRITA. I don't know him.

PAPÁ JUAN. What?

CURRITA. No . . . I 've never seen him. When he used to come to Arenales I was always away at school. But I heard so much about him . . . here and at home and everywhere . . . that I made up my mind, Papá Juan, not to look at another man . . . seriously . . . till I 'd first seen Trino in flesh and blood. And I won't. I think he must be different from everybody else. Once, for a whole night, some one walked up and down outside our school with a guitar . . . singing love songs. The nuns did n't know whether to be angry or to laugh. They were very good songs. We lay in bed and bit the sheets to keep from laughing. That was Trino! Whenever people talk of him I feel happy and my heart begins to beat. And time and again you 've told me how good and brave and clever he is. So you 're to blame, too. And you told me he 'd once tried to shoot himself for the sake of some woman. And then I was quite sure I loved him. For a man who 'd do a thing like that . . . can't be an ordinary sort of man, can he?

PAPÁ JUAN. Well, there were practical advantages in it . . . from your point of view.

CURRITA. Why?

PAPÁ JUAN. Why, if he 's done it once he won't do it again . . . you may feel pretty sure. It 's an experiment one 's not apt to repeat.

CURRITA. How can you joke about it! What sort of a woman can she have been . . . not to love Trino!

PAPÁ JUAN. But, my dear child . . . you don't know anything about him.

CURRITA. Yes, I do. I may n't ever have seen him . . . but I know all about him. I wish he knew half as much about me.

I tell you, Papá Juan . . . when I wrote him the letter the other day, asking him to come to your birthday, I wrote him such a letter . . .!

PAPÁ JUAN. But that was my letter . . . you rascal!

CURRITA. And when his answer came saying he would, and Aunt Marciala read it . . . I seemed to see the words dancing round the room like little flames . . . and I shook and I could n't stop shaking. If I 'd been a bird you 'd have heard every feather rustle. But you can't ever tell with a woman, can you?

PAPÁ JUAN. Currita, Currita . . . you 're making me very happy! And there 's nothing you can tell me about Trino . . . who has had his way . . . his own royal way with me . . . ever since he was so high.

CURRITA. You get your own way with him sometimes, don't you?

PAPÁ JUAN. Nobody will ever get their way with Trino.

CURRITA. We 'll see about that, Papá Juan!

PAPÁ JUAN. Trino! That rascal of a Trino!

CURRITA. Shall I go and get that picture of him . . . the one in the big room?

PAPÁ JUAN. Run along. I see I 'll have no peace till you do.

CURRITA. I won't be a minute.

She starts to go. He calls her back.

PAPÁ JUAN. Currita!

CURRITA. Yes?

PAPÁ JUAN. Nothing . . . nothing. Ah . . . but my little light 's a little nearer . . . is n't it?

CURRITA. Is it? Mine seems a little nearer . . . sometimes.

She runs off.

PAPÁ JUAN. Who 'd ever have thought of it? Such a child! Currita and Trino! Who 'd ever have dreamt of it!

Trino appears, and sees Papá Juan.

TRINO. Papá Juan . . . Papá Juan!

The surprise is rather much for Papá Juan.

PAPÁ JUAN. Trino! It can't be.

TRINO. But it is. I 'm the first to arrive.

PAPÁ JUAN. But . . . such a surprise! I 'm almost . . . I 'm quite . . .! It 's you, you rascal?

TRINO. Who else?

PAPÁ JUAN. Yes . . . yes, it is! At this very moment too! There . . . let me get my breath . . . that 's all right. Well . . . have you seen the children?

TRINO. No.

PAPÁ JUAN. Not seen the children . . . not seen Marciala and Evaristo?

TRINO. Oh . . . those children! Yes, I 've seen them . . . been having a talk to them. I 've been here quite a while.

PAPÁ JUAN. Think of that now . . . think of that! Having a talk . . . and so were we . . .! Think of that!

At this moment Currita returns. But her eyes are on the picture of Trino she is carrying and she does not see the real Trino till she finds herself close to him. When she does she gives a cry, half of amazement, half of fear. Instinctively she hides the picture. But she stands staring.

TRINO. What is it? What 's the matter?

PAPÁ JUAN. It 's nothing . . . it 's nothing.

TRINO. Don't be frightened of me, Currita. Are n't you Currita?

CURRITA. Yes. Trino?

TRINO. Yes . . . I 'm Trino. How do you do?

CURRITA. I 'm quite well, thank you. How do you do?

They shake hands; he smiling, she as if under a spell. And Papá Juan says, half to himself. . . .

PAPÁ JUAN. If this is n't God's work . . . why, it 's good enough to be!

ACT II

Doña Marciala is sitting there, alone and at her ease; and Eulalia's voice can be heard. She is singing the famous Jota from "La Bruja." The sound comes nearer.

Even as the birds in the springtime
Sing of the sorrow of loving. . . .

DOÑA MARCIALA. Now whatever is the matter with that young woman?

The song goes on.

> So I this jota am singing
> To comfort me in my sadness.
> Even as the birds in the springtime. . . .

And Eulalia appears.

EULALIA. Oh! I did n't see you!

DOÑA MARCIALA. I heard you, though.

EULALIA. I 'm afraid you could n't help it . . . and I know what it sounds like. Shall I give you the key of the china closet? I 've taken out the thick dinner-set . . . the one with the little blue edge. . . .

DOÑA MARCIALA. That 's right.

EULALIA. . . . and put it in the pantry. Frasquita helped me.

DOÑA MARCIALA. Thank you, my dear. Yes . . . now the young people have begun to arrive my best china 's safer on its shelves. Sit down for a little.

EULALIA. I was going over to the farmyard to see if La Tordilla has laid an egg.

DOÑA MARCIALA. Well . . . you can go presently. Rest a minute. Did you put out the bed-linen?

EULALIA. Yes. What a whiff of lavender when you open the cupboard!

DOÑA MARCIALA. I always say there 's no sweeter scent than the scent of clean white linen.

EULALIA. I took two sets from the lower shelf.

DOÑA MARCIALA. Bless you . . . you 're a wonderful help.

EULALIA. Oh . . . don't thank me, please! I 'm so happy here. I 'm like a child with a new toy. But something marvellous must be going to happen . . . an earthquake or a comet or something . . . for Mother to leave me in peace here a whole week.

DOÑA MARCIALA. Is n't leaving you here marvel enough for you?

EULALIA. Oh . . . if I could only live with you and go home for a week now and then . . . instead of coming here for a week and living at home! Aunt Marciala . . . I want to kiss you.

DOÑA MARCIALA. Do, my dear.

> *Rosa — one of Carmen Campos' many daughters — appears from the right. She wears a big apron and her sleeves are turned up.*

ROSA. Señorita.

DOÑA MARCIALA. What is it?

ROSA. I 've done those rooms on the top floor. What 's next?

DOÑA MARCIALA. Have you polished the floors?

ROSA. No, Señora.

DOÑA MARCIALA. Well . . . do.

ROSA. Yes, Señora. Oh . . . and is any one to have the small attic?

DOÑA MARCIALA. No . . . I don't think we 'll need it.

ROSA. Had I better take a turn at it in case?

DOÑA MARCIALA. No harm.

ROSA. Then I 'll do that now.

> *With which Rosa disappears.*

EULALIA. Is Uncle Raphael going to stay at Monte Mayor the whole afternoon?

DOÑA MARCIALA. I don't know. They 're all there. When visitors arrive I like them to go and pay their respects to Our Lady of Monte Mayor the very first thing. Once that 's done this house is Liberty Hall, as my father says. But first let them make their little pilgrimage.

EULALIA. I never saw Uncle Evaristo so bowed down with care. They were a cartload! Twelve children!

DOÑA MARCIALA. And imps of Satan . . . every one of them!

EULALIA. Uncle Raphael has grown fat, has n't he?

DOÑA MARCIALA. I 'd never have known him. A perfect elephant! And such a handsome man as he used to be! He lets himself go. Well . . . what can you expect . . . when his wife 's no better!

EULALIA. She 's very kind.

DOÑA MARCIALA. Very kind . . . and as lazy as a toad!

EULALIA. Were n't you asking for Currita just now? Here she is.

DOÑA MARCIALA. Currita?

EULALIA. Yes.

Currita comes through the garden. Greetings and kisses.

CURRITA. Good afternoon, Aunt.

DOÑA MARCIALA. Bless you!

CURRITA. How are you, Eulalia?

EULALIA. Bless you, my dear!

CURRITA. Just as I left home your mother arrived. Poor Papa! She looked like giving him a terrible time.

EULALIA. Oh dear . . . oh dear . . . I 'm so sorry! She told me last night that she meant to have a talk to him!

CURRITA. But where 's Papá Juan?

DOÑA MARCIALA. I think he must have gone for a walk with Trino.

CURRITA. I don't doubt it! Trino . . . Trino! Now he 's here I might not exist. I 'd like to see the last of Trino.

EULALIA. I should n't.

CURRITA. No . . . nor should I. But I like saying so. I ask you, though! I came here this morning to see Papá Juan. Out with Trino! This afternoon . . . Papá Juan and Trino are out! But I simply must see him. There 's a letter to be answered. Where have they gone?

DOÑA MARCIALA. My child . . . I 've no idea.

CURRITA. Can I have Manuel to come with me to find them?

DOÑA MARCIALA. But if we 've no idea where they are . . .! Answer the letter yourself. You 've the confidence of the Crown.

CURRITA. Well, I shall. And if I answer it wrong . . . Papá Juan can blame Trino. I 'll go to the study, then.

DOÑA MARCIALA. Now don't untidy everything.

CURRITA. No, I won't. Come along, Eulalia. Shall I leave my shawl here? No! Yes! No! Yes . . . I will!

DOÑA MARCIALA. Where have your wits gone wool-gathering?

CURRITA. Come along . . . I 've a secret to tell you.

EULALIA. Oh . . . what about?

CURRITA. About you, of course.

EULALIA. But how can it be about me?

CURRITA. Then it must be about me . . . or perhaps it's about both of us. Never mind! Come along.

EULALIA. I'm coming.

The two girls go out together to the right, laughing and chattering their happy nonsense.

DOÑA MARCIALA. Currita . . . she's like a lizard on a wall! And the other child . . . so happy . . . poor little thing!

Don Evaristo comes through the garden. He is very hot and very, very cross.

DON EVARISTO. If ever they catch me going out with them again . . . !

DOÑA MARCIALA. What . . . back already?

DON EVARISTO. Yes.

DOÑA MARCIALA. By yourself?

DON EVARISTO. Yes.

DOÑA MARCIALA. But where's Raphael? And where are the children?

DON EVARISTO. Where I left them . . . the whole tribe of them! Let them plague their parents. It's a parent's duty to put up with it, perhaps. It isn't mine. And I won't put up with it. I say I . . . !

DOÑA MARCIALA. Evaristo . . . Evaristo! In the name of the Twelve Apostles, I do beg of you. . . .

DON EVARISTO. Marciala! In the name of the Eleven Thousand Virgins, let me assure you. . . .

DOÑA MARCIALA. Keep calm. My dear . . . age is telling on you.

DON EVARISTO. Nonsense . . . it's not age that's telling on me. . . .

DOÑA MARCIALA. And sit down. You're quite exhausted.

DON EVARISTO. I will not sit down. I'm very hot, I shall catch cold if I sit down.

DOÑA MARCIALA. Very well, my dear . . . then stand up.

DON EVARISTO. You don't know what those children are like.

Ill-mannered young . . . !   Mischievous young . . . !   It was
bad enough getting there.   We 'd no sooner packed them in their
carriage than they cried because they wanted to walk . . . and
after two minutes walking they were crying to be back in the
carriage.   And when we got up the hill to the church and stopped
where the orange trees are . . . Raphael was the very first to start
stealing the oranges.   And his wife lay down on the grass and
showed her legs . . . yes, she did ! . . . and they 're not meant
for show, I assure you.   And as to the Holy Virgin in the church
. . . not a soul went near her !   Then one wretched child . . .
who should have been promptly smacked . . . found the garden
gate where the notice is put up: " No Admittance " . . . read it
. . . went right in . . . and began picking the flowers.   And two
or three more of the little fiends followed him.   So I went to their
father . . . and all he said was that his children invariably wanted
to do the one thing they were told they must n't.   I could stand no
more of it, Marciala.   So I grinned at them and said : " Well, as
you 've all made yourselves quite at home and as I 've lots to do
in Arenales, I 'll leave you."   And I left them.   And I had to ride
back upon Gasparón's fruit waggon . . . well, you know what
that 's like !   And, if you please, Marciala, you will never again
ask me to take any one anywhere.

DOÑA MARCIALA.   I thought it 'd do you so much good to get
out in the country for a little.   I should sit down now, if I were you.

DON EVARISTO.   My God . . . what a family !   And I 'm sure
there 's lots I have n't told you.   I shall remember it in a minute !
Yes . . . one little beast started eating those poisonous berries.
And his father only laughed.

DOÑA MARCIALA.   You 're past the age for junketings . . .
that 's the truth, I 'm afraid.

DON EVARISTO.   I 'd like to have seen you there.   You 'd have
had a fit !   Savages !   Heathen savages !   And look at my cigar
case [*which is empty*].   That 's Raphael !   Could n't finish one
without lighting another from it.

DOÑA MARCIALA.   Good !   Now you keep it empty for a little.
Cigars are very bad for you.

DON EVARISTO.   Not so bad as sweets are for you.   I 've caught you before now . . . eating them on the sly.

DOÑA MARCIALA.   Nonsense!

DON EVARISTO.   Well . . . what 's the news here?

DOÑA MARCIALA.   None.

DON EVARISTO.   Where 's Papá Juan?

DOÑA MARCIALA.   Out for a walk.

DON EVARISTO.   With Currita?

DOÑA MARCIALA.   No . . . with Trino.

DON EVARISTO.   Don't you think this gadding around is very bad for him?

DOÑA MARCIALA.   Yes, I do.   He had a nasty little turn of giddiness this morning . . . well, you saw!   But what 's the use of talking?   He takes no notice.

DON EVARISTO.   Bless him!   And where 's Eulalia?

DOÑA MARCIALA.   She 's as happy as a bird.   She 's in your study.

DON EVARISTO.   In my study?   What 's she doing in my study?

DOÑA MARCIALA.   I don't know.   She and Currita went off there.

DON EVARISTO.   But what 's Currita doing in my study?   God bless my soul . . . I 'll put a padlock on the door!   What on earth is she doing in my study?   Little tornado!

And off he goes to see.

DOÑA MARCIALA.   So crotchety, poor dear!   Well . . . I must get out those moulds for the quince cheese.

She leaves her repose in her comfortable chair and goes off to the right to do so.   In a moment we hear and see Papá Juan and Trino returning leisurely through the garden laughing and talking as they come.

PAPÁ JUAN.   Hey . . . yes!   Always up to your nonsense!

When they are well in the room Trino comes to a determined halt.

TRINO.   Look here, Papá Juan . . . are n't you tired yet?

PAPÁ JUAN.   Not a bit.

TRINO. Then I am!

And he flings himself into a chair.

PAPÁ JUAN. Well . . . so am I!

And he sits down too.

I was just bragging. Hey! Did you tell Manuel to take the carriage to meet our little priest?

TRINO. I did, Señor! And Manuel is doing it.

PAPÁ JUAN. Did we enjoy our walk?

TRINO. I did . . . thoroughly.

PAPÁ JUAN. One of the walks I like best. That bit of the river bank 's so pretty.

TRINO. Yes. A river 's a magical thing. It can cast a spell on my restlessness, even. And, lying under the trees there, the ripple of the water might be a woman's voice. Such peace in the sound of it!

PAPÁ JUAN. Hola! Hola! Will you be kind enough to inquire for me whether Doña Francisca Saavedra del Monte Guevara y Perez Cañas Garzón Cedillo y Lozano is in the house?

TRINO. Who on earth is that, Papá Juan?

PAPÁ JUAN. She is otherwise know as Currita.

TRINO. Currita! Who 'd have thought of it! What makes you suppose she 's here?

PAPÁ JUAN. If you 'd eyes in your head you would n't ask. There 's her shawl.

Trino takes up the shawl as if it were not quite an ordinary shawl.

TRINO. Is it? Currita's shawl! Then it 's a new one. I 've not seen her wear it, anyhow. You know . . . a shawl 's a delightful thing . . . and a most significant thing. It 's apparel for a queen . . . and for a peasant. Yes . . . a shawl 's a most charming thing.

PAPÁ JUAN. And this one 's Currita's, moreover!

TRINO. What 's that?

PAPÁ JUAN. That was an aside. You know . . . they have them in plays. You were n't supposed to hear it.

TRINO. But I did!

He puts the shawl down and takes a thoughtful turn or two
about the room. After a moment Currita comes back. She
looks a little crestfallen.

TRINO. Here 's Currita.

PAPÁ JUAN. Hola, Currita!

CURRITA. Oh . . . so you 're back at last, both of you!

TRINO. We 're back at last. And what 's the news with you?

CURRITA. I 've been getting a scolding from Uncle Evaristo.
Oh, such a scolding!

PAPÁ JUAN. What for?

CURRITA. Because I went to his study to write a letter. I 'll
tell you about that in a minute. But I did n't write the letter.
I started to draw a picture instead. It was to be an allegorical
picture: Love, from the Creation through the Ages . . . and its
victims from Adam down to Trino.

TRINO. Down to me?

CURRITA. Down to you.

PAPÁ JUAN. What a subject for an allegory! But why down
to Trino?

CURRITA. Because you say Trino 's the typical man of his time.
Well . . . you know about that and I don't. So of course I had
to take all Uncle Evaristo's nice coloured pencils to draw the
Allegory . . . and he came in and found me. And if I 'd lit a
bonfire on the floor he could n't have made more fuss.

PAPÁ JUAN. But where is this Allegory?

CURRITA. He tore it up.

TRINO. What a shame!

CURRITA. Oh . . . it would have been a masterpiece!

TRINO. I 'm sure of it.

PAPÁ JUAN. By such an artist!

CURRITA. But I can describe it to you. There was Adam . . .
all alone . . . and very, very bored with the Garden of Eden.
And up in one corner I put God . . . asking most politely for his
rib to make it into a wife for him. And Adam with his arms up
in admiration saying . . . " Lord God, if that 's what you can do
with one rib, take the lot! "

Papá Juan and Trino burst out laughing.

PAPÁ JUAN. Hey . . . you 're a madcap!

TRINO. But what 's the use of chalks for that? It ought to be a fresco. And where did I come in, may I ask?

CURRITA. Oh . . . I had n't got to you!

TRINO. But where was I to come in?

CURRITA. It would have ended with you.

PAPÁ JUAN. How were you going to do him?

CURRITA. He 'll be angry, if I say.

TRINO. I could n't be . . . with you.

CURRITA. Will you promise not to be angry?

TRINO. I 'll be angry if you think you need my promise not to be angry.

CURRITA. I was going to make you very pale . . . with black eyes . . . looking at a woman's picture . . . and with a pistol to your head. Are n't you angry?

TRINO. You need n't go on.

PAPÁ JUAN. Yes . . . I 'm afraid he 's angry after all.

CURRITA. I said he would be. Forgive me.

TRINO. No . . . I 'm not angry. But I did n't think you knew of that.

CURRITA. Oh, yes . . . I knew. I won't speak about it . . . ever again, though.

PAPÁ JUAN. No . . . I should n't. We never like to be reminded of the silly things we 've done.

TRINO. I don't object . . . well, I don't to Currita's reminding me. No . . . that 's not the sort of folly it stings one to remember. Indeed . . . I rather like to be reminded that at any rate I 'm no longer such a fool as to . . .! Fancy wanting to blow your brains out at twenty because a woman deceived you.

CURRITA. She did . . . did she!

TRINO. As if one had ever a right to say: " Well, life has no more to give than this . . . so I want no more of it!"

PAPÁ JUAN. Good, Trino . . . good! Life never owns to a failure. The longer the winter the nearer the spring! And I 've seen a hundred of each. So I ought to know. Hey?

TRINO. Bless you, Papá Juan!

PAPÁ JUAN. And I don't doubt it 's been just by believing that, that I 've lived to see so many of them. For I 've never yet sat down to say: "Why, what 's the good of going on?" "Go on" . . . life never stops saying it. You die once. But you 're born every morning when you open your eyes.

TRINO. Yes, indeed.

PAPÁ JUAN. Why, think of it! If you 'd killed yourself for the sake of that woman . . . you would n't be sitting now looking at this pretty sight that 's before you.

CURRITA. Papá Juan . . .

PAPÁ JUAN. But I give you fair warning that this young allegorist . . .

CURRITA. Papá Juan . . . what are you saying?

PAPÁ JUAN. Tut tut! Don't shake your head at me. I 'm grown up. I shall say what I like! . . . that this young symbolist finds something to admire in that exploit of yours.

TRINO. Really?

PAPÁ JUAN. Yes, indeed!

TRINO. Dear me! How does that come about, Currita?

CURRITA. Now you 're both going to make fun of me.

TRINO. No . . . I 'd like to know what you find to admire.

CURRITA. Oh . . . don't take it so seriously. I 'll tell you. There 's nothing very strange about it. I do admire what you did . . . yes, I do! For whatever you may say . . . at least it was n't commonplace . . . it was n't sordid. Trino, you don't know what it means when you 're young and you want things to happen, to have to live here in this town where nothing ever happens! All there 's to hope for here is that when the church clock has struck three it 'll strike four in an hour's time . . . and after that you live for another hour in the hope that it 'll strike five. If they 'd only ring that poor bell for a fire alarm now and then I 'm sure it would be so pleased. There are days when I feel I shall die, Trino, if something does n't happen . . . something a little glorious . . . or a little desperate. Yes, I suppose it was silly of you to try and shoot yourself. But I 'm not a bit sorry

you tried, Trino. I 'd only be sorry . . . if you 'd succeeded.
Yes, then I 'd have been sorry . . . very sorry.

*A silence falls; though Papá Juan looks mischievously from
Trino to Currita and from Currita to Trino. From the
right comes Eulalia, breaking the spell. She carries some table
linen, ironed and folded.*

EULALIA. Currita.

CURRITA. What is it?

EULALIA. Aunt Marciala wants you.

CURRITA. What for?

EULALIA. She has something to ask you.

CURRITA. But what?

EULALIA. She did n't say. Are n't you going?

CURRITA. Yes, I 'll go. Don't you know what it is?

EULALIA. Have n't an idea!

Eulalia goes out again. Currita is in no hurry to follow her.

CURRITA. Now what can she want with me?

PAPÁ JUAN. If I may advise . . . I should go to her and
say: "Aunt Marciala, what is it you want with me?" She will
probably tell you . . . and so the mystery will be solved.

CURRITA. Yes . . . that is an idea, is n't it? I 'm off!

*She is, but her little feet might be made of lead. Silence falls
again, till Trino suddenly breaks it.*

TRINO. Papá Juan.

PAPÁ JUAN. What is it?

TRINO. I wish your birthday were over.

PAPÁ JUAN. I don't wish it were over . . . but I wish it were
here. Five days yet! And once or twice it has come to me that,
after all, I may n't see the day.

TRINO. Oh . . . don't say that.

PAPÁ JUAN. Well . . . death 's enough of a woman . . . and
enough of a jade . . . to play a trick on me if she can. But I
think I 'll be too clever for her . . . just as you were, Trino.
Why do you wish my birthday were over?

TRINO. I want to get away from here.

PAPÁ JUAN. What 's wrong? Is n't your bed comfortable?

TRINO. Papá Juan . . . I have something to tell you that will surprise you very much. I 'm in love with Currita.

PAPÁ JUAN. Dear me, dear me, dear me! That is most surprising.

TRINO. Deeply . . . desperately . . . and quite hopelessly in love.

PAPÁ JUAN. Yes . . . that 's the usual thing. But why run away? If you 'd fallen in love with Aunt Filomena, now . . . why, yes, I 'd recommend bolting. But with Currita . . . is it really so hopeless?

TRINO. But I don't want it to be anything but hopeless, Papá Juan. I object to falling in love. And I most particularly object to falling in love with Currita. Such a charming child . . . pretty . . . imaginative . . . !

PAPÁ JUAN. In fact if it had to be some one . . . you 'd really prefer Filomena?

TRINO. Do please try to understand.

PAPÁ JUAN. I 'm trying. But it 's not very easy.

TRINO. Who am I to go knocking at the gate of that fairyland Currita calls her heart? I 've had no luck in love affairs. I 've never yet told a woman I loved her but she did n't have to suffer for it somehow.

PAPÁ JUAN. Really! Dear me! Have you ever been in love?

TRINO. Oh . . . a hundred times.

PAPÁ JUAN. But that 's to say you 've never been in love at all. Trino, Trino . . . we talk so much about it! But your poets and romancers may say what they please . . . there 's only one genuine sort . . . the love that has life and yet more life for its end. If that 's what love means to a man and a woman, they can hear, if they 'll listen when they 're alone together, a voice . . . is it? . . . very far off. No, nothing so certain as that! It 's like music sounding in space . . . and calling to them . . . calling: " Life give me life." You 've never heard that?

TRINO. No.

PAPÁ JUAN. You 'll know it when you hear it.

TRINO. Love must be fruitful, you mean . . . or it 's not love?

PAPÁ JUAN. Does the sun shine on the earth in vain? Ah, Trino, believe me . . . I was the same at your age . . . everything else is just playing at love.

TRINO. Playing at love!

Manuel appears in the garden.

MANUEL. Don Juan.

PAPÁ JUAN. Come in, Manuel.

MANUEL. It 's Antoñón . . . the one from Chorrito . . . says he wants to speak to you.

PAPÁ JUAN. Antoñón . . . why, to be sure!

TRINO. What Antoñón 's that?

PAPÁ JUAN. He 's a fine fellow. He 's a cousin of ours . . . and he runs a little market garden. I 'll take you to see it.

TRINO. A cousin of ours, is he?

PAPÁ JUAN. Yes, a cousin. His father was Gumersindo Álvarez del Monte . . . who was a first cousin twice removed of my father's. He was an innkeeper . . . had his inn down by Christ Church. Nothing left of it now. All forgotten . . . innkeeper and inn! Even Christ gets forgotten in these days!

MANUEL. What am I to tell him, Señorito?

PAPÁ JUAN. Tell him? Why . . . show him in, of course.

MANUEL. As you say, Señorito.

Manuel departs, disapprovingly, to do so.

TRINO. I 'll leave you with him. I 'll be in the Patio.

He goes out to the left. Currita, coming in at that moment from the other direction, sees him go; and a little regretfully.

CURRITA. Oh. . . .

PAPÁ JUAN. We 're getting on! Here 's Antoñón now!

CURRITA. Papá Juan.

PAPÁ JUAN. Well . . . what did your aunt have to say to you?

CURRITA. She wanted to find out something that I did n't mean she should. And she did n't.

PAPÁ JUAN. Hola! Was it some secretarial secret?

CURRITA. I 've had a letter from Gabriela.

PAPÁ JUAN. You have!

CURRITA. Yes, I have, Señor! And I went to the study to

answer it.   She wants to know why you keep sending to say she must come for your birthday when she has written to you twice to say that she will.

PAPÁ JUAN.   Written to me twice?

CURRITA.   That 's what she writes to me.   So if the letters ever came . . . there 's been a little juggling somewhere.

PAPÁ JUAN.   I see!   Well . . . that kind of conjuring trick does n't amuse me.   I shall speak to those children of mine.

Manuel now comes back with Antoñón, who has been described to us already.   But he is now dressed as is fitting for so important a visit.

ANTOÑÓN.   God be with all here.

PAPÁ JUAN.   Come in, my dear Antoñón, come in!   How are you?

ANTOÑÓN.   I 'm well, I thank you.   And I hope you 're quite well, Don Juan.

PAPÁ JUAN.   Look at me!

ANTOÑÓN.   And you, Señorita?

CURRITA.   Very well, thank you.   And how 's your wife . . . how are your girls?

ANTOÑÓN   Doing themselves credit, I hope.

CURRITA.   And the children?

ANTOÑÓN.   Wearing out shoe-leather.

CURRITA.   Give them my love.

ANTOÑÓN.   I will.

CURRITA.   God be with you.

ANTOÑÓN.   And with you, Señorita.

Currita is going the way Trino went when Manuel's voice checks her.

MANUEL.   Señorita Currita.

CURRITA.   Now, what is it you want?

MANUEL.   I don't want anything.   But your maid 's come to say that your mother says you 're to go home at once.

CURRITA.   To go home at once?

MANUEL.   That 's what she said, Señorita.

PAPÁ JUAN.   Is anything wrong?

CURRITA. Is anything wrong, did she say?

MANUEL. Well . . . she was all of a grin . . . so there should n't be anything very wrong. But she says you 're to go home at once.

CURRITA. Heavens above us! Very well . . . I 'll go. Some days I simply have no luck. I won't be long, Papá Juan.

She settles her shawl and goes off through the garden. Manuel follows her.

ANTOÑÓN. She has a way with her . . . that girl of Don Joaquín's. And it 's a way of her own too.

PAPÁ JUAN. Yes . . . she has a way with her.

ANTOÑÓN. Not a bit less the young lady for it either? She reminds me . . . well, she reminds me of my spring radishes. They 're tender . . . but they 've a tang to them.

PAPÁ JUAN [*His appreciative little chuckle*]. Hey! Well now . . . sit down.

ANTOÑÓN. You 're very kind.

He sits down.

PAPÁ JUAN. And put your hat down too.

ANTOÑÓN. It 's not in my way, thank you.

PAPÁ JUAN. Give it to me, then.

So Papá Juan takes the hat, puts it on a chair and then settles himself again. Antoñón takes a long silent look at him.

ANTOÑÓN. Don Juan, are you really as old as they say you are . . . or are you taking us all in?

PAPÁ JUAN. You must ask the good priest who christened me.

ANTOÑÓN. Where is he now?

PAPÁ JUAN. Ah . . . he has been waiting up there for me this many a year! He was a good man . . . and he was good to me. Don Manuel Martínez y Argote his name was. And he said he was descended from the poet, Don Luis de Góngora y Argote. But we all used to call him Papa Mousetrap . . . because he 'd invented a most infernal machine . . . it slaughtered them in thousands.

ANTOÑÓN. And you keep your memory!

PAPÁ JUAN. Hey! And so your folks are all well?

ANTOÑÓN. They 've no time to be ill.

PAPÁ JUAN. I dropped in to see them the other day. And your garden 's a marvel. I 'm jealous. Mine 's nothing like so good.

ANTOÑÓN. They get the same sunshine. But yours eats up food and looks pretty. I look to mine to feed me.

PAPÁ JUAN. That 's true . . . that 's very true! It has not been such a bad year, though, for either of us.

ANTOÑÓN. No, we 've had rain, thank God!

> Rain in May
> Gives us bread every day.

PAPÁ JUAN. Yes, yes!

> Rain in May,
> That 's the way
> To a muddy road,
> But a garden gay.

Well, well! Did your María tell you why I wanted you to come and see me this afternoon? Will you and she and your children give me the great pleasure of your company to dinner here on the twenty-fifth instant to celebrate my hundredth birthday?

Antoñón does not answer.

PAPÁ JUAN. Come, come, come! What does this mean?

ANTOÑÓN. Señor don Juan del Monte, in this world of ours there always have been, have n't there, the rich and the poor? Now I daresay it 's hard to do your duty by riches . . . by your poverty I know it is. Not that I want to be rich . . . I don't. I 'm better off than some rich men I know . . . because I 'm content to be poor. Yes, in spite of what the song says:

> When a poor man is n't sober
> They call him a drunken old sot,
> When a rich man 's half seas over:
> What humour the gentleman 's got!

I take no shame for being poor. My friend Alonso . . . that 's married to Carmen Campos . . . says a day 's coming when all the poor will be rich. Moonshine! But if ever it does and I live

to see it . . . I won't be rich, I promise you. No . . . poverty
for me! Better be a rich poor man than a poor rich one any day.
D 'you follow me?

PAPÁ JUAN. Partly, Antoñón . . . partly.

ANTOÑÓN. And don't you think with me that cotton frills look
wrong on a silk skirt? Set me and my wife and children down
at your dinner table . . . we 'd be like that.

PAPÁ JUAN. Why?

ANTOÑÓN. Because this world 's been rolling one way too long
for it to roll the other way just because we want it to . . . as I
say to my friend Alonso.

PAPÁ JUAN. Well . . . with due respect to you and your friend
Alonso . . . on my hundredth birthday it 'll roll just for once the
way I think it should. You 'll come to dinner . . . and your
wife and children too . . . with their cotton frills on! And we 'll
all be delighted to see you.

ANTOÑÓN. Señor don Juan del Monte . . .

PAPÁ JUAN. And now what is it?

ANTOÑÓN. If Jesus Christ came into the world to set these
things right . . . and if he could n't. . . .

PAPÁ JUAN. I want no more of your moralizings, Antoñón.
You 're not the only poor man that 's coming to dine with me.

ANTOÑÓN. No?

PAPÁ JUAN. No, indeed. I 've a little grand-nephew serving
his king and country . . . he 's a drummer boy. And you should
read the letter he wrote me!

ANTOÑÓN. But the rest don't live in Arenales. In a place like
this where everybody knows everybody and they all get gossiping
and backbiting . . . let a poor man sit once at a rich man's table
. . . why, that 's the end of the world!

PAPÁ JUAN. This world won't end to satisfy them. And if a
little thing like that 's going to end it . . . well, the sooner it
ends the better. And we 'll build one with more sense in it out of
the bits . . . where a rich man and a poor man can have dinner
together without a lot of fools to make a fuss about it.

ANTOÑÓN [*grimly ironic*]. But that 's the sort of mad idea

my friend Alonso has.   That 's what he says to me . . . and in
so many words.

PAPÁ JUAN.   I know.   But he says it when he 's drunk . . . and
I say it when I 'm sober.   And he thinks he 'll bring it to pass by
shooting people . . . and I only want to shake hands with them.
That 's the difference between us.   So shake hands with me now
. . . and say you 'll come to my party.

They shake hands.

ANTOÑÓN.   Don Juan . . . when a man 's as good as you I
suppose he does n't need to think he 's any better than other men.

PAPÁ JUAN.   Why . . . if our gardens have the same sun to
shine on them . . . so have we.   Promise you 'll come.

Antoñón does not answer.

PAPÁ JUAN.   Promise.

ANTOÑÓN.   But there 's more than me to reckon with.

PAPÁ JUAN.   What . . . are n't you master in your own home?

ANTOÑÓN.   Oh, I 'm its master . . . but it 's got a mistress.
I have my way in the house . . . because that 's my wife's way
too . . . as long as it 's understood that in some things she gets
her way.   I 'll tell you.   There 's a lady . . . who 's your relative
and mine . . . and with all the world and his wife . . . and with
my wife more than most . . . she 's like this.

*He strikes his fingers together.   We recognise the gesture; so
does Papá Juan.*

PAPÁ JUAN.   No need to name her!

ANTOÑÓN.   What she 's got against us I don't know . . . no
more does María . . . and we don't either of us care.   But whenever that lady passes our door she spits on the ground . . . and,
what 's more, she treads it in.

PAPÁ JUAN.   What a quaint thing to do!

ANTOÑÓN.   Ah, you may laugh.   But when my wife sees her
do it she sees red.   And time and again, I tell you I 've had a
trowel ready to throw at that good lady's head.   For after all,
Don Juan del Monte . . . spitting on the ground . . . if you feel
that way towards anybody . . . that 's one thing.   But treading
it in after . . . that 's going rather far!

PAPÁ JUAN. Well . . . you come to my party and you 'll have your revenge. For she 'll have to sit and swallow her insults then . . . mouthfuls of them!

ANTOÑÓN. Don Juan . . . you do me an honour in asking me and I 'll not let you ask me again. The folk from Chorrito will be there.

PAPÁ JUAN. Good!

ANTOÑÓN. But if I may give a bit of advice . . . when you 're setting out that dinner table put Doña Filomena at one end of it and my wife at the other.

PAPÁ JUAN. Hey! Hey!

ANTOÑÓN. For all I know my friend Alonso 's day of universal brotherhood may dawn . . . but, even so, we shan't see the sun rise on universal sisterhood in a hurry.

PAPÁ JUAN. Hey!

ANTOÑÓN. Good-bye, then . . . and thank you, Señor don Juan del Monte.

PAPÁ JUAN. Good-bye and thank you, Antoñón. I 'll come to the gate with you.

ANTOÑÓN. No . . . indeed . . . please!

PAPÁ JUAN. Nonsense . . . go ahead!

ANTOÑÓN. You do me too much honour.

As they pass out into the garden who should arrive but Doña Filomena.

PAPÁ JUAN. Afternoon, Filomena.

DOÑA FILOMENA. Good afternoon.

And, seeing Antoñón she really does seem to spit. Moreover, she treads it in.

ANTOÑÓN. There . . . what did I tell you?

PAPÁ JUAN. Go along, man, go along. Back in a minute, Filomena!

Papá Juan and Antoñón disappear. Filomena is furious.

DOÑA FILOMENA. And I must wait, if you please, the convenience of that . . . market gardener! And I imagine these things, do I! I might be a scullery maid! I shall begin to think I am a scullery maid soon.

Eulalia's voice is heard. She is singing the same song.

DOÑA FILOMENA. Eulalia . . . singing! Her sulks she kindly keeps for me. Sing away, my child . . . sing away!

This last to Eulalia herself, who has just appeared. At the sight of her mother she has stopped singing very promptly; and her face falls. Doña Filomena's expression would indeed hardly dispose any one to either mirth or melody.

EULALIA. Oh, Mamma! When did you come?

DOÑA FILOMENA. Sing on, Eulalia, sing on! No hypocrisy, please! The moment I 'm out of your way you 're happy enough, it seems.

EULALIA. That was n't why I was feeling happy . . . just for the moment, Mamma.

DOÑA FILOMENA. Don't prevaricate, Eulalia. Your sisters at home, no doubt, are dancing and singing, too, because I 'm out of their way.

EULALIA. If they are, I can't help it.

DOÑA FILOMENA. Eulalia, how dare you!

EULALIA. You 've just come from Currita's, have n't you?

DOÑA FILOMENA. I have just come from Currita's. And I opened their eyes to some purpose, I think.

EULALIA. What about?

DOÑA FILOMENA. As I mean to here.

EULALIA. Oh, Mamma . . . please!

DOÑA FILOMENA. It 's useless to "Oh Mamma" me. The matter 's most serious.

EULALIA. But what is it?

DOÑA FILOMENA. Nothing you can be supposed to understand. Ask me no more. Call your uncle and aunt here immediately.

EULALIA. Uncle Evaristo 's asleep.

DOÑA FILOMENA. Wake him up. Where 's Trino?

EULALIA. He 's in the patio . . . reading a novel.

DOÑA FILOMENA. Some nasty free-thinking stuff, I expect! Tell him to stop reading it and come here. Most instructive to hear what our young revolutionary has to say to this!

EULALIA. Revolutionary! Oh . . . what is it all about?

DOÑA FILOMENA. Nothing, I have told you, that you can understand. Will you do as I bid, please?

EULALIA. Yes, I will. Mamma . . . I pray God to make you different.

DOÑA FILOMENA. What? What's that?

EULALIA. I do. I pray to God to make you quite, quite different. You do nothing but quarrel with every one . . . and it makes me perfectly wretched.

DOÑA FILOMENA. Eulalia . . . how dare you?

EULALIA. You scold . . . and you stir up strife . . . and you think the worst of every one. And you never go anywhere but you bring trouble with you. And it makes me wretched. For I'm your daughter . . . your own flesh and blood, as you're always telling me. And I'd so like to be proud of you and have people say nice things about you. And you should hear what they do say the moment your back's turned! It's dreadful!

And Eulalia departs in floods of tears.

DOÑA FILOMENA. The girl's losing her mind! A very good thing I came. These hysterics! . . . we'll have no more of them!

Papá Juan comes back through the garden singing to himself.

PAPÁ JUAN.

"When King Fernando lost his crown . . ."

DOÑA FILOMENA. An odd visitor to find with you, Papá Juan. Are you buying your vegetables from him for the famous dinner?

PAPÁ JUAN. No . . . he's coming to help eat it.

DOÑA FILOMENA. That man!

PAPÁ JUAN. Yes. Why not? He's a cousin of ours.

DOÑA FILOMENA. My daughters and I are to sit down to dinner with a market gardener?

PAPÁ JUAN. Yes . . . that's what he is . . . and he keeps pigs besides. But I daresay he won't bring the pigs with him. I'll ask him not to.

DOÑA FILOMENA. Is this, may I ask, to be a family dinner party or a heathen orgy?

PAPÁ JUAN. I don't know of any heathen that are coming.

I don't know that we 've got any heathen in the family. I rather wish we had.

DOÑA FILOMENA. Once and for all, please . . . if that man and his brood are to be there I shall be conspicuous by my absence.

PAPÁ JUAN. Once and for all, thank you . . . he and his brood will be there . . . and so will you be.

> *Eulalia passes across the room. She is still very depressed and she gives Papá Juan a most appealing look.*

DOÑA FILOMENA. Neither I nor my girls.

PAPÁ JUAN. You and your girls both.

DOÑA FILOMENA. You flatter yourself, Papá Juan.

PAPÁ JUAN. No, I do not. Now, don't you be a goose, Filomena. I 've known you since the day your mother brought you in the world . . . and I knew her from the day her mother brought her into the world. I know all about you . . . and I know you mean to come to my dinner.

DOÑA FILOMENA. I say no more . . . I say no more! Silence is golden. I say no more!

> *So Papá Juan takes a little turn round the room and rather mockingly hums his song again.*

PAPÁ JUAN.

"The braggarts threw their bombs-o!"

But apart from the pleasure you find in our society . . . and now that you 've rallied a little from the shock of meeting the market-gardener . . . to what do we owe the honour of this visit, Filomena?

DOÑA FILOMENA. I will tell you . . . when the rest of the family have assembled.

PAPÁ JUAN. Oh, . . . indeed!

DOÑA FILOMENA. Including that infidel Trino.

PAPÁ JUAN. Is he, now?

DOÑA FILOMENA. I particularly wish him to be present. I shall then have to mention a certain name . . .

PAPÁ JUAN. What name?

DOÑA FILOMENA. Not often mentioned here . . . and its owner might well be considered unmentionable.

PAPÁ JUAN. What name, please?

DOÑA FILOMENA. Gabriela.

PAPÁ JUAN. Gabriela. How lucky! I was just about to mention her myself. Good! Here's Marciala. And here's your infidel, too.

Doña Marciala and Trino have arrived from the left.

DOÑA MARCIALA. Hola, Filomena!

DOÑA FILOMENA. Good afternoon, Marciala.

TRINO. How are you, Aunt Filomena?

DOÑA FILOMENA. Thank you, I am well . . . Señor.

TRINO. What have I done to be called Señor!

DOÑA FILOMENA. I have not, I think, had the pleasure of seeing you since the morning of your arrival . . . when you passed me without a word.

TRINO. Did I?

DOÑA FILOMENA. I think so.

TRINO. Fancy! I thought it was the other way about.

Doña Marciala makes a sign to Trino to drop the subject.

DOÑA FILOMENA. Yes, Marciala . . . I saw you do that.

PAPÁ JUAN [*His chuckle*]. Hey!

DOÑA MARCIALA. Well, what is it, Filomena . . . what have you to say to us?

DOÑA FILOMENA. We will wait for Evaristo, if you please.

Don Evaristo comes from the right; half awake and in a very bad humour.

DON EVARISTO. Here's Evaristo. What's the matter? [*Sighting Filomena.*] Oh . . . I smell trouble!

DOÑA FILOMENA. You don't say you are happy to see me, I notice.

DON EVARISTO. No, I don't, Filomena. Because, when I do you call me a hypocrite for my pains.

They all sit down and there is a pause.

PAPÁ JUAN. Well . . . we're all here.

DOÑA FILOMENA. Yes . . . we are all here.

DON EVARISTO. Why must I be woke up?

DOÑA FILOMENA. When the honour of your family is at

stake, you 'd prefer, I should think, to have your eyes opened to it!

DOÑA MARCIALA. Filomena . . . what are you talking about?

DOÑA FILOMENA. Ask Papá Juan.

PAPÁ JUAN. Papá Juan has something to say about it on his own account. Now, Marciala . . . and Evaristo! Have there been any letters from Gabriela?

Don Evaristo looks at Doña Marciala, she at him. But they neither of them say a word.

PAPÁ JUAN. Thank you. I see there have been.

Doña Filomena coughs; a most expressive cough.

DON EVARISTO. You 'd better explain, perhaps, Marciala.

DOÑA MARCIALA. Papá . . . up to now we 've done whatever you asked us to do . . . and you know we only want to please you. But when it comes to Gabriela . . . there we must draw the line.

DON EVARISTO. Yes . . . there, I am afraid, we must draw the line.

PAPÁ JUAN. Must we? And why?

DON EVARISTO. Well, now, Marciala . . . why? Why . . . should you say?

DOÑA FILOMENA. Allow me to tell you why. Because I don't set foot in the same house with such a woman . . . that 's one reason. And though there may be no pure young minds here to contaminate . . . am I to bring my daughters to rub shoulders with . . . with a strumpet?

PAPÁ JUAN. Come, come, now!

DOÑA FILOMENA. Strumpet . . . I repeat! Does even the atheist demand that of me?

They all — except Papá Juan — look round for the atheist.

TRINO. Who . . . may I ask . . . is the atheist?

DOÑA FILOMENA. I think you know!

PAPÁ JUAN. Don't let us waste time, please, talking nonsense.

DOÑA FILOMENA. Far be it from me to do so! This is my last word. If Gabriela comes to your party, my girls and I stay away.

PAPÁ JUAN.   Well, we 'd still have the market-gardener! Listen to me, please. Gabriela 's coming and you 're coming . . . and that 's all about it.

DOÑA FILOMENA.   An outrage!

DOÑA MARCIALA.   No, Papá, no! For once Filomena is right.

DOÑA FILOMENA.   For once . . . for once! I thank you! Have I never been right before?

DOÑA MARCIALA.   Well, you are now, Filomena . . . and that 's all that matters for the moment. Papá . . . do consider. Gabriela 's been unfortunate . . . weak . . . we 'll call it what you like. But don't ask us to receive her here. It 's not on our own account. We must think of others . . . and of the example. What a scandal in the town! And the treatment she 'll expose herself to if she comes . . . have you thought of that? Will it be a kindness to her?

DON EVARISTO.   Marciala is right . . . I 'm afraid she 's right.

DOÑA FILOMENA.   And I . . . for once!

DON EVARISTO.   For once.

DOÑA FILOMENA.   Psha!

PAPÁ JUAN.   No . . . you 're wrong . . . all three of you.

DOÑA MARCIALA.   Papá . . .!

DOÑA FILOMENA.   How would the anarchist settle it?

She gazes at Trino.

TRINO.   Oh . . . am I an anarchist, too?

DOÑA FILOMENA.   To whom else does the term apply?

TRINO.   Well, the anarchist . . . to justify his title . . . would first place a bomb under your chair. . . .

DOÑA FILOMENA [*to the company and the universe in general*]. D 'you hear that?

TRINO.   A very little one . . . just big enough to make you jump. Next I should tell you all . . . and I do . . . that Gabriela 's fault is not a crime to be punished as you wish to punish it. When it 's love brings a woman to grief . . . I 'd be gentle.

DOÑA FILOMENA.   It is easy to see that you have no belief in God.

TRINO.   How do you make that out?

DOÑA FILOMENA.   Is it or is it not against God's law for a woman to bear children till she 's married?

TRINO.   And what about the women who won't bear children when they are married?

DOÑA FILOMENA.   I am not here to quibble.

PAPÁ JUAN.   Trino 's right.   Are you going to punish Gabriela when what God did was to send her a child?   She was weak . . . that I know.   But wicked . . . no, she was n't.   To be here with us all again may save her from more weakness . . . and from wickedness, too.   She must come.   Don't deny it me.   In my hundred years I 've seen much of the ill of life . . . I 've seen more of the good.   And just for this one day I want us all to be together . . . rich and poor . . . happy and unhappy . . . strong and weak . . . yes, if you like, wicked and virtuous, too. Is it worth while to make differences?   In another hundred years we 'll all be together again . . . and there 'll be no difference then.

A little pause.

TRINO.   Don't worry, Papá Juan.   You shall have your way. Shan't he?

DOÑA MARCIALA.   Yes, Trino.   Yes, Papá, yes.   We 'll say no more about it.

TRINO.   There . . . you see!   Yours to command . . . ours to obey.   If you want the whole world to your party the whole world shall come.   And when I keep my hundredth birthday I 'll have the whole world to mine.   Except Aunt Filomena!

DOÑA FILOMENA.   I 'll see to that!

TRINO.   And now I 'm off to find out if the pony-chaise is ready.   We 've to go to meet the little priest.

PAPÁ JUAN.   That 's true . . . I forgot.

TRINO.   In two minutes!

As Trino vanishes, Currita appears.   They exchange greetings.

CURRITA.   Hola!

TRINO.   Hola!

CURRITA.   Well!   You do all look glum.   Whatever has happened?

DOÑA FILOMENA.   One thing we may be sure will always happen. I shall be thrust aside . . . I shall be given the go-by.   For whatever else is not a crime . . . poverty is.   I foresaw this . . . I foretold it.   Well . . . I hope you are all satisfied.

She rises majestically.

CURRITA.   Oh dear!

DOÑA MARCIALA.   Now where are you off to?

DOÑA FILOMENA.   To rescue my precious child.

She goes out to the left, stifling an indignant sob.

CURRITA.   Oh . . . but she's a cross to carry!

DON EVARISTO.   The flower of our flock!

DOÑA MARCIALA.   She shan't take that poor child home and make her miserable.   I'll see that she does n't.

Doña Marciala disappears after her good sister-in-law, fire in her eye.   But poor Don Evaristo sits drooping in his chair.

CURRITA.   Uncle Evaristo . . . oh, what is the matter?

DON EVARISTO.   Currita . . . if these vexations continue . . . I really think that I may die before your dear aunt, after all.

With which he pulls himself together a little and departs.

CURRITA.   What has happened . . . oh, do tell me, Papá Juan?

PAPÁ JUAN.   They 're all to be here, Currita . . . every single one.   I 'm so happy about it . . . you can't think.   Gabriela . . . and Antoñón and his children, too.   I shall have them all round me just for once.   Can you understand what that means to me?   And now I must be off with Trino.

CURRITA.   You 're always off somewhere with Trino, are n't you?

PAPÁ JUAN.   Tut tut!   Don't look like that.   I take Trino with me . . . but I leave Trino here.

CURRITA.   Do you?   How do you?

PAPÁ JUAN.   Ah!

Trino returns.

TRINO.   'Tention!   Quick march.

PAPÁ JUAN.   Quick march it is!

CURRITA.   But I must know what the quarrel was about. Gabriela?

TRINO. Yes. But it was n't a quarrel . . . nothing so lively. We all just found ourselves in one of those nasty, damp fogs of bigotry . . . and cowardice . . . and selfishness . . . in which well-meaning people get so hopelessly lost. But if it had come to fighting . . . I was ready for 'em! In this house Papá Juan's will is law . . . and if he can't enforce it I can. Have n't I told you that I 'm a parcel of all the Del Montes that ever were? Very well! When I speak with all their voices at once let every one listen and hold their tongues. Papá Juan shall have his party . . . such a party! And if any one is missing . . . well, it shan't be Gabriela.

PAPÁ JUAN. Bravo, Trino!

CURRITA. Bravo!

TRINO. Set us to do the impossible, Señor . . . and the impossible is done.

CURRITA. Oh, yes, Papá Juan . . . ask us to do something quite, quite impossible.

TRINO. You 're his darling, Currita . . . and nothing 's too good for you. Ask me to steal from its belfry that bell which annoys you and to melt it into bullets and to have a shot at myself every morning with one of them to relieve the monotony of your existence . . . and I 'll do it . . . I 'll do it with pleasure.

PAPÁ JUAN. Hey!

CURRITA. Oh, Trino, it must be wonderful to be as foolish as you are!

TRINO. Quick march now, Papá Juan.

PAPÁ JUAN. Yes . . . quick march.

TRINO. We shan't be long, Currita.

CURRITA. No . . . don't be long.

Trino and Papá Juan — he leaning on Trino's arm — start off through the garden.

PAPÁ JUAN. Not a single one missing . . . I shall have them all around me . . . think of it!

Currita stands looking after them.

CURRITA. His little light! Oh . . . I hope I shall always see it too.

ACT III

*Carmen Campos is putting the room straight.   Far off in the garden,
where the birthday party is in full swing, we hear a man's
voice singing — Carmen pauses to listen . . .*

> Señor don Juan del Monte
> Has come to his hundredth birthday,
> May Heaven shower graces upon him
> For he has sown wisdom and goodness.

CARMEN.   He can sing! Who wrote all the words for him, I
wonder.   That 's the tenth verse or more.
  *In the doorway on the left there suddenly appears Alonso,
  Carmen Campos's husband.   He also, it is evident, has been
  celebrating the occasion.*

CARMEN.   Alonso!

ALONSO.   Yes . . . here is the missing guest.

CARMEN.   Who let you in?

ALONSO.   Manuel let me in . . . my proletarian comrade . . .
my brother in revolution.

CARMEN.   That I 'm sure he is n't.   Who told him to let you in?

ALONSO.   His sense of the importance of the occasion told him.
Is Alonso Parra . . . your very own husband . . . is he not to
press the hand of Don Juan del Monte this day?   Stand in my
path if you dare.   Let Bishops and Archbishops stand in my path
if they dare.

CARMEN.   Now, none of your silly talk!   To begin with, Doña
Marciala does n't want you here.   She never knows what you 'll
do or say next.   In the second place . . . nor do I!   Go away
and leave us in peace.

ALONSO.   In what do I offend?   Name it.   Set forth the offensive thing.

CARMEN.   You 've been drinking . . . and you smell of drink.
That 's one offensive thing.

ALONSO.   I have drunk what was due to my sense of the importance of the occasion.   And I do not imagine . . . I say I do not

upon which the sun shines . . . and the moon and the stars will shine a little later . . . as they have never shone before. It is an occasion, I told them, of peace and of concord . . . upon which Alonso Parra himself abrogates his principles and does homage to Don Juan del Monte. Why? Because upon this occasion Don Juan del Monte has gathered around him the rich and the poor and made no difference between them. And because Don Juan del Monte has made rivers of gold and silver to run in Arenales . . . rivers of refreshment to the poor. That's what I told my friends. And my words so moved them . . . that it was the unanimous sense of the meeting that I should come and say it all over again to the company here assembled. And I have come to do so. And I venture to think it will astonish them.

CARMEN. Well, it might! But you and your Liberty Lovers reckoned without me. And you won't do so. And that's flat.

The song in the garden goes on . . .

> What have you there on your bosom
> That smells so sweetly?
> Orange flowers from the Indies
> And green rosemary.
> What smells so sweetly?
> Orange flowers
> And white rosemary.

ANTOÑÓN. I should n't stop him, Carmen Campos. He's had a drop . . . and he'll talk a lot of nonsense. But it won't be noticed. For the fact is that some of them out there are talking a lot of their own sort of nonsense too . . . because they 've had a drop. There's one good lady I 've just come here to get away from. She's had half a drop . . . and she was crying over me!

ALONSO. That's disgusting . . . that's most disgusting!

ANTOÑÓN. People should learn to carry their liquor with dignity. Wine or no wine makes no odds to me. I did n't want to come away. It's pretty to see them all there . . . as gay as a Manila shawl. God bless Don Juan del Monte!

CARMEN. Nothing 's ever been seen like it in Arenales.

ANTOÑÓN. Nor anywhere else, Carmen Campos. A Don Juan del Monte 's not born every day . . . and when he is he does n't often live to be a hundred . . . and when he does he does n't give a party like this.

ALONSO. My very words . . . the very words I had in mind to say!

ANTOÑÓN. Well, now I 've said them . . . so you need n't. I 'm a pretty tough customer, let me tell you. I 've no use for sentiment. I earn my living hard . . . and the weather and my crops are all I 've time to care about. But I tell you this, too, Carmen Campos . . . and you, "Comrade Alonso." When Don Juan del Monte took his place to-day at table . . . with us all sitting round him . . . well, any one that wanted to see me cry had only to look at me.

CARMEN. I 'm sure I could n't have seen you. I was crying too much myself.

ANTOÑÓN. Forgetting all our quarrels . . . and forgetting all our troubles . . . simply at the sight of that old man there. And each time I looked at him he seemed more of a miracle to me.

ALONSO. Most happily expressed, Comrade! But why? Because when all are equal . . . all are content!

CARMEN. Can't you stop grinding out that same old tune?

ANTOÑÓN. But it 's the children's corner I can't keep away from. The young rascals! Did you see Rafaelita . . . that 's the little dark one in red . . . stand up and say her piece of poetry to Don Juan? God knows I 've five to feed already . . . but I 'd take her home with me. If the angels in heaven were n't listening to her . . . well, they missed a treat!

ALONSO. There are no angels in heaven. That 's a scientific fact.

CARMEN. A lot you know about what 's in heaven . . . and a lot you 're likely to.

ALONSO. Carmen Campos . . . you are an ignorant woman. You can't read or write . . . you have no culture . . . you are incapable of understanding such books as my friend the barber

DOÑA FILOMENA. Is n't it a miracle? Here we all are . . . so happy and so loving! Just like dear disciples! Eating from the same dish . . . drinking from the same cup! What are you laughing at, Antoñón?

ANTOÑÓN. It 's the cup that does it! I know that miracle.

DOÑA FILOMENA. Don't you make fun of me now. D' you mean to say you think I 've had a sip?

ANTOÑÓN. Two sips, Señora. But it shan't go any further.

DOÑA FILOMENA. You 're a wag! No, Antoñón, no . . . that could n't make me happy. True happiness, remember, comes from within. It can only come from a loving heart . . . like mine! But when I 'm happiest, Antoñón, I 'm still a little sad . . . thinking of that dear partner of my joys and sorrows, who is no more.

ANTOÑÓN. Miss your husband sometimes, do you?

DOÑA FILOMENA. Always. And I ask . . . why does not God take me to him? For then he 'd be happy too.

ANTOÑÓN. I should n't worry, Señora. I don't doubt the good God knows what 's best for both of you. I 'm going back to the garden.

Doña Filomena sits forlorn.

DOÑA FILOMENA. Don't leave me, Antoñón.

ANTOÑÓN. Come along then. Better take my arm. You might slip.

DOÑA FILOMENA. Shan't we take a stroll first . . . by ourselves . . . till I 'm composed?

ANTOÑÓN. Just as you say.

DOÑA FILOMENA. Oh . . . the children are singing now . . . the darlings! Like the song of birds . . . is n't it . . . oh, is n't it?

The sound of the song floats in.

> Who tells tales of the charcoal seller?
> Who tells tales of the charcoal girl?
> Who 's that saying that I am married?
> Who 's that saying that I 'm in love?

The little widow, the little widow,
The little widow they want to wed;
To the Count de Cabra, the Count de Cabra,
To the Count de Cabra she 'll be led.

I do not love the Count de Cabra,
The Count de Cabra — ah, poor me!
I do not love the Count de Cabra,
The Count de Cabra, but only thee.

ANTOÑÓN.   Very like birds.   And if my two among 'em only were birds they would n't be so hard on their shoe leather.

DOÑA FILOMENA.   You 're such a wit!   Why, who 's this? It 's not Papá Juan?

ANTOÑÓN.   Yes . . . it 's Papá Juan.

Passing into the garden, they meet, first Trino, and then Papá Juan on Doña Marciala's arm.

DOÑA FILOMENA.   There 's nothing wrong with Papá Juan?

TRINO.   No, nothing at all.   But he 's getting very excited . . . and we must n't run risks.   So I 've brought him . . .

DOÑA FILOMENA.   Dear Trino!   Always so thoughtful . . . always so wise!

TRINO.   Am I?   Why, of course . . . so I am!

DOÑA FILOMENA.   Dear Papá Juan!

PAPÁ JUAN.   Hola, Filomena!   Been drinking my health again, have you?

DOÑA FILOMENA.   What a day for us all . . . what a day . . . what a day!

DOÑA MARCIALA.   We know, Filomena.   You go back to the others now.   I 'll be there in a minute.

DOÑA FILOMENA.   Dear Marciala!   I 've never been so happy. I 've laughed so much . . . and I 've cried so much.

ANTOÑÓN.   And her heart is full!

DOÑA FILOMENA.   Come along, Antoñón.

She disappears.   Papá Juan is in great glee.

PAPÁ JUAN.   What miracle is this, Antoñón?

ANTOÑÓN.   I 'll tell you.   It 's the miracle that came after the miracle when the Lord turned the water into wine. So it 's quite all right, of course. She 's a dear sweet lady . . . and I 'm her bosom friend. But the truth is, Don Juan . . . I like her better when she spits.

Doña Filomena re-appears.

DOÑA FILOMENA. Antoñón . . . I 'm waiting.

ANTOÑÓN. Coming, Señora, coming.

They both disappear into the garden.

TRINO. Well . . . you 'll be quiet here.

PAPÁ JUAN. What 's that?

TRINO. Aha . . . you 're my prisoner! Just for a little . . . then we 'll take another plunge into the vortex.

DOÑA MARCIALA. Yes, Papá . . . one can have too much of a good thing. You 've been very excited. And you 'll please stay here quietly with Trino till I come back.

PAPÁ JUAN. Very well . . . I 'll be good . . . I 'll do just what you tell me. [*After a pause.*] Marciala?

DOÑA MARCIALA. Yes, Papá.

PAPÁ JUAN. What about the flowers . . . the flowers from the dinner table?

DOÑA MARCIALA. That 's all right. I had them sent off to the cemetery at once.

PAPÁ JUAN. Who took them?

DOÑA MARCIALA. Carmen Campos's two girls. Don't worry now. Everything you wanted done is being done.

PAPÁ JUAN. But they won't know where your mother's grave is . . . will they?

DOÑA MARCIALA. Of course they know . . . where Mamma's grave is . . . and Santita's . . . and where they all are! You are not to worry.

TRINO. The very best thing you could do would be to take a little nap.

PAPÁ JUAN. No. I can't do that.

DOÑA MARCIALA. Papá . . . it 'd be so good for you.

PAPÁ JUAN. No . . . I can't take a nap . . . and I won't take a nap. You run along and keep things going . . . and I 'll

have a talk to Trino. They 're to go on dancing, now. And the
children can sing again . . . and they can have games . . . and
they are to sit up as late as ever they like. What 's the use of
my living to be a hundred years old if the children can't enjoy
themselves?

DOÑA MARCIALA. Very well. You stay here with Trino and
I 'll see to it all. St . . . Trino!

She turns at the window and beckons to him.

TRINO. Yes.

DOÑA MARCIALA. Don't leave him alone.

TRINO. I won't. But nobody will come.

DOÑA MARCIALA. He ought to take a nap.

TRINO. I know he ought.

PAPÁ JUAN. I hear you! You 're just a devil of a nuisance to
me . . . you two. Take a nap . . . take a nap . . . take a nap!
My birthday . . . that I 've been looking forward to . . . and
counting on . . . and then when it comes I 'm to waste a whole
lot of it by going to sleep! I never heard of such nonsense. Run
along.

*So Doña Marciala runs along. Trino stands very still and
out of Papá Juan's sight. Perhaps he will go to sleep after
all. But no!*

PAPÁ JUAN. Trino.

TRINO. Yes.

PAPÁ JUAN. How 's the world wagging with you?

TRINO. Pretty well.

PAPÁ JUAN. Only pretty well?

TRINO. Very well.

*Trino sits near him now. Trino does seem a little depressed.
Papá Juan, though, begins to think over his party . . . and
he chuckles.*

PAPÁ JUAN. Hey! Raphael made a good speech. A bit vulgar . . . he is a bit vulgar . . . but a good speech. And he
took it out of Evaristo. Hey! And Currita made a very good
speech . . . a very very good speech when you drank my health.
Did you write it for her?

TRINO. No . . . I could n't write anything half so good.

PAPÁ JUAN. Could n't you?

TRINO. Why, nobody but Currita could have written it . . . for there 's only one Currita.

PAPÁ JUAN. That 's very true. Currita! Half angel and half imp! And whose happiness . . . and torment . . . is she to be . . . that 'll be the next question. What 's that you said?

TRINO. I did n't say anything.

PAPÁ JUAN. Well, take my advice . . . and hurry up and say something. Are you off to-morrow?

TRINO. No . . . I don't think so. But I 'll pack up and be off now . . . if you don't stop talking and try to rest.

PAPÁ JUAN. Well, I shan't. So good-bye. Sorry to lose you!

There is a short silence.

PAPÁ JUAN. Gabriela too! I 'm afraid they were all a bit patronising to Gabriela. And Filomena was so sure it would n't do for her to come. But did you see her when Raphael told her it was her turn to make a speech? Can't ever keep his head, Raphael! Did n't answer him . . . gave us a look . . . and then bent down and kissed her child. Not a bad speech, that!

TRINO. She could n't have made a better. I want to talk to you later about Gabriela. We must see what can be done.

PAPÁ JUAN. And did you ever see such a child! As pretty as a flower and as quick as a kitten! These children that slip in by the back door . . . queer, is n't it! Nature seems to know she must treat them better . . . because we shall treat them worse. Now, listen to me, Trino . . .

TRINO. No, I won't listen to you.

PAPÁ JUAN. Why not?

TRINO. I have told you that I want you to keep quiet.

PAPÁ JUAN. Well . . . you talk then and I 'll listen.

TRINO. No, I won't talk either. I don't mind singing you to sleep.

PAPÁ JUAN. I have told you I 'm not going to sleep. You 're a very obstinate fellow! Nothing 's going to happen to me . . . don't you worry. And if you don't talk, I shall. Ah, Trino, Trino . . . even you can't quite understand what this day's coming has meant to me! And now it's here . . . and I see them, as I've longed to see them . . . children and children's children and their children around me . . . suddenly it all seems strange that such a glory should be mine . . . that I should have travelled this long road when so many have dropped by the way. When I think of my dead, Trino, it is very strange indeed to be alive.

TRINO. Dear Papá Juan . . . don't let us talk of death.

PAPÁ JUAN. Why not . . . for it's death that I'm facing now! There is where life lies for me now. Why should I fear to face it . . . the peace of it . . . of the new life of the soul?

He sits lost in thought for a little. The children's voices can be heard again singing far off.

PAPÁ JUAN. What singing is that?

TRINO. The children . . . out there in the garden. Does it disturb you?

PAPÁ JUAN. No, no!

TRINO. Still . . .

He goes into the garden, and after a little the voices die away.

PAPÁ JUAN. Trino! Now where's he gone? Got it fixed in his head that I must take a nap! Half a glass of wine and Filomena's flinging her arms round Antoñón . . . and Trino telling me twenty times over that I must take a nap. What children!

Trino tiptoes back and gives a cautious look to Papá Juan, so still in his chair, his eyes closed even. But . . .

PAPÁ JUAN. If you think I'm asleep I'm not!

TRINO. I'll draw the curtains . . . there's a lot of light comes in.

PAPÁ JUAN. You can draw what you like.

So Trino draws the curtains. The children's voices have died away. The room is dim and silent. Trino sits down and quietly takes a book.

TRINO. That's better. He is asleep! Had to get him out of that turmoil! Glad of a little peace myself!

He dips into his book. Silence. After a moment Currita peeps through the curtains.

CURRITA. Can't one have both? I like people to love me . . .

TRINO. And you like to talk a bit too.

CURRITA. Well . . . talk a bit yourself if you don't want me to. You 're not at Mass.

TRINO. I 'd as soon listen.

CURRITA. You 're a wonderful listener!

TRINO. When you 'll talk to me!

There falls a little silence between them.

CURRITA. Shall I go on talking then?

TRINO. Please.

CURRITA. I like listening too, you know.

TRINO. Do you?

CURRITA. Sometimes.

TRINO. Then listen, Currita. . . .

Papá Juan stirs in his sleep again; and they turn to him, to hear him say faintly . . .

PAPÁ JUAN. Trino . . . Trino!

CURRITA. Ah . . . but he 's dreaming of you now!

TRINO. No . . . of us both.

PAPÁ JUAN. Trino!

CURRITA. D' you think so?

TRINO. What makes him, I wonder?

CURRITA. We 'll ask him when he wakes. We 'll ask him what his dream was.

TRINO. That 's the most wonderful thing about him, you know. Asleep or awake, he can still dream. With so much to look back on he can look forward still. A hundred years old and still full of hopes and longings . . . and I 'm thirty, and I 'd come to doubt if I 'd any left. One feels pretty small beside him. Think of it . . . how he has planned for his birthday and his party! You 'll see . . . now it 's over he 'll find something else to set his heart on.

CURRITA. Oh, he 's found that already.

TRINO. Has he? D' you know what it is?

CURRITA. Yes . . . I know.

TRINO. What is it, then? Tell me.

CURRITA. No, I can't.

TRINO. Why not?

CURRITA. I 'd rather not tell you.   So don't ask me, please.
At this juncture Papá Juan wakes up and sits watching them.

TRINO. But what harm can there be in your telling me?

CURRITA. No harm.   But . . . well, I 'm not going to tell you, that 's all.

TRINO. I shall ask Papá Juan, then.

CURRITA. No . . . you 're not to . . . you 're not to!

TRINO. But you 're going to ask him his dream.
He has taken her hands in his.

CURRITA. But that 's quite different . . . really!   Oh . . . let me go, Trino.

TRINO. Must I let you go?

CURRITA. Please . . . Oh, Papá Juan . . . Trino!
For Papá Juan has risen and is coming towards them.

TRINO. Papá Juan.

CURRITA. There!   We woke him . . . talking.   I said we should.

PAPÁ JUAN. It was n't you that woke me.

CURRITA. Really!

PAPÁ JUAN. No . . . voices much further off.   Can you hear that singing, Trino?

TRINO. Not the children . . . I stopped them.

PAPÁ JUAN. No . . . further still . . . much further.   Listen! From somewhere beyond the world.
Trino remembers.   Currita is close to him.   He puts his arms round her.

TRINO. Yes . . . yes!   Now I hear it.

PAPÁ JUAN. Can you hear the music, Currita?

CURRITA. No.

TRINO. I hear it.

CURRITA. No . . . I hear nothing.

PAPÁ JUAN. As long as he hears it . . . you will . . . when the time comes.

CURRITA. Shall I?   Are you sure?

AMARANTA.
CONSTANZA.
MÓNICA.
INÉS.
CONCHITA.
A DRESSMAKER'S ASSISTANT.
A SISTER OF MERCY.

FORTUNATO.
DON VICTORIO.
ALBERTO.
A BLIND MAN.
AN OLD GENTLEMAN.
GORGUERA.
A LAME BEGGAR.

FORTUNATO

THE FIRST SCENE

Alberto Hidalgo is a young Madrid architect. We are in his study. It is well, though very simply furnished. There is a door on the right, another on the left. Through the glass of the enclosed balcony at the back, the pale clear sky of a December morning can be seen. On our left is Alberto's writing-table; a calendar hangs on the wall near it. There is a small electric stove alight in one corner.

Mónica, the housemaid, comes in, followed by Don Victorio. If there is one thing upon which Mónica prides herself more than another — and she is tolerably self-satisfied upon all accounts — it is her education and intelligence. Don Victorio is a gentleman who lives by his wits; but at the moment, if one may judge by the look of him, not very successfully. For in this bitter weather he is wearing a light summer suit and a straw hat, and both are of the shabbiest. No wonder his teeth are chattering!

MÓNICA. Walk in.

DON VICTORIO. Tha-tha-tha-tha-tha-thank you! Oh . . . it's good to be in a warm room again!

MÓNICA. Call this warm? Now the drawing-room is warm. As cold as Iberia . . . I call this.

DON VICTORIO. S-s-s-s-s-Siberia! Perhaps I could go into the drawing-room, then.

MÓNICA. Yes, you can.

DON VICTORIO. Is your mistress in the drawing-room?

MÓNICA. Yes, she is.

Don Victorio launches into an apostrophe.

MÓNICA. Well, Señor . . . I showed him in . . . to the Señora . . . and the Señora's mother . . . who was with the Señora . . . and there he is still.

ALBERTO. And why did you show him in?

MÓNICA. I had my orders.

ALBERTO. You were told to show him in?

MÓNICA. I had my orders.

ALBERTO. Very well. Be sure you 're there when he goes . . . and let me know when he 's gone.

MÓNICA. You may rely on my doing so, Señor.

And Mónica, supremely self-satisfied, departs.

ALBERTO. What a fool!

He sets to work again. His wife appears. Constanza is pretty and gentle, and looks, indeed, like the angel of pity of Don Victorio's apostrophe.

ALBERTO. My dear! Why . . . why did your mother recommend us that idiot of a woman for a maid?

CONSTANZA. She means so well.

ALBERTO. She has the brains of a hen. But if only she was n't so pleased with herself! I don't know what silly thing she 'll do next.

CONSTANZA. We must be patient. It 's her first place. And she tries so hard. But do you know what she did just now?

ALBERTO. Yes, I do. Let Don Victorio in . . . and showed him in to you, what 's more. And says you told her to.

CONSTANZA. I particularly told her not to.

ALBERTO. So I supposed. Well . . . is he going on as usual?

CONSTANZA. I 've left him with Mother. Am I interrupting you?

ALBERTO. You are!

CONSTANZA. Are you working?

ALBERTO. I am! Well . . . what is it?

CONSTANZA. I want to ask you something.

ALBERTO. I know you do . . . and I know what it is, too.

CONSTANZA. How do you know?

ALBERTO. I don't have to be very clever, do I, to know what 's going to happen when that humbug gets let in to see you and your mother?

CONSTANZA. Oh, don't call him that, Alberto! After all he does n't beg because he likes begging.

ALBERTO. And what's to-day's tragedy?

CONSTANZA. He has been walking the streets looking for work . . . as usual.

ALBERTO. As usual!

CONSTANZA. He was hardly inside the room before he broke down completely.

ALBERTO. I 'm sure he did! Then . . . let me see: "Oh, my benefactress, I kiss your feet . . . I have not come for money . . . if I ask you for a penny, turn me out of the house."

CONSTANZA. I believe you were at the keyhole.

ALBERTO. What an odd thing it is! He never comes for money . . . but he never leaves without it.

CONSTANZA. Don't be so cynical. You should have seen him shivering by the fire. The poor man was half dead with cold.

ALBERTO. He might make a good living as an actor.

CONSTANZA. And don't mock at misfortune. You should have heard the tale he told us. Two of his children are down with the measles . . . and last week the house caught fire. The servant has been stealing things and a cat scratched his sister and they think it 's mad. His father has got St. Vitus's dance, and his wife's brother tried to throw himself out of the window and put out his eye.

ALBERTO. Thank you . . . that will do! Why take in the daily paper! This leaves it nowhere.

CONSTANZA. D' you think he 's not telling the truth?

ALBERTO. Of course he is n't.

CONSTANZA. I think he may exaggerate a little. But don't let us be too hard on him for that. We might do the same in his place. We don't know what it means to be without a roof to cover us or a dinner to eat.

ALBERTO. Come, come . . . I'm not such a callous brute, am I?

CONSTANZA. You 're a dear. And you 're the most generous of men. You give away far more than you ought to.

ALBERTO. Quite! And so do you. We both do. If we gave it to deserving people and it did any good . . .! But Madrid is the swindlers' paradise. From now on not a penny do I part with till I 've proved that the case is genuine. Look here . . . by this morning's post!

He holds up three letters.

CONSTANZA. Is n't it dreadful?

ALBERTO. This man says he 's promised work in Malaga . . . and will I pay his fare there . . . for if I don't he 'll starve.

CONSTANZA. Poor thing!

ALBERTO. Here 's a woman says the doctor has ordered her daughter Malt Extract and if she does n't get it she 'll die.

CONSTANZA. Poor thing!

ALBERTO. And here 's one raising money to buy herself a type-writer to support life on.

CONSTANZA. Poor thing!

ALBERTO. The subscription list is headed by the Prime Minister, the Mayor of Madrid, and the President of the Academy. Likely, is n't it!

CONSTANZA. No . . . I suppose not. Still . . . one never knows!

ALBERTO. And just now when I popped my head out of the front door, there was a man selling chestnuts who wanted money to buy a barrow; a workman out of work who wanted boots and a shirt or so; two Sisters of Charity asking help for an insane asylum, and a Friar collecting funds to build an alms house for the sane. This sort of thing would bankrupt a millionaire. And I 'm a wretched architect who 's had a little luck . . . though it has n't run to building ourselves a house yet. Not to mention, my dear, not to mention . . . and you know it as well as I do . . . that when people are really in want they are far likelier to hide away and hold their tongues about it than to indulge in these antics that Don Victorio obliges us with.

CONSTANZA. I know . . . I agree. We ought to set our faces

against it. You 're very generous and I 'm very easily taken in. But just this once . . . don't you think we might . . .? Because whether it 's all true or not . . . he 's crying. And when people cry, somehow I 've got to believe them.

ALBERTO. Simpleton!

CONSTANZA. Besides . . . I 've not told you yet what his real trouble is.

ALBERTO. Well?

CONSTANZA. And I 'm sure this is true.

ALBERTO. Even so, my dear, we cannot keep on giving money to every one that asks us.

CONSTANZA. I agree . . . I 've said so. No need to get so excited, beloved!

ALBERTO. Well, what 's his real trouble?

CONSTANZA. Their landlord's going to turn them into the street this very morning if they don't pay their rent.

ALBERTO. God's will be done!

CONSTANZA. So he 's going round . . . getting a little here and a little there . . . to try to make it up.

ALBERTO. Very well! He must get a little here, then, I suppose.

CONSTANZA. Darling . . . how good you are!

ALBERTO. But on one condition.

CONSTANZA. Yes.

ALBERTO. That this is the last penny Don Victorio has out of us.

CONSTANZA. The very last.

ALBERTO. And what 's more . . . that we give not a penny to any other beggar till this month 's past.

CONSTANZA. I promise you.

ALBERTO. *I* promise you.

CONSTANZA. You are good.

She gives him a kiss.

ALBERTO. I owe that, I fear, to Don Victorio's skill as a beggar!

CONSTANZA. Goose!

ALBERTO. Now I must get on with my work.

Constanza is just going out when Mónica appears.

MÓNICA. If you please, Señor . . .

CONSTANZA. Yes . . . what is it?

MÓNICA. No, Señora . . . it is the Señor I wish to speak to.

CONSTANZA. I see!

Constanza goes out much amused.

ALBERTO. Well, what is it . . . what is it?

MÓNICA. I wish to make no mistakes, Señor, in the discharge of my duties. There is a ring at the front door. If it is the gentleman that came yesterday, what do I say to him?

ALBERTO. What gentleman that came yesterday?

MÓNICA. I think you will remember, Señor, that I brought you in his card . . . and he asked for it back . . . and you said it smelt of herrings.

ALBERTO. Quite! Well, if it's that gentleman say I greatly regret I cannot see him now . . . but I will write.

MÓNICA. That is understood then. And if it is the gentleman that came the day before yesterday . . .

ALBERTO. Heavens! Who was it came the day before yesterday?

MÓNICA. He was short and he was fat and he was shaved. And he had a white waistcoat on and black boots. And he did n't live in Madrid. Because printed on his card there was . . . was it León or was it Burgos?

ALBERTO. Or Córdoba?

MÓNICA. Yes, it was Córdoba. I knew it had a cathedral.

ALBERTO. Good! Well, if the gentleman from Córdoba should come. . . .

MÓNICA. That also is understood, sir.

ALBERTO. But what is understood?

MÓNICA. That you cannot see him either . . . but that you will write.

ALBERTO. Not at all. I want to see him . . . and you are to show him in.

MÓNICA. That's what I thought, Señor.

Mónica is retiring, self-conscious and efficient, when Alberto stops her.

ALBERTO. It really is understood, is it?

MÓNICA. There is no great difficulty in understanding it, I think.

ALBERTO. I agree.

MÓNICA. If it's the gentleman that came yesterday he's to go away and you'll write . . . and if it's the gentleman that came the day before yesterday I'm to show him in.

ALBERTO. Quite so!

MÓNICA. Then I think that's all, Señor.

And with perfect assurance she goes to open the door. It is hardly worth Alberto's while to set his mind to his work again. Instead, with a glance to the door by which his wife went and another to that by which Mónica has vanished, he murmurs. . . .

ALBERTO. Ah . . . soft hearts! Thick head!

Whereat Mónica returns and resolutely announces. . . .

MÓNICA. The gentleman that called yesterday.

Alberto rises in wrath.

ALBERTO. But haven't I just this moment told you . . .?

Fortunato's appearance interrupts him.

FORTUNATO. Good morning.

ALBERTO. Good morning.

Fortunato is really a most ridiculous creature; one does not know whether to pity him or laugh at him. And as he stands there, so shabby, so humble, and so depressed, it is only too easy to guess what his errand is.

MÓNICA. And can I do anything more for you, Señor?

Alberto goes up to the creature and says with concentrated passion. . . .

ALBERTO. Didn't I tell you plainly that this was the gentleman I didn't want to see?

MÓNICA. Yes, Señor . . . you did. But I felt so sorry for him.

ALBERTO. Another soft heart! God is too good to me! Go away, do.

This last he flings out loudly, so loudly that poor Fortunato meekly inquires . . .

FORTUNATO. Me?

ALBERTO. No. You!

This to Mónica, who is quite unabashed.

MÓNICA. Yes, Señor. Also the telephone is ringing. And as I wish to make no mistakes . . . if this should be the gentleman. . . .

ALBERTO. Whoever it is . . . tell him I 've gone to China.

MÓNICA. Yes, Señor. As you say.

Mónica departs; and Alberto, recovering himself a little, surveys his unbidden guest; but, one fears, not too sympathetically.

ALBERTO. Now . . . please tell me. . . .

FORTUNATO. I gathered . . . I could n't help gathering . . . that you did n't mean to see me.

ALBERTO. I happen to be very busy just now. . . .

FORTUNATO. Then . . . another day perhaps. . . .

ALBERTO. No . . . as you are here. . . .

FORTUNATO. You 're very kind.

ALBERTO. Sit down.

FORTUNATO. But I must n't disturb you.

ALBERTO. Never mind.

FORTUNATO. But I am disturbing you . . . and annoying you. Another day! [*And he turns to go, but turns again to say rather wistfully.*] Except that . . . another day . . . well, it 'll be just the same, I 'm afraid.

ALBERTO. You 'd far better tell me now what it is you want of me.

FORTUNATO. You are most kind. First, I 'm so sorry to call on you dressed like this. . . .

ALBERTO. That 's no matter.

FORTUNATO. I 'm ashamed to be seen in these trousers . . . but they 're the only ones I have.

ALBERTO. Quite so!

FORTUNATO. And the coat 's just as bad . . . and my boots are n't much better. . . .

ALBERTO. And your hat and your shirt are nothing to speak of.

FORTUNATO [*with a wry smile*]. No . . . my shirt is nothing at all to speak of.

It is evident that this is literally true.

ALBERTO. Well . . . I 'm glad you can joke about it.

FORTUNATO [*blankly*]. Joke! I did n't mean to. I 'm very sorry. I 'd better come back another day.

ALBERTO. No, no . . . say what you have to say . . . and say it now.

FORTUNATO. You really are most kind. I knew your father. We were in the same office once.

ALBERTO. Yes . . . you told me that in your letter. And I remember your name.

FORTUNATO. Your father . . . God rest his soul! . . . thought well of me in those days. I 'm very much afraid that 's the only claim I have on you. I lost my place there four years ago. The head of my department had a nephew and . . .! Really, it was a perfect scandal . . .!

ALBERTO. Yes . . . we won't go into that. Tell me what I can do. What is it you want?

FORTUNATO. Work.

ALBERTO. What sort of work?

FORTUNATO. Anything. I 'm a clerk by rights. Book-keeping besides . . . double entry. A little French. But in these four years I think there 's nothing I 've not tried. I was a bricklayer's labourer for a bit . . . I carried the bricks up the ladders. But I can't stand heights . . . I never could. And I used to shake so that at last I fell off and nearly killed myself. From sheer fright.

ALBERTO. You were n't used to the job.

FORTUNATO. No . . . it was fright. I 'm afraid I 'm a dreadful coward. Once I got a place as night-watchman in a shop that has been several times burgled . . . and only God knows what I went through there. But I could n't see those that depended on me starve, could I? I 'm only telling you this to show you there 's really nothing I won't do. Nothing!

ALBERTO. Well . . . I 'll think it over . . . I 'll see what I can suggest. There's nothing I know of at the moment. But I'll think it over . . . I'll see what can be done.

FORTUNATO. You are most kind. I do hope you forgive me for coming. You have n't any children of your own, perhaps.

ALBERTO. No.

FORTUNATO. Then you won't understand. . . .

ALBERTO. You have?

FORTUNATO. Yes. Five. And they're all quite young. Five mouths to find food for. Food! I do assure you, I lie awake at night sometimes wondering where our next day's meal is to come from and saying the word over and over till . . .! But I've no right to trouble you with all this.

ALBERTO. No . . . go on!

FORTUNATO. One loves one's children better than anything in the world. But one might love them twice as much and it would n't make up to them for bringing them into the world and letting them starve there. I beg your pardon!

> *This last is an apology for the large tear which rolls down his cheek and which he wipes away.*

ALBERTO. Don't give way. And don't torment yourself. I'll find you a job as soon as ever I can.

FORTUNATO. I pray to God it may be soon, Señor. For it has come to this: My wife has to stay indoors now because she has n't clothes to put on. We've sold the very bed we slept on. We've nothing left to sell.

ALBERTO. I'll find you work. I promise. You're not to worry any more.

FORTUNATO. I am deeply, deeply grateful.

> *There is a pause. Fortunato does not get up to go.*

FORTUNATO. And . . .! But . . .!

ALBERTO. Yes?

FORTUNATO. I . . .! Really, I'm so unused to begging.

ALBERTO. But I've promised to find you a job.

FORTUNATO. Yes. But . . .! The fact is . . .!

ALBERTO. Oh, to be sure! A little something to go on with?

FORTUNATO. If you could see your way!

Poor Fortunato lowers his eyes with shame. But Alberto suddenly stiffens, remembering the talk with his wife.

ALBERTO. No! No . . . I can't!

FORTUNATO. No?

ALBERTO. I 'm very sorry. I 'm not a rich man . . . I 've a thousand obligations . . . and I can't. I 've promised to find you work . . . and that 's all I can do.

FORTUNATO. Of course . . . I understand . . . I 'm most grateful . . . I 've no right to . . .! I would n't have come at all . . . except that things seemed so hopeless. And I won't detain you . . . and I 'm really most grateful. May I come back in a day or two?

ALBERTO. Yes . . . come back in a week.

FORTUNATO [*despairingly*]. In a week! Thank you. May God reward you! In a week! I 'm most grateful. Good morning.

Fortunato fades away. Alberto has an impulse to call him back. But he resists it.

ALBERTO. No, no . . . when I 've just said I would n't! I must find out about him. But I strongly suspect that old fraud in there has just got what this fellow deserved. Oh . . . Mónica!

For Mónica has looked into the room.

MÓNICA. Señor?

ALBERTO. Who was it on the telephone?

MÓNICA. Señor de Galíndez.

ALBERTO. What did he want?

MÓNICA. He said he had the cheque ready for you . . . and were you at home, please?

ALBERTO. And what did you say?

MÓNICA. Just what you told me. That you 'd gone to China.

ALBERTO. Good! Good!

He takes up a paper-knife with what appear to be most sinister intentions.

MÓNICA. Was n't that right?

ALBERTO. Be off! And don't let me see your face again.

Mónica departs in indignant silence. At the same moment

torn off the calendar. She repairs the omission, and reads to-day's.

CONSTANZA. "Society is a conspiracy of knavery against honesty . . . Leopardi." Oh, how shocking! "One half the world gets up in the morning determined to cheat the other half before bedtime . . . Anon." How cynical!

SCENE TWO

A street corner in a quarter of Madrid where there are still more empty lots than houses, so that our main view is of hoardings and advertisements. The corner itself, however, is occupied by a little wine shop. Down one street comes a blind fiddler, playing as he comes. He stops before he reaches the corner and leans against the wall, still playing. Down the other street comes Don Victorio, beaming, rubbing his hands, less from the cold now than from satisfaction with a good job done. He slips into the wine shop, and after a moment slips out again, wiping his mouth and yet more cheery. He looks round and then waves and whistles a pre-concerted signal to some one at some other corner. Then while he waits he falls to whistling an obbligato to the blind man's tune. Gorguera appears in response to the signal. He is Don Victorio's confederate and hanger-on. He is poorly dressed, but he wears a good thick overcoat; and he carries a big cape which Don Victorio promptly takes and wraps round him. When their talk is well on its way the blind man stops fiddling, though he stays leaning against the wall.

DON VICTORIO. Thank you, my lad . . . I've been wanting this badly.

GORGUERA. What luck?

For answer Don Victorio delicately breathes in his face.

DON VICTORIO. A petty vair! Luck enough for the price of that!

GORGUERA. You're a corker!

He wrings his chief and mentor enthusiastically by the hand.

DON VICTORIO. I am the Moses of Madrid . . . I draw water
from the rocks. But . . . curse it ! . . . on a day like this and
dressed like this I 'd make the statues down the Prado feel sorry
for me.

GORGUERA. And . . . combeen ?

DON VICTORIO [*holding out his five fingers*]. Sink !

GORGUERA. You 're a corker !

And again he wrings his hand.

DON VICTORIO. I asked for four pesetas seventy-five. Odd
sums sound well . . . and of a morning there 's mostly no change
in a house till the cook gets back from market. And *I* could n't
give change, could I? So it was Sink, my boy !

GORGUERA. You are a corker !

He wrings his hand yet again.

DON VICTORIO. Well, what have you been up to? What about
that letter to Don . . . to that priest ?

GORGUERA. I took it . . . I gave it him myself. He kept
on looking at me while he read it . . . and then he stared at me
as if he 'd stare right through me . . . and I 've to go back to-
morrow.

DON VICTORIO. Impudence ! A letter . . . full of Latin . . .
and asking help for a poor sick niece . . . and signed by a brother
priest. And you 're to go back to-morrow? Ah . . . you 've
got a lot to learn, my lad !

GORGUERA [*humbly*]. I know it, Don Victorio.

Don Victorio fetches two more letters from his pocket.

DON VICTORIO. Well . . . you 'd better take these other two
before we get our lunch. Let 's see . . . the black-edged one 's
for the widow. How did I sign it? Sinforiano Núñez. How
does that sound?

GORGUERA. Fine !

*Don Victorio, before he licks the envelope, glances through
the letter again with all an author's pride.*

DON VICTORIO. "The boyhood friend of him who has just
passed away." Curse it . . . when a man 's not cold in his
grave the least a widow can do is to stump up something for his

FORTUNATO. But you 've got to find it work first, have n't you?

DON VICTORIO. Are n't you still in that same old office?

FORTUNATO. No. I wish I were!

DON VICTORIO. Well . . . at least you don't catch cold once a week sitting in those draughts. I never met such draughts!

FORTUNATO. It 's draughtier in the streets looking for a job.

DON VICTORIO. Did they chuck you out?

FORTUNATO. Yes.

DON VICTORIO. I 'm damned! You were the only man there that ever did any work as far as I could see.

FORTUNATO. It was just my luck.

DON VICTORIO. This country 's going to the dogs . . . I 've been saying so for years. The men who work are the only men who don't get on. I found that out. Work! I know a trick worth two of it. And what are you doing now?

FORTUNATO. Well . . . I 've done a little of everything these past four years. Selling lottery tickets . . . and penny toys. No good!

DON VICTORIO. I know. Your stars get crossed sometimes.

FORTUNATO. I 'm afraid I have n't got a star. Last year I put every penny I could scrape together into a business. It failed. And that was the last straw.

DON VICTORIO. What sort of business?

FORTUNATO. Selling ices. My wife made the ices. I rented a little pitch down by the Prado . . . and, oh, the rent I had to pay! It was in May . . . just when the warm weather was starting. But on the day we started . . . it snowed! Yes, I do assure you, it snowed.

DON VICTORIO. Man alive . . . why had n't you looked at the weather forecast?

FORTUNATO. I never thought of that. But it snowed and snowed. And every one that passed was shivering and swearing. And when they saw my stall with "Ices for Sale" on it . . . they said such things to me! Ten quarts my wife had made. And we had to eat it all ourselves or waste it. And the children nearly died of it. Better for them if they had, I suppose.

DON VICTORIO. Well, it was bad luck, Fortunato. I say . . .
what the devil did your parents give you such a name for? That
was tempting providence.

FORTUNATO. So I sold the stall and put the money into candles.

DON VICTORIO. Candles! Why candles?

FORTUNATO. I 've a friend who 's a sexton . . . and he meant
to let me stand at the cemetery gates to sell candles.

DON VICTORIO. That 's a gloomy trade.

FORTUNATO. Then we found out the Archbishop was forbid-
ding it . . . because it 's superstitious.

DON VICTORIO. Quite right. So it is! And you could n't
eat the candles.

FORTUNATO. We very nearly had to.

DON VICTORIO. No . . . you 've had no luck.

FORTUNATO. And since then it has been dreadful.

DON VICTORIO. No prospects?

FORTUNATO. No.

DON VICTORIO. Here . . . I 'll give you a tip. Ever heard
of Don Alberto Hidalgo?

FORTUNATO. The architect?

DON VICTORIO. Yes. He 's got a wife. She 's soft . . . any
one can get round her. You go there.

FORTUNATO. But I 've just been there.

DON VICTORIO. Did n't you get anything?

FORTUNATO. Promises.

DON VICTORIO. Ah! I 'm afraid that 's because I 'd just been
there before you.

> *He cannot help feeling — and even showing — a certain pride
> in this.*

FORTUNATO. You?

DON VICTORIO. Me!

FORTUNATO. They gave you something, did they?

DON VICTORIO. Thrust it on me!

FORTUNATO. No . . . I 've no luck. But how do you manage
it? What do you do . . . what do you say?

DON VICTORIO. Well . . . it can't be taught. It just comes

to me. I talk a lot . . . and I look miserable . . . and I cry.
And if there 's a hole in my coat I take care they see it. And I
kiss their hands. That 's the great thing. Cry a lot and kiss
their hands. If you can't get hold of their hands . . . kiss something that belongs to them. Kiss the furniture. Kiss anything.
Keep on crying and kissing things and don't come away till you 've
got what you want.

FORTUNATO. But can you cry . . . on purpose?

DON VICTORIO. And to order! Name your requirements.
Anything from one tear slowly trickling down the nose . . . to a
perfect flood. I can foam at the mouth too.

FORTUNATO. But is n't that being a . . . being rather a . . .

DON VICTORIO. Fraud?

FORTUNATO [*most apologetically*]. Yes.

DON VICTORIO. Why . . . of course it is!

FORTUNATO. I really should n't like to do it . . . even if I
could.

DON VICTORIO. Look here . . . if you 're going to be imprac-
tical you 'll never get on. When you set out to do a thing do it
as well as you can and make a success of it. That 's common
sense. I 've got my dinner to-day and you have n't. And as
to the rights and the wrongs of the thing . . . did I ask to be
born into this world? No. Then I 'm owed a living here . . .
and if I can't get it one way I will another. That 's only reason-
able!

FORTUNATO. Well, it may be . . . I don't say. But I 'm
really afraid I could n't.

DON VICTORIO. Very well! Then I 'm sorry for you, that 's
all. Look here, though . . . we 're old friends. I 've got a
young fellow lunching with me at La Perica's. He 's my assistant . . . I 'm teaching him his trade. Enough for two is
enough for three. Come along.

FORTUNATO. Thank you . . . oh, thank you . . . you 're
very kind. But I think I won't. I don't think I could eat . . .
with the children at home having nothing. I 'm sure you understand.

DON VICTORIO. Well . . . there 's not enough for a regiment, I 'm afraid. I 'll be off then. See you again some time!

FORTUNATO. Some time.

Don Victorio goes down the street, turning for a last glance at Fortunato, and saying. . . .

DON VICTORIO. That 's a depressing fellow . . . say what you like!

He disappears. Fortunato, left alone with the blind man (who has fallen asleep on his campstool) for the first time in our acquaintance with him, braces himself up a little.

FORTUNATO. He 's a scoundrel . . . that 's what he is . . . a scoundrel. And it pays to be a scoundrel! For I might have had what he cheated them out of! It 's not fair . . . it 's not fair. And me without a penny . . . without a penny in the world! Very well then . . . from now on I don't care what I do. I 'll beg . . . here in the street . . . from the next person I see. From the very next. . . .

As he says it his eye falls on a young woman coming down the street, a dressmaker's assistant she might be, by the look of her. He hesitates till she has passed him. Then with an effort he takes off his hat and says. . . .

FORTUNATO. Señorita.

THE YOUNG WOMAN. Were you speaking to me?

FORTUNATO. Yes. No. Yes.

THE YOUNG WOMAN. Well . . . what is it?

FORTUNATO. I . . .!

He gesticulates vaguely, unable to utter another word.

THE YOUNG WOMAN. Out with it! I can't stop here all day.

FORTUNATO. No, no . . . do listen.

THE YOUNG WOMAN. Are n't I listening?

FORTUNATO. Won't you be so kind as to . . . to . . . to . . .

THE YOUNG WOMAN. Well . . . what?

FORTUNATO. . . . to tell me the way to the Calle Juan de Mina.

THE YOUNG WOMAN. The Calle Juan de Mina. That 's a long way from here. It 's over by the North Station.

FORTUNATO. No . . . it 's near the Stock Exchange.

THE YOUNG WOMAN. Yes . . . you 're right . . . it is near the Stock Exchange.

FORTUNATO. You go down past the Stock Exchange . . . and the first on the left is Philip the Fourth . . . and the next is Lealtad . . . and the next is Juan de Mina.

THE YOUNG WOMAN. Well . . . if you know . . . what did you ask me for?

FORTUNATO. Oh! I . . . I just thought I 'd like to make sure.

THE YOUNG WOMAN. No, you did n't. You thought you 'd like to get acquainted with me . . . that 's what you thought. An old scarecrow like you, too. Shame on you!

And she goes on her way, leaving Fortunato utterly crushed.

FORTUNATO. I 'm no good at it. I knew I should n't be.

Now an old gentleman is turning the corner. He stops by the blind fiddler and puts a piece of money in the tin plate, muttering as he does so . . .

OLD GENTLEMAN. Bless my soul . . . here 's another of 'em. What 's Madrid coming to!

As this looks promising Fortunato resolves on another effort and addresses the old gentleman hat in hand.

FORTUNATO. Señor.

OLD GENTLEMAN. Eh?

FORTUNATO. For God's sake, Señor . . . a little help. I 've a wife and children . . .

OLD GENTLEMAN. Ah, yes . . . the same old tale! And if I give a penny to one . . . the rest of you swarm round like flies. No . . . I 'm sorry . . . I can't.

FORTUNATO. It 's the first time I 've ever begged . . . like this.

OLD GENTLEMAN. I 'm glad to hear it. And let it be the last. You 're a fit man, are n't you? You 're not blind . . . or crippled. Why don't you work?

FORTUNATO. I can't get work.

OLD GENTLEMAN. Nonsense! That 's what all you loafers say. Look for it . . . and keep on looking. No, I can't help you.

And I can't stop here talking to you. I 've lots to do . . . most urgent business. Deuce take these beggars!

> *He goes on his way. During this talk a Sister of Mercy has also passed along and has paused to put a coin or two in the blind man's plate. Fortunato stands looking after the old gentleman.*

FORTUNATO. Urgent, is it? Not so urgent as mine! Well . . . that 's that! That 's no good. What else can I do? What else can I try . . . except stealing! Very well then . . . I 'll steal. Yes, I will. I 'll steal sooner than see them go hungry!

> *He sets off in desperation. But passing the blind man, he catches sight of the coins in the tin plate, and stops, transfixed.*

Holy Virgin, Queen of Heaven! What a chance! Is he asleep? Yes, he is. No one would see me. Oh, but I can't . . . I can't: I could never look any one in the face again. Oh . . . the Devil should n't be let tempt me like this. Saints in Heaven help me!

> *He has a dreadful struggle with himself; but after a second or so he manages to tear himself from the spot. Round the corner, though, he stops again, temptation still strong.*

But why should n't I? It 's not as if it was for myself . . . it 's for them. And he may be a fraud like that other fraud. I don't doubt he is.

> *He creeps back a few steps.*

Besides . . . whoever gave it him . . . did n't give it him, so to speak. They just meant to be charitable. And I need it as much as he does . . . more than he does . . . because of the children. I 'll do it. I will do it. And I 'd better do it now or there 'll be somebody coming. Very well . . .!

> *He slips round the corner, gives a quick glance about him, snatches the coins from the plate and retreats, shaking all over, the coins tight in his clasped hand.*

I 've done it. I 've done it! And nobody saw me.

> *He feverishly stuffs the coins in his pocket. But his pocket must have a hole in it, for they come falling down his trouser-leg and go rolling about the street. If a bomb had exploded Fortunato could not be more frightened.*

Oh! . . . Holy Souls in Purgatory!

He goes down on hands and knees and chases the coins.

One . . . two . . . where 's the other? Here! But nobody saw me . . . I 'm sure.

He gets up again and stands a moment to recover equanimity.

I must pull myself together . . . I must n't be a fool. Nobody saw me. Not so bad, then, for a first try! Not so bad . . . if nobody saw me!

He laughs mirthlessly. But the noise has wakened the blind man, who calls in his feeble voice. . . .

THE BLIND MAN. Conchita! Conchita . . . are you there?

At this Fortunato starts trembling again, and turns to watch the blind man who bends over to feel in his tin plate. Finding it empty, he sighs.

THE BLIND MAN. No luck! Conchita! Conchita . . . where are you?

FORTUNATO. She 's not here. There 's nobody here . . . except me.

THE BLIND MAN. Thank you, Señor. You 're very kind.

Finding himself taken for a passer-by, and for a gentleman at that, Fortunato manages, if a little feebly, to sustain the character.

FORTUNATO. Kind! Do you do well out of your fiddle?

THE BLIND MAN. Oh no, Señor . . . not well. But I scrape along . . . thanks be to God!

FORTUNATO. Ah . . . quite so! Thanks be to God . . . as you say.

THE BLIND MAN. You 're pretty well starved with the cold when you get home at night . . . but as long as you 've earned a bit of something for the children.

FORTUNATO [*his voice shaking a little*]. Oh . . . you 've got children, have you?

THE BLIND MAN. Yes, Señor . . . three children.

FORTUNATO. Three. Well . . . I 've got five.

THE BLIND MAN. Ah . . . but you don't have to worry, I daresay, over feeding them and clothing them.

FORTUNATO. No . . . no, of course not. [*Then, under his breath*]. I can't . . . I can't!

> *This last is wrung from him as he stands clasping and unclasping the coins in his hand.*

THE BLIND MAN. What 's that?

FORTUNATO. I . . . I did n't speak. Well, my friend . . . here 's a little something . . . something for the children.

> *He presses the coins into the blind man's hand and then heaves a mighty sigh . . . as if relieved of as mighty a burden.*

THE BLIND MAN. God reward you, Señor, God reward you! It 's very good of you to spare it.

FORTUNATO. Not at all . . . not at all! I can spare it . . . I can spare it.

> *Conchita has returned by this, and stands staring in open-mouthed amazement at Fortunato's lordly almsgiving. The blind man becomes conscious of her.*

THE BLIND MAN. Conchita!

CONCHITA. Yes . . . I 'm here. Demetria says if you want some you must come and get them. She would n't trust me . . . she would n't!

THE BLIND MAN. Come along, then.

CONCHITA. All right.

THE BLIND MAN. Bring the stool.

CONCHITA. I 've got it.

THE BLIND MAN. Good-day to you, Señor.

FORTUNATO. Good-day . . . good-day!

> *The Blind Man and Conchita go their way along the street.*

THE BLIND MAN. What 's he like?

CONCHITA. Sh! You could have knocked me down with a feather. He looks the asking sort . . . not the giving. I don't think he 's quite right in his head. You do meet some odd people, though, if you go about.

> *They go on their way; and the Blind Man, to lose no chance, begins again on his fiddle.*

FORTUNATO. Why . . . I could n't feel happier if I 'd my

pockets full of money! What 's to be done now, though? Beg
. . . again?

> *He turns to go along the other street. Meanwhile a ragged
> old cripple has encountered the blind man and Conchita; and
> Conchita, it seems, could n't help telling him of this wonderful
> occurrence.*

THE CRIPPLE. That him?

CONCHITA. That 's him.

> *She goes after her father while the cripple hurriedly pursues
> Fortunato.*

THE CRIPPLE. Señor. . . .

> *His hat is off and his hand outstretched for alms. But For-
> tunato, hearing the step, has turned and his hat is off too and
> his hand almost outstretched. And we leave the two looking at
> each other in mutual amazement as the sound of the blind
> man's fiddle dies away.*

SCENE THREE

> *A little garden — though really we can hardly dignify it by that name
> — in the suburbs of Madrid. A few shrubs, a few struggling
> flowers are all it boasts. Its chief feature is the bare brick wall
> that bounds it, its most noticeable furnishing a curious board,
> set up like an easel and of the height of a man, standing against
> this wall. A couple of kitchen chairs complete the picture.
> Fortunato and the maidservant, Inês, appear. Inês is a
> melancholy young woman; later we shall learn why. For-
> tunato looks very weary.*

INÉS. This way.

FORTUNATO. Thank you.

> *He sighs.*

INÉS. You 're tired.

FORTUNATO. Yes . . . I 'm a little tired.

INÉS. Take a chair.

FORTUNATO. Thank you. Is this supposed to be Madrid
still? I feel I 'm half way to Toledo.

INÉS.   Did n't you come by tram?

FORTUNATO.   No . . . no . . . I was in rather a hurry. That 's to say, I prefer walking.   And looking about and wondering where the house was . . . why, I was here before I knew!

INÉS.   You want to see Señora Amaranta?

FORTUNATO.   Do I?   The advertisement did n't have any name to it.   It just said: Assistant Required.

INÉS.   It was Señora Amaranta put it in.

FORTUNATO.   This is her house, then?

INÉS.   No . . . she boards here.   Doña Catalina Antonelli . . . it 's her house . . . takes boarders.   They 're mostly professionals . . . and foreigners.   Señora Amaranta . . . she 's an Argentine.

FORTUNATO.   An Argentine!

INÉS.   I 'll tell her you 're here.

She returns to the house to do so.

FORTUNATO.   Well . . . something may come of it.   That 's a glum girl!   Yes . . . if God is good to me!   And since I gave that money back I 've felt quite hopeful.   Here she is again . . . glummer than ever!   I 'm too late . . . as usual.   They 've engaged somebody.

Inés reappears.

INÉS.   Señora Amaranta says will you wait, please.

Fortunato gives a long-drawn sigh of relief.

FORTUNATO.   Ah!

Inés gives a long-drawn sigh — of despair, it would seem.

INÉS.   Ah!

FORTUNATO.   Anything wrong?   You won't think it rude of me asking.   But you seem very low in your mind.   What 's the trouble?

INÉS.   Life.

FORTUNATO.   Oh . . . of course!   But anything in particular?

INÉS.   Yes . . . I 've got a sorrow.   Have you?

FORTUNATO.   Many of them.   Ah!

INÉS.   Ah!

They sigh in unison this time.

AMARANTA.   And you 're hard up?

FORTUNATO.   Look at me.

AMARANTA.   Down to your last penny?

FORTUNATO.   My very last.

AMARANTA.   The wolf at the door!

FORTUNATO.   A whole pack of them! [*He laughs feebly at this rather feeble joke.*]   I have n't laughed since I don't know when.

AMARANTA.   Well . . . we must see what we can do for you. Are you an artist?

Fortunato stares.

FORTUNATO.   Oh, no, Señora! That is . . . not so far as I know. But I 'm willing to try. No . . . I 'm a clerk by profession . . . that is, I was. I 've not had much work for four years.

AMARANTA.   Four years! That 's bad.

FORTUNATO.   It has been! I really don't know how we 've pulled through. And . . . are you an artist, Señora?

AMARANTA.   But . . . don't you know me?

FORTUNATO.   Know you! Yes . . . of course . . . in a sense. But. . . .

AMARANTA.   I am Amaranta the Invincible.

FORTUNATO [*who is obviously leagues from knowing her*]. Oh . . . of course! Your face . . . and your voice . . .! Who could mistake it?

AMARANTA.   Yes, indeed! I am an artist. I am at the head of my profession. That is why envy and calumny pursue me. I come of a race of artists. We die for our art.

FORTUNATO.   Really! You don't say so!

AMARANTA.   My dear papa . . . crossing Niagara upon a tight-rope . . . stumbled and fell. The thundering cataract was his tomb. What a glorious end! Don't you think so?

FORTUNATO.   Oh . . . most!

AMARANTA.   My brother Hannibal . . . a godlike creature . . . and as noble in soul as in body . . . was eaten by his six black panthers. And Aristides, the youngest of us . . . perished in the urn.

FORTUNATO. The urn! What urn?

AMARANTA. He was famous . . . world famous . . . for his fasting . . . sealed in a crystal urn. But once . . . when he'd endured for a fortnight . . . his strength failed . . . and he passed away.

FORTUNATO. That's an art I do know something of! I might do well in an urn!

AMARANTA. It is not a subject for humour. I follow in my mamma's footsteps.

FORTUNATO. Indeed! Might I ask what she died of?

AMARANTA. Dear Mamma died of old age.

FORTUNATO. Good! I mean . . . well . . . one's thankful it was no worse. Might I ask, too, what it is you want me to do? As long as it's anything I can do. . . .

AMARANTA. A child could do it.

FORTUNATO. I'm glad of that.

AMARANTA. I must put you through a few simple tests.

FORTUNATO. Yes, of course. I write quite a good hand . . . I know a little French . . . I can do bookkeeping by double entry. . . .

AMARANTA. These pleasantries are out of place.

She rises majestically and majestically departs, leaving Fortunato bewildered.

FORTUNATO. Pleasantries! What does she mean? What does the woman do? What does she want of me? I can't walk a tight-rope. Well . . . I could but fall off! But I hope it isn't panthers.

Señora Amaranta returns, Inês following her. She is her pleasant self again. She carries a rifle over her shoulder, and Inês has a tray with some indistinguishable small objects on it. At the sight of the rifle Fortunato's eyes open painfully wide. But with a smile and nod to him she passes on to examine that strange board standing against the wall. Fortunato makes a little dash towards Inês and asks desperately.

FORTUNATO. For pity's sake tell me. Who is she? What is she?

INÉS. What is she? She 's the world's champion shot.

FORTUNATO. Good God!

*Having adjusted that strange board Amaranta the Invincible
turns to him with a smile.*

AMARANTA. Now we 're ready. Come along.

FORTUNATO. Where?

AMARANTA. Here. You stand straight in front of the target
. . .

FORTUNATO. The target! ! !

AMARANTA. And you 've nothing to do but to keep calm.

FORTUNATO. Calm!

AMARANTA. And cool. Cool as a cucumber!

FORTUNATO. I feel as cold as ice.

*She now takes a box of very large wax matches from Inês' tray,
strikes one and hands it to him.*

FORTUNATO. Thank you, I . . . I 'm not smoking.

AMARANTA [*reprovingly*]. Come, come . . . this is business,
Hold it at arm's length, please.

*She leaves him to do so and takes her own stand fifteen paces
from him.*

FORTUNATO. But . . . but what is it you 're going to do,
please?

AMARANTA. Shoot out the lighted match.

*And with ease and precision she takes aim. But in a twink-
ling Fortunato has saved her the trouble; he has blown it out.*

FORTUNATO. No, no . . . it 's out . . . it 's out!

*Amaranta the Invincible lowers her rifle and looks at him
sternly.*

AMARANTA. What is this? Are you afraid?

FORTUNATO. Not at all. Afraid . . . oh, dear no! Well
. . . perhaps . . . yes . . . just a little afraid.

AMARANTA. Do you realise that you insult me by saying that?
But you do it in ignorance. It is excusable. You evidently do
not know me.

FORTUNATO. That . . . that is so, Señora. I confess it. I
do not know you.

AMARANTA.   I can reassure you, I fancy.   Have you good eyes?

FORTUNATO.   Excellent.

She beckons him to her and then points towards some tree not far off.

AMARANTA.   Do you see the top branch of that tree . . . and a spray of bloom at the end of it?   The flower at the very end has four petals . . . can you see that?

FORTUNATO.   Yes.

AMARANTA.   I 'll take one of them off.

She shoots and apparently does so.

AMARANTA.   What do you say to that?

FORTUNATO.   I 'm struck dumb.

AMARANTA.   And you 're not afraid any longer?

FORTUNATO.   How . . . how . . . how could I be?

AMARANTA.   Then go and stand in front of the target.

She takes up her position again and waits for him.

FORTUNATO.   You don't mind my suggesting it . . . have you ever thought of trying it with a candle stuck in a bottle, now?

AMARANTA [*looks at him coldly*].   Where, then, would be the credit of extinguishing it?

FORTUNATO.   I should have thought it would come to about the same thing.

AMARANTA.   Really?   That 's not a very sensible remark. Where would be the risk . . . where would be the thrill?   Who wants to see me snuff out a candle stuck in a bottle?   But held in your hand or an inch above your head so that if I make the slightest slip I kill you on the spot . . . there 's a thrill in that! That 's what the public pay to see.

FORTUNATO.   Yes . . . of course . . . they would!

AMARANTA.   Suppose dear Papa, instead of slinging his tight-rope over mighty Niagara had crossed some wretched little gutter of a river . . . can't you see the difference?

FORTUNATO.   Yes . . . he 'd have got a ducking . . . but he 'd be alive now.

AMARANTA.   Why did great crowds gather round to watch those first aeronauts vanish into the sky?   Because death was waiting

for them there. Is n't danger the very salt of life? Yes . . .
your own danger. In your youth, no doubt, you loved some fair
woman who was another's. Did n't you?

FORTUNATO. No . . . really . . . I don't remember. . . .

AMARANTA. Was n't it her greatest charm that, at any minute,
her husband might come in and kill you in her very arms?

FORTUNATO. The fact is, you know . . . I 've never been at
all like that. I 'm for a quiet life . . . I always was.

AMARANTA. Well . . . let 's get back to business. Light your
match, please. Square to the target. Arm out to its full extent.

*Fortunato gets the match lit and his arm out. But try as he
will, it shakes like an aspen. Amaranta's rifle is to her
shoulder again, but she lowers it in despair.*

AMARANTA. Heavens, man . . . keep still! If you shake
like that how can I help shooting you?

*This is too much for poor Fortunato. He flings down his
match in despair.*

FORTUNATO. Señora . . . I . . . I 'm afraid I shan't suit
the place. My nerves would never stand it. I 'm sorry. You
must excuse me.

*Amaranta is now very angry indeed, coldly, impersonally
angry.*

AMARANTA. I see. Thank you . . . I quite understand!
You came here without knowing who I was. And the moment
you learn I am Amaranta the Invincible . . . all the slanders
you 've heard about me set you quivering like a jelly.

FORTUNATO. I do assure you, Señora . . . I have n't heard any
slanders about you.

AMARANTA. Nonsense!

FORTUNATO. Not a slander.

AMARANTA. Nonsense, I tell you . . . when Madrid is ringing
with them! Ringing with the lie that I shot Sabatino by bungling
a new trick with him!

FORTUNATO. Oh . . . they say that, do they?

*Fortunato and Inês exchange a glance, and hers is a guilty
glance.*

AMARANTA. A drunken good-for-nothing who dared to fall in love with me! And when I sent him about his business . . . what else did he expect, pray? . . . the fool goes and shoots himself. Is that my fault? I 'm sure he 's no great loss. But what a chance for my enemies! And they take it! I know what 's being said of me. That my eye 's out . . . that my nerves are shaky . . . that I 'm going to pieces. I know what the audience were thinking last night . . . I could feel it. And I 've had three contracts sent back to me. But I 'll show them! I 'll astonish them. Before I leave Madrid they shall see what shooting is. I 'll shoot as I 've never shot before. Now what have you to say?

FORTUNATO. Nothing, Señora . . . nothing. I think I 'd better go.

AMARANTA. Then go. You have the impertinence to distrust me! I have shot at men for twenty years . . . and never singed a hair of their heads. Do you know what the Spread-Eagle is? I cover that target with a sheet and I place you against it . . . so. And I draw a pattern round you with bullets as if I drew it with a pencil. I have done that five hundred times and more to my own mother . . . the dearest thing on earth to me. To my own mother! And when she walked away from the target scatheless the audience would go mad with delight. Be off with you! And don't come whining to me about your five starving children again. You 're a coward.

She turns to go. But a convulsion seems to seize Fortunato.

FORTUNATO. My children! Señora. . . .

AMARANTA. What now?

FORTUNATO. Wait . . . wait! Yes . . . I 'm a coward . . . I always have been. But I 'll do it. In spite of that . . . I 'll do it.

AMARANTA. That 's right!

FORTUNATO. I did n't think I could. But I can. Here I am . . . spread-eagled! Draw your pattern. Go on!

He spreads himself ecstatically against the target, like another St. Sebastian.

AMARANTA. Splendid! Quite still, please.

And she takes a masterly aim.

FORTUNATO. I 'll be still! And my children will have bread.

AMARANTA. Steady!

She fires. We hear the ping of the shot on the target. Fortunato gives a yell; his knees collapse.

AMARANTA. What is it?

INÉS. Oh . . . what has happened?

Fortunato feels himself very carefully all over.

AMARANTA. Well?

FORTUNATO. Nothing.

AMARANTA. So I should hope!

FORTUNATO. Nothing at all. A little nervousness . . . to begin with. But I 'm quite myself now. Fire away, Señora . . . fire away.

With a slight touch of arrogance he spreads himself once more upon the target.

AMARANTA. You 're a hero.

FORTUNATO. Not at all . . . not at all! But most kind of you to say so.

AMARANTA. Steady!

She fires again; and but for a slight twitch Fortunato manages to keep it up.

AMARANTA. Steady!

She fires a third time. We might almost think Fortunato was enjoying himself.

FORTUNATO. And my children will have bread!

AMARANTA. Steady!

She fires again.

FORTUNATO. My children will have bread!

AMARANTA. Steady!

FORTUNATO. My children. . . .

She goes on firing; Fortunato rejoicing still.

The Lady from Alfaqueque

(La Consulesa)

A COMEDY IN TWO ACTS

(1914)

THE STREET CRIES OF ALFAQUEQUE

FERNANDITA.
BLANCA.
ADORACIÓN.
ROSITA.
PALOMA.
ALBERTA.
DON PASCUAL.
FELIPE RIVAS.
NICOLÁS.
NOBLEJAS.
REALITO.

THE LADY FROM ALFAQUEQUE

ACT I

*Pascual and Fernandita are a happy married couple who live in the
Salamanca quarter of Madrid; and the scene of this comedy
is a sitting-room in their flat. It is not a very large room;
it is not extravagantly furnished, but everything is in good
taste. There are doors right and left and at the back a glass-
enclosed balcony which looks out upon a garden. The balcony
holds a couple of dozen plants, some of which are in flower.
They are Fernandita's own care; and among them (the glory
of them) are a camellia and an orange tree. But it is evening
now, and the doors of the balcony are shut. On the walls hang
various views of Alfaqueque, the town in Andalusia where
Fernandita was born and brought up. The room is lit by a
lamp which can boast the distinction of having once lit a room
in Alfaqueque. And at the moment Don Pascual is sitting
alone reading his evening paper beside a little table, the handi-
work of a citizen of Alfaqueque who is (as we shall hear later)
temporarily sequestered in gaol. In fact, the chief thing evident in our good friends' home is their loyalty to the wonderful
town of Alfaqueque. Don Pascual is a man slightly over fifty,
an able man, a kindly man, with something gallant, as of the
seventeenth century hidalgo, about him. His reading is inter-
rupted by the appearance of Rosita, a handsome young woman,
one of the servants. She also comes from Alfaqueque and is
amazingly proud of that simple fact. She carries herself as
the queen of a carnival night, and her smile of self-satisfaction
seems permanently painted on her face.*

ROSITA. Señor.

DON PASCUAL. Yes?

ROSITA. There's a gentleman to see you.

DON PASCUAL. Did n't he give you his name?

ROSITA. I did n't ask him. I 'm afraid I never shall get used to answering the door. It 's a thing one must be brought up to, I suppose. And the moment he set eyes on me he stared like a dumb thing. I 'm sure I don't know why!

DON PASCUAL. Dear me! Where 's Alberta, then?

ROSITA. She 's somewhere about.

DON PASCUAL. Ask her to come here, please.

Rosita merely puts her head out of the door and calls . . .

ROSITA. Alberta!

Alberta appears in response. She is a handsome young peasant girl from the North, turned servant in Madrid.

ALBERTA. Did you want me, Señor?

DON PASCUAL. Will you see who it is at the front door, please . . . and if it 's the young man that called this morning, show him in.

ALBERTA. Yes, Señor. [*Then to Rosita as she passes her.*] Of course it 's wonderful to have a duchess to help you. But you have to do all the work!

With which she departs.

ROSITA. Did you hear that, may I ask, Señor? That 's how she goes on the whole time. Anybody could see, I should think, that I 'm not accustomed to service. And one is n't born knowing things, is one?

DON PASCUAL. Certainly not, Rosita, certainly not!

ROSITA. Not to mention the slight difference of having Manolito of Alfaqueque for one's father . . . a jeweller and an artist . . . instead of Atanasio of Talavera de la Reina . . . a man that makes the baskets you carry coal in. That goes without saying, I should suppose!

DON PASCUAL. Nevertheless, Rosita, you are right to remark it!

Realito appears at the door. He is the son of an Andalusian chemist, and has come to seek his fortune in Madrid. He has a new suit on, and it is much too tight for him. He is praying that this present ordeal may be a short one.

REALITO. Señor.

DON PASCUAL. Come in.

REALITO. Good evening.

DON PASCUAL. Good evening.

ROSITA [*not to be left out*]. Good evening.

REALITO. I hope you are well, Señor.

DON PASCUAL. Yes, thanks. Was it you left a letter from Señor Donoso this morning?

REALITO. I had the honour . . .

DON PASCUAL. That 's right, then. Sit down.

REALITO. Thank you.

DON PASCUAL. You can go, Rosita.

ROSITA. I 'm going!
She departs, very much at her ease, and smiling most affably upon the newcomer.

DON PASCUAL. So you 've come to Madrid to seek your fortune?

REALITO. That 's right. What is there to do in a country town nowadays? You lounge about and take too much to drink. . . .

DON PASCUAL. You can do that in Madrid if you want to.

REALITO. I suppose so. It 's the same wine wherever you drink it. But it does n't taste the same here. There 's no fun in drinking a drop too much here.

DON PASCUAL. No? Well, now . . . what are your plans . . . and what can I do for you? I 've not much influence, I fear. I 'm the manager of a chocolate factory. It 's not a Government department . . . though some people seem to think so, by the way they ask me for employment in it.

REALITO. Señor Donoso said you 'd a lot of influence.

DON PASCUAL. Take that with a pinch of salt. Still . . .! What do you want to do . . . and what can you do? That 's the question.

REALITO. I 'll do anything. I 've got to earn my living.

DON PASCUAL. Quite so. But is n't there something you 're particularly good at?

REALITO. I 've got two hands and five fingers on each of them . . . same as any man.

DON PASCUAL. You 'll need some better recommendation than that, I 'm afraid. Have n't you been trained for any profession?

REALITO. No, Señor. I tried for a degree at College. But I did n't get it. And what use is a profession to a man?

DON PASCUAL. Not much money in them, certainly. Do you write a good letter?

REALITO. I don't know. I 've never thought about it. I can say what I 've got to say. My cousin Benito now . . . he writes a good letter. And a beautiful hand.

DON PASCUAL. Can you do typewriting?

REALITO. No, Señor. My cousin Benito . . . he does typewriting.

DON PASCUAL. What about French? Can you speak French?

REALITO. I did start on French. But after three lessons I stuck.

DON PASCUAL. Rather soon, was n't it?

REALITO. It was the verbs I could n't manage. My father said : " Learn it without verbs, then . . . it won't make so much difference."

DON PASCUAL. That was your father's point of view, was it?

REALITO. So I tried it without the verbs . . . but it was n't any easier. Benito speaks French. You should hear him.

DON PASCUAL. I fear it 's Benito that should have come looking for a job.

REALITO. But he 's got a job . . . and a very good job . . . in Seville. And he 's just going to be married to the prettiest girl you ever saw. He has all the luck.

DON PASCUAL. Quite so! Well . . . I 'll write a line now to Señor Donoso . . . and I 'll have a talk to him about you tomorrow.

REALITO. Thank you, Señor . . . thank you very much.

Don Pascual is leaving the room when his wife comes in.

DON PASCUAL. Oh . . . Fernandita!

FERNANDITA. Yes?

REALITO [*bowing*]. Good evening.

FERNANDITA. Good evening.

DON PASCUAL. This young man has just brought me a letter of introduction from Bautista Donoso.

REALITO. Señora.

FERNANDITA. So glad. . . .

DON PASCUAL. My wife.

REALITO. Your servant.

DON PASCUAL. I 'll leave you to entertain him while I write my letter.

> *And he goes off to do so. Fernandita is a woman of fifty or nearly, and one of the best and sweetest women in the world. Sometimes she seems a little stupid — when she is n't. Sometimes she seems so and is. She was born — as we already know — in Alfaqueque, and she does it honour. And although she has lived in Madrid these twenty years, from her soft Southern accent, you 'd think she had arrived here yesterday. Nor have Madrid fashions had any influence over her. She dresses and does her hair as she would if she lived in Alfaqueque; and this, though it may be quaint, gives her great charm and distinction. Her heart is in Alfaqueque, in that small corner of the earth where she was born.*

FERNANDITA. Do sit down again.

REALITO. Thank you.

FERNANDITA. It 's cool to-night, is n't it?

REALITO. Coolish!

FERNANDITA. And only the beginning of October! You 're from Andalusia?

REALITO. Yes, Señora. You can tell it by the way I speak, I suppose.

FERNANDITA. I thought you were. I was born there.

REALITO. I could tell that. No use trying to hide it.

FERNANDITA. I don't want to hide it. I 've lived in Madrid for twenty years. But I might live here fifty and. . . .

REALITO. I know! I 've been here three days. You can guess what it feels like to me.

FERNANDITA. Where exactly do you come from?

REALITO. Alminares.

FERNANDITA.   Alminares! I used often to go there when I was a girl. And I 've a great friend there.

REALITO.   Who 's that?

FERNANDITA.   Esperanza Ruiz.

REALITO.   Esperanza Ruiz! But she 's related to me. One of my cousins, that is . . . a niece of my father's . . . is married to one of her cousins.

FERNANDITA.   Fancy that! But who is your father then?

REALITO.   Feliciano Real.

FERNANDITA.   Feliciano Real!

REALITO.   Yes, Señora.

FERNANDITA.   The chemist at Alfaqueque?

REALITO.   Yes, he was. He has moved now to Alminares. He got on the wrong side in politics.

FERNANDITA.   Oh, I remember him so well! We used to call him . . .! You won't mind?

REALITO.   No, Señora, no.

FERNANDITA.   We used to call him little Pot-belly.

REALITO.   Ha, ha! I 'm little Pot-belly's son.

FERNANDITA.   But then . . . you were born in Alfaqueque?

REALITO.   Why, of course I was! I was christened at San Gregorio's. And I grew up there.

Fernandita is as pleased as if she had won a prize in a lottery.

FERNANDITA.   You come from Alfaqueque! But we 're compatriots.

REALITO.   Are we?

FERNANDITA.   Yes . . . I 'm from Alfaqueque. I used to live in the House with the Two Fountains . . . that was my home.

REALITO.   Then you must be. . . .

FERNANDITA.   Fernandita Osorio.

REALITO.   Think of that! I never dreamt! I am glad to see you.

And he jumps up to shake her warmly by the hand . . . by both hands.

FERNANDITA.   And I 'm very glad to meet you, Señor.

REALITO.   Oh . . . please don't call me that! Why, I used

to play in your garden when I was a boy.   And I used to go and
see the pig-killing.   Holy Saints . . . but it is good to find you
here.   [*He is so happy about it that he even forgets his new clothes.*]
Why ever did n't Señor Donoso tell me who Don Pascual had
married?

FERNANDITA.   He 'd never think of it.   And what is your own
name, Señor?

REALITO.   Oh . . . please . . . not Señor!   I 'm Feliciano
. . . like my father . . . and his father . . . and his grandfather . . . and his great-grandfather.   And if I marry and have
a son. . . .

FERNANDITA.   Then he 'll be Feliciano, too.

REALITO.   It 's no use changing things just for the sake of
change . . . is it?   But I 'm always called Realito.

FERNANDITA.   Well . . . there 's no place in the world like
Alfaqueque, is there?

REALITO.   No.   Of course, the people in Alminares always
tell you . . .!   But who cares what they say?

FERNANDITA.   They may say what they like.   Alfaqueque
. . . why it 's like a silver cup when you stand on the hill looking
down at it.   I believe the Holy Virgin herself scattered flowers
in the valley there.   And the houses are so white and clean!   And
the windows with their lattices!   And the fields with the sun
on them!

REALITO.   Oh yes . . . yes!

FERNANDITA.   Where else can you see such a sky?   And the
water ice-cold from the wells.   I sometimes think Heaven must
be very like Alfaqueque.   The worst day in the year there is
better than the best one anywhere else . . . I know that!

REALITO.   D' you remember those little almond cakes they
make there?   Now those are cakes!

FERNANDITA.   Oh, as to cakes . . . and sweets . . .!   To
begin with you can't get cinnamon like ours even in Granada.
Or lemons . . . no, not even in Utrera.

REALITO.   And the honey cakes!

FERNANDITA.   And the walnut paste!   And the spice cakes!

REALITO. Oh, don't talk to me about the spice cakes! Once I ate sixty-seven for a wager. And it nearly killed me. I got so hot inside I thought I should burst into flames.

FERNANDITA. Sixty-seven! I don't wonder! But let me tell you something. I get all the Alfaqueque sweets . . . and cakes . . . here in Madrid. There's a friend of mine . . . she comes from Alfaqueque . . . Adoración Martínez she's called . . . and she's a perfect genius at making them. Yes . . . wherever I lived there'd be no place like Alfaqueque for me. It makes me happy . . . just to sit and think of it. And sometimes I get a parcel . . . one of my friends there will send me some palm grapes . . . or a big loaf of brown bread . . . or some palmitos . . . or some prickly pears. It's a red-letter day when a parcel comes.

REALITO. I'm sure it is!

FERNANDITA. Look at my pictures. They're all of Alfaqueque.

REALITO. Why . . . so they are! I didn't notice. I was a bit nervous when I first came.

FERNANDITA. Look at them now, then. Take a good look. One at a time!

He does not need bidding.

REALITO. That's very good of the Campo Real! And the Campillo! There . . . that's where I was born.

FERNANDITA. D'you call this good of the Torre del Moro?

REALITO. Very good. Just like it! And there's the Calle las Cruces. And the Santuario. Every bit of Alfaqueque!

FERNANDITA. And my husband's got a big coloured photograph . . . which takes it all in . . . hanging in his study.

REALITO. Olé! People talk about Madrid! I tell you . . . Madrid's a disappointment to me. Oh . . . one can't compare Alfaqueque to it, I know. But Cadiz now. Once you've seen Cadiz there's nothing in Madrid need astonish you. After all . . . as I was saying last night to a Madrid man in the boarding-house here . . . what does it amount to? What has Madrid got that Cadiz hasn't? More streets . . . more houses . . ,

and they may be a bit higher here and there. Lots of statues
. . . but nobody remembers who they 're of. Oh yes . . . more
carriages up and down the Paseo . . . and more pictures in the
Museum. But really that 's all there is to it.

FERNANDITA. I know . . . I know! Madrid 's never ending.
And so tiring! But Alfaqueque. . . .

*At this point in comes Blanca, looking for her work-bag, which
she has left on a chair. She is a beautiful girl, gentle and
graceful. Seeing a stranger she bows to him, with a . . .*

BLANCA. Good evening.

REALITO [*jumping up*]. Good evening.

BLANCA. I 'm so sorry . . . I 've been looking everywhere
for my work-bag. I must have left it . . . yes, here.

She has found it and is going.

FERNANDITA. Blanca!

BLANCA. Yes?

FERNANDITA. This is a compatriot of ours.

BLANCA. Indeed?

REALITO. Delighted.

BLANCA. How d' you do?

REALITO. Your daughter . . . is it?

FERNANDITA. No . . . just a friend. I 've no children.

REALITO. But you 're from Alfaqueque too?

BLANCA. Yes . . . though I left there so young I 'm afraid it
does n't show. I was brought up in Madrid. Why . . . what
a stroke of luck for you, Fernandita! A visitor from Alfaqueque
. . . and a new excuse to talk about it. Have you both been
singing alleluias to the honey cakes and the brown bread and the
green trees and the water from the wells?

FERNANDITA. There . . . that 's how they make fun of me
. . . because I still love my home!

Blanca kisses her affectionately.

BLANCA. Well . . . who could help it! So glad to have met
you.

This last to Realito as she goes towards the door again.

REALITO. The pleasure 's mine. My name 's Feliciano Real

. . . but I'm called Realito.   My father's the chemist in Almi-nares now . . . 4 Calle del Pozo.

BLANCA.   Yes?   Good-bye for the present.

She disappears.

REALITO.   Our compatriot is a very charming young lady! Who is she?

FERNANDITA.   She's Blanca Solis.   Her mother was Josefa Mariño . . . Frasquita's niece . . . the ugly Frasquita . . . Torremocha's cousin . . . the one that married Pasquita Merengue.

REALITO.   Oh, to be sure!   I remember her mother.   Does she live in Madrid now?

FERNANDITA.   Yes . . . since she married again.   She was left a widow, poor woman . . . and then she went and married the most dreadful man you can imagine.

REALITO.   From Alfaqueque?

FERNANDITA [*very indignantly*].   No, indeed!   We don't have such men in Alfaqueque.   He detests his step-daughter . . . and he treated her so vilely that just to get away from him she got engaged.   And that only made matters worse. . . .

REALITO.   I say!

FERNANDITA.   I felt so sorry for the child.   Something simply had to be done.   And one day I went and fetched her here.   And here she'll stay till she's married . . . in January.

REALITO.   That was very kind.

FERNANDITA.   Not that I like the man she's marrying.   He's a bit of a brute.   But she'd marry a convict, I believe, sooner than go and live at home again.

REALITO.   I suppose so!

FERNANDITA.   Poor girl . . . she'd no other refuge.   My husband says anybody can find food or clothing or shelter here as long as they come from Alfaqueque.   He calls this house the Alfaqueque Legation . . . and he calls me the Minister Plenipo-tentiary from Alfaqueque.

REALITO.   That's good . . . that's very good!

At this moment there appears in the doorway Don Salustiano Rodríguez Noblejas.   He is a clerk in a Government office;

by no means in a very grand position there. He is the politest
person imaginable.

NOBLEJAS. May I come in?

FERNANDITA. Come in, Noblejas.

NOBLEJAS. Good evening.

REALITO. Good evening.

NOBLEJAS. I 'm not disturbing you?

FERNANDITA. Not a bit.

NOBLEJAS. And how are you, Doña Fernandita?

FERNANDITA. Very well. And you? And how 's Paloma?

NOBLEJAS. She 's very well, I thank you. And your good
husband . . . is he well?

FERNANDITA. Very well indeed. He 's in his study.

NOBLEJAS. Should I intrude, d' you think, if I joined him
there?

FERNANDITA. I fancy he 's expecting you.

NOBLEJAS. Then in that case . . . if you 'll excuse me . . .

FERNANDITA. Why, of course!

NOBLEJAS. You 're very kind [*with a bow to Realito*], Señor!

REALITO. Not at all!

At the door he turns to bow again.

NOBLEJAS. Your servant, Señor. Doña Fernandita . . . your
most humble servant.

And he bows himself out. Emboldened by Fernandita's
friendliness, Realito has his word to say.

REALITO. He 's not from Alfaqueque either . . . no more than
your young lady's stepfather is!

FERNANDITA. No . . . we don't grow his sort there either, do
we? I did n't introduce you. You 'd have had to stand and
exchange compliments for a quarter of an hour. There never was
anybody so polite. My husband swears that he said to the priest
who christened him: "Please be so very kind as to take the chill
off the water."

Realito has a good laugh at this.

Poor fellow . . . he 's a clerk in the Pensions Office . . . and
he has one of the inside flats here. Pascual finds him a little extra

DON PASCUAL.   No, no! It scared him for a moment.

FERNANDITA.   I keep telling Alberta not to wax the floors so much. Waxed floors . . . horrid things anyhow. Why not good clean tiles . . .?

DON PASCUAL.   Such as we find in Alfaqueque!

FERNANDITA.   Now are you going to get that boy a job?

DON PASCUAL.   It won't be very easy.

FERNANDITA.   Surely . . . something in the factory?

DON PASCUAL.   My poor factory! He'd not be much use there, I fear . . . unless we paid him to come and eat chocolate! But I'll do my best. Still . . . I fear he's not the hero of your dreams who's to come from Alfaqueque.

FERNANDITA.   Never mind. Find him something small to start with.

DON PASCUAL.   He looks strong enough. I know a man on the railway. Shall I get him a job as a porter?

FERNANDITA.   Pascual! A nice refined boy like that!

DON PASCUAL.   True! Well . . . now I must go and attend to our other nice refined friend. Poor old Noblejas!

On his way out he encounters Rosita. There is a slight cloud on the young woman's face, though her self-satisfaction can still shine through it.

ROSITA.   Señora.

FERNANDITA.   What is it?

ROSITA.   I wish to be searched.

FERNANDITA.   What?

ROSITA.   Searched, if you please, from top to toe . . . as if I were a common factory hand. My trunk as well . . . and my bed! Everything belonging to me!

FERNANDITA.   But what am I to search you for?

ROSITA.   We've been doing the silver. There's a fork lost. Alberta looks at me as if she thought I'd taken it. Señora, when a girl grows up surrounded . . . as I've been at my father's . . . by necklaces and earrings and jewelry of all sorts, will she, I ask you, soil her fingers or her conscience . . . with a fork? I ask you, Señor.

DON PASCUAL. Don't! Forks are no affair of mine.

FERNANDITA. I never heard of such a thing!

ROSITA [to Don Pascual]. Is my word to be doubted? Shall I strip myself here and now?

FERNANDITA. Silly child! I know you better than that, I should hope . . . and all your family besides. Such nonsense!

She goes out determinedly to put the matter straight.

ROSITA. But the fork's not the worst of it, Señor.

DON PASCUAL. Indeed! What is?

ROSITA. I hardly liked to tell the Señora. To think that I should do such a thing! It comes of being so unused to service. [*Then with the sweetest smile.*] I had the best coffee cups on a tray just now . . . and as I got to the dresser the clock struck. That always makes me jump. And I jumped. And down they dropped!

DON PASCUAL. Were any broken?

ROSITA. Every one. Every single one. When I jumped.

DON PASCUAL. The Señora will jump when she hears of it! Can't you keep your wits about you, young woman?

ROSITA. Don Pascual . . . how can I carry heavy trays with hands like mine? They used to say in Alfaqueque that I'd hands like the Virgin of the Santuario.

DON PASCUAL. Did they really? Why, then, of course, it follows that you cannot carry trays!

As he once more opens the door to go he hears a voice — it is the voice of Nicolás — saying loudly and obstreperously. . . .

NICOLÁS. Good evening! Can't you hear me? Yes . . . I said good evening.

DON PASCUAL. Blanca's young man! No . . . really! . . . I don't feel up to him!

And he escapes in the opposite direction.

ROSITA. He does take some things so seriously . . . does Don Pascual! So unlike dear Father! Whatever went wrong . . . he'd always a smile for you. And I'm his own daughter in that . . . thank goodness!

Nicolás now appears. He is a Madrileño through and through. Further he is a very cross-grained young man. Besides this, he is a bit of a bounder. He is his uncle's favourite nephew, and his uncle is rich. He is studying for a profession he never means to practise; and he thinks, because he has money in his pocket, that he can be as rude to everybody as he likes.

The smile Rosita gives him is worthy of her father.

ROSITA. Hola! How are you?

NICOLÁS. Here . . . you must n't say Hola to me. Tell Señorita Blanca I 've come.

ROSITA. You are irritable, are n't you!

NICOLÁS. Here . . . you must n't talk to me like that! Tell the Señorita I 'm waiting.

ROSITA. Well . . . if it comes to that . . . don't order me about.

Rosita departs, her nose in the air.

NICOLÁS. A nice sort of girl to have round the house! Gets cheekier every day!

Ill-humoured, impatient, he paces up and down waiting for Blanca, who arrives at last, sweet and gentle, and as different as can be from this young man she means to marry.

BLANCA. Welcome.

NICOLÁS. Don't be theatrical.

BLANCA. How do you do, then . . . if you like that better.

NICOLÁS. I don't like affectation.

BLANCA. I was in the middle of a letter to Mamma.

NICOLÁS. To your mother.

BLANCA. To Mamma.

NICOLÁS. To your mother!

BLANCA. I said . . . to Mamma.

NICOLÁS. To your mother!! I 'm not going to call her Mamma. Let 's be clear about it. So why should we call her Mamma?

BLANCA [*laughing*]. Very well . . . to my mother. It makes no difference to me. You seem very upset. Are n't you well?

NICOLÁS. As well as I ever am. I got out of bed the wrong side. And when I get in the tram to come here . . . the first vexing thing happens!

BLANCA. If that was the first you must have got out of bed rather late.

NICOLÁS. Is that a joke?

BLANCA. Well . . . what happened in the tram?

NICOLÁS. Oh, nothing, my dear girl . . . nothing! I was grossly insulted, that was all. The trams themselves are a disgrace. You crawl along. No smoking allowed. No spitting allowed. Wait till the car stops. Don't speak to the driver. Keep your ticket ready. Beware of pickpockets. Use coal-tar soap. Drink Solares water. You might as well be back at school again.

BLANCA. I know . . . it's shocking.

NICOLÁS. And then, if you please, two little whipper-snappers of second-lieutenants . . . just into their uniform . . . began giggling at me. I wasn't going to stand that. I was starting to teach them manners . . . and the tram stopped . . . and we all three tumbled out. And if there hadn't been a policeman there . . . anything might have happened. But if they'd been a couple of generals I wouldn't have had them giggling at me. Well . . . that was nothing, I suppose!

BLANCA. But, Nicolás, you're always getting into these disputes . . . with people in trams . . . or with the men watering the streets . . . or with some one because he walks the wrong side of the pavement. Why?

NICOLÁS. Because I'm a man and not a child . . . to be pushed and ordered about. And because I like to see things done properly. What a country!

BLANCA. I know. But keep calm . . . and sit down.

NICOLÁS. I don't want to sit down. And a nice little upset I had with the porter here.

BLANCA. With the porter too!

NICOLÁS. That's the first thing that happens to annoy me.

BLANCA. No . . . the second.

NICOLÁS. Thank you. There 'll be a third soon, it seems!
You 're in a charming mood this evening.

BLANCA. Am I? I 'm sorry.

NICOLÁS. This porter here has got some grudge against me.
He 's never there to work the lift. I have to ring and ring. I
shall write and complain about him . . . and he 'll lose his place.
His dog, if you please, was asleep in the lift . . . and he just
did n't want to disturb it. And the seat all covered with hairs!
[*He picks a few off his trousers.*] I will not stand this sort of
thing . . .!

BLANCA. Oh, come . . . forget it! And sit down and talk
to me. Won't you, please?

He obeys; for really she is so gentle and charming.

NICOLÁS. All right!

BLANCA. How 's your uncle?

NICOLÁS. Just the same. He 'd try the patience of a saint.
Rolling in money . . . and keeps me tied to that wretched desk.
You wait till I get hold of it!

BLANCA. Now, Nicolás, you 'll do as I tell you about that.

NICOLÁS. Oh! Shall I!

BLANCA. It 's all nonsense, this notion of selling the business
and buying a country place.

NICOLÁS. I shan't sell it. I shall put in a good manager. But
if you think I 'm going to spend the rest of my days selling cloth
by the yard . . . you 're mistaken. I mean to enjoy my life.

BLANCA. I want you to. But there 's more to be thought of.
You can have a good time without neglecting your business, can't
you? And the master's eye . . .

NICOLÁS. Don't try your village wisdom on me!

BLANCA. We 've not only ourselves to think of. At least . . .
we shan't have, shall we?

NICOLÁS. Now look here, Blanca, don't start any of that nonsense.

BLANCA. What do you mean?

NICOLÁS. What I say! And it 's not the first time I 've had
to say it. If it 's children you 're thinking of . . . no, thank you!

BLANCA. You can't seriously mean that, Nicolás!

NICOLÁS. Of course I do. What do you know about it? Good God . . . who wants children, I'd like to know! Little nuisances . . . cutting their teeth and catching measles . . . and having stomach-aches . . . and you sit up half the night with them. . . !

BLANCA. I hate to hear you talk like this, Nicolás . . . even in fun.

NICOLÁS. Do you?

BLANCA. Yes. I want to have children. And why should I be ashamed to tell you so? It has always been my dream to have children.

NICOLÁS. Nonsense!

BLANCA. But what else is marriage for?

NICOLÁS. Now don't start being clever.

BLANCA. There's nothing very clever in that.

NICOLÁS. Be practical. Children are a nuisance and that's all about it. They tie you by the leg. You can't take them a holiday with you . . . you can't leave them at home. If you even take a child to a theatre it yells and has to be carried out. And when they grow up they either spend all your money or they turn on you because you won't let them. No, thank you!

He strides up and down grumbling to himself. Blanca sits watching him. She can hardly help smiling at his surly foolishness, though she manages to look stern enough when he meets her eye. At this moment Fernandita returns, never expecting to find herself in the midst of a battle. But she sizes up the situation quickly enough.

FERNANDITA. What . . . another quarrel!

BLANCA. Just for a change.

NICOLÁS. No need to be sarcastic . . . as well as foolish!

FERNANDITA. Now . . . now!

BLANCA. You see what he's like. I might as well be at home again.

NICOLÁS. Don't you compare me to your stepfather, now.

FERNANDITA. But what's it all about?

BLANCA.   Simply because I said . . .

NICOLÁS.   Now don't twist things.

BLANCA.   Tell it yourself, then.

FERNANDITA.   What was it?   Come!

NICOLÁS.   Blanca, if you please, announces that when she's married she wants to have children.

FERNANDITA.   Well . . . that's natural enough, is n't it?

BLANCA.   Why, of course!

NICOLÁS.   Of course not!

BLANCA.   I repeat . . . and I 'll shout it from the house tops if you like: When I 'm married I wish to have children.

NICOLÁS.   I don't.

BLANCA.   And I do.

FERNANDITA.   Well, you can't have it both ways!   You must agree about it somehow.

BLANCA.   That's how we quarrelled . . . trying to agree.

NICOLÁS.   It's impossible, it appears, to be happily married unless you have children!

FERNANDITA.   No . . . it is n't impossible.   But. . . .

NICOLÁS.   Of course not!   You 've none.

FERNANDITA.   No.

NICOLÁS.   Very well, then!

FERNANDITA.   Why God gave me none I don't know . . . nor why He gave you such a wicked temper. . . .

NICOLÁS.   Never mind my temper!   You 've no children, so you 're all for other people having them . . . and having to put up with them.   That's what it comes to.   Nothing so easy to bear as other people's troubles!   [Suddenly, rounding on Blanca.] Ask your mother how she has liked having children . . . and getting to look like a sack of potatoes.

BLANCA.   Oh . . . this is too much!   How dare you speak like that about my mother?   Let me tell you that all the happiness she 's had in her life she owes to her children.

FERNANDITA.   That's true enough.

BLANCA.   It's not her children that have made her miserable.

FERNANDITA.   No, indeed!

BLANCA.   And I 'm the only one that had better never have been born.   For if I 'd not been I could n't have come to know you.

FERNANDITA.   And that 's very true.

NICOLÁS.   Yes . . . you must needs back her up, must n't you?   And every one 's bound to be right except me.   Stand by each other as long as there 's a man you can get the better of. That 's women all over!   [*Rounding once more on Blanca, only to discover now that she is in tears.*]   Yes . . . and now cry!   It only wanted that!   I 'd better go out and take a walk.

BLANCA.   Do!

NICOLÁS.   It 'll give you a chance to cheer up.

BLANCA.   And give you a chance to cool down.   Good-bye.

FERNANDITA.   Now, now . . . don't part like this.   What a storm in a tea-cup!   You want to have children and he does n't. Very well then, you must compromise.   That 's what married life is . . . compromise.

BLANCA.   Oh, let me alone, please!   Day after day . . . it 's always the same . . . he does nothing but make me wretched!

And she runs from the room, crying bitterly.

FERNANDITA.   You 're not going to leave her like this . . . surely!

NICOLÁS.   It 's all put on.   She only does it to upset me.   I know her.   But she won't get round me.   And the sooner it 's plain that I 'm to be master the better.   D' you think it a proper sort of thing for her to talk to me about having children?

FERNANDITA.   Who else should she talk to about it, pray?

NICOLÁS.   Well!!   I 'm off.   A pleasant evening for me . . . this!

On his way out he encounters Noblejas, whose politeness is very detaining.

NOBLEJAS.   Ah . . . Señor Don Nicolás . . . and how are you?   Delighted to see you, I 'm sure.   And how is your very good uncle?

NICOLÁS.   Thank you.   He 's well.   And I 'm well.   We 're all well.   And as I see you a dozen times a day we need n't

stand here bowing and scraping like dancing masters . . .
need we?

And off he goes.

FERNANDITA. Did you ever know such manners? They must
have fed that young man as a baby on tintacks soaked in vinegar.

NOBLEJAS. I own to being a little surprised . . .

FERNANDITA. A pleasant partner for a lifetime, won't he be?

NOBLEJAS. . . . for I don't think I gave him any cause. . . .

FERNANDITA. Poor girl . . . poor girl!

NOBLEJAS. . . . and it is the very first time that I have been
subjected to such. . . .

FERNANDITA. Some women seem cursed from their birth.

NOBLEJAS. But can I be of any service?

FERNANDITA. I must cheer her up a little, if I can.

NOBLEJAS. For if there's anything I can do. . . .

FERNANDITA. Though . . . poor child! . . . what is there
one can do for her?

*Fernandita, her mind on Blanca, goes out, quite oblivious to
his fluid politeness, and leaves him indulging in it.*

NOBLEJAS. You have only to command me. Need I assure
you . . .?

*Adoración comes in to find him still automatically bowing to
vacancy, as it seems. She is a rather more than middle-aged
lady, visibly ravaged by the privations and struggles of her life,
but with her spirit ardent and unbroken still. Like Fernandita
she comes from Alfaqueque; and to Fernandita, whom she
adores, she owes most of her bread-and-butter nowadays. For
with her husband's help (he was a clerk in a Government office
and lost his place in some political landslide) she makes the
famous Alfaqueque sweets. Fernandita buys them and sees
that other people buy them too. At this very moment Adoración
has a basket of them on her arm. She is very humbly dressed
with a black shawl round her shoulders and a veil over her head.*

ADORACIÓN. How do you do, Salustiano? Ah, dear me!
What a joy it is, is n't it, just to breath the air of this house?
Fragrant with lavender!

NOBLEJAS. And how do you do, Adoración . . . queen of confectioners! How are things with you?

ADORACIÓN. I must n't grumble. And with you?

NOBLEJAS. I must n't grumble. Your husband 's quite well?

ADORACIÓN. Very well, thank you.

NOBLEJAS. And your brother-in-law . . . he 's well, I hope?

ADORACIÓN. Yes.

NOBLEJAS. And your children . . . all well?

ADORACIÓN. Very well.

NOBLEJAS. And there 's nothing wrong with your sweets, I 'm sure!

ADORACIÓN. Thank you . . . they were never better. Try one.

NOBLEJAS. No, no, I was n't hinting at . . . .

ADORACIÓN. Try one . . . try one! You won't get another such anywhere but here. I 've just left four dozen in the dining-room for dear Fernandita. And I hope they 'll be some comfort to her in the midst of her worries. Poor darling . . . with everybody plaguing her and imposing on her! Have you heard Rosita's latest?

NOBLEJA . No . . . what has she done?

ADORACIÓN. A whole set of coffee cups . . . priceless . . . one of dear Fernandita's most treasured possessions . . . her great-grandmother 's . . . smashed to atoms!

NOBLEJAS. Dear me . . . dear me!

ADORACIÓN. You may well say so. What a girl! She may come from Alfaqueque. But if ever she gives a thought to anything except her looking-glass I 'm mightily mistaken. An idle minx!

NOBLEJAS. Rosita?

ADORACIÓN. Rosita! And I 'm only waiting for the day when they 'll show her the door. Who does she think she is, pray? If she 's told to sweep a room . . . why, she can't soil her hands with such work! If she 's asked to make a bed . . . what, a jeweller's daughter make beds! The result is she does nothing at all. And when she does do anything you wish she had n't. Heavens above us . . . is she the only person who 's a little down in the world!

NOBLEJAS. No, Adoración, no. But I 'd so much rather not talk like this of her behind her back.

ADORACIÓN. Look at me! I 've kept my carriage . . . two horses and two men on the box. And I make sweets for a living . . . yes, and carry them round to my customers, too. And Shanks's mare is all I 've to ride . . . when I can't afford a tram. And my husband . . . well, I think you know . . . when he was in the Treasury, never a thing done till his advice was asked! And now he spends his days beating eggs. Not precisely what he was born to, I think.

NOBLEJAS. No, no . . . by no means!

ADORACIÓN. Very well then! Don't let that young woman try on any of her airs with me . . . that 's all. God forgive me for being uncharitable! But she 's a twisty one, that 's what she is . . . a twisty-twiddler!

NOBLEJAS. A what?

ADORACIÓN. A twisty-twiddler. And they 'll find it out sooner or later.

NOBLEJAS. I don't in the least understand. . . .

ADORACIÓN. So was her sister . . . and her cousin Pilar. So 's her mother's cousin . . . and her sister-in-law. She 'll turn out just the same. I see it in her eye.

NOBLEJAS. But what exactly is a twisty-twiddler . . . and how do you see it in her eye?

ADORACIÓN. It 's going crooked instead of straight . . . and for the love of it, what 's more.

NOBLEJAS. I see. And all the family are the same?

ADORACIÓN. Every one. They twisted her on to poor Fernandita just to get rid of her.

NOBLEJAS. That was kind of them!

ADORACIÓN. It makes me stiff with rage to see how people impose on the blessed creature. D' you see this thing? (*It is the cheap little three-legged table by which Don Pascual sat reading.*) A gentleman from Alfaqueque, who 's taking a little holiday in gaol, sent this to her. Would she give fifty pesetas for it? From Alfaqueque! So of course she did. Oh, once I get started about her. . .!

NOBLEJAS. It's all quite true.

ADORACIÓN. But . . . you see . . . it's only since we came to know her that we've been able to look life in the face again. I remember it so well . . . the House with the Two Fountains where she was born. I declare it must be holy water flows from them. And, you know . . . Don Pascual, he was just an ordinary man till she married him . . . and now he's a perfect saint. God bless her!

NOBLEJAS. God bless her.

ADORACIÓN. She'll be your earthly providence if you come from Alfaqueque.

NOBLEJAS. Or from Pancorbo.

ADORACIÓN. Where's that?

NOBLEJAS. I come from Pancorbo.

ADORACIÓN. And she does things so delicately! The other day my husband came to see Don Pascual on business. And when he got out in the street again he thought his hat did n't fit very well. But he took no more notice till he got home. Then what d' you think he found? Fernandita had tucked twenty-five pesetas in the hat-band.

NOBLEJAS. That must have made it very heavy.

ADORACIÓN. No, not in silver, silly man! A note for twenty-five pesetas. And God knows it came that day like a shower of rain in summer.

Noblejas has his own hat in his hand; as if absent-mindedly he runs his fingers round inside it, in case . . . by any chance. . . .

NOBLEJAS. That was a charming thought. But . . . I don't see how she had the chance to. . . .

ADORACIÓN. Quite simple! He hangs his hat on the hatstand when he arrives.

NOBLEJAS. Does he now . . . does he?

Noblejas eyes his own hat . . . and possibly the future too.

ADORACIÓN. Well . . . she does n't seem to be coming. I'll

just run in and say good-night and give her a kiss.   Good-bye,
Noblejas.

NOBLEJAS.   Good-bye.   God bless you, Adoración.

ADORACIÓN.   I don't get a good night 's sleep unless I 've had
a glimpse of Fernandita.

*As she goes she almost collides in the doorway with Don
Pascual.*

ADORACIÓN.   Don Pascual . . . Don Pascual . . . now don't
you scowl at me!   I 'm only going to say good-night to Fernandita.   Saint Fernandita . . . yes, that 's what she is.   And this
house is her shrine.

Off she goes, all aglow with enthusiasm.

DON PASCUAL.   More Alfaqueque!   What . . . and are you
still here?

*It is said half in joke — but only half; and Noblejas is a
little hurt.*

NOBLEJAS.   If my presence is unwelcome I sincerely regret it.

DON PASCUAL.   No, no . . . I did n't mean that, Salustiano!

NOBLEJAS.   But as I was going out Adoración came in . . .

DON PASCUAL.   Quite so.

NOBLEJAS.   And she always has her little song of praise to sing.
And so have I . . . so have I!

DON PASCUAL.   Well . . . we 'll take it as sung, shall we?
We meet to-morrow.

NOBLEJAS.   God willing.   If not . . . we bow to His will.

DON PASCUAL [*half to himself*].   Your best bow, I 'm sure
. . . to the Almighty.   Till to-morrow then.

NOBLEJAS.   Till to-morrow . . . believe me, yours to command.

DON PASCUAL.   I do believe you.

NOBLEJAS.   You are too good.   Will you make my adieux,
please, to Doña Fernandita?   Good-night.   Your most obedient!

He bows himself out.

DON PASCUAL.   I really prefer Adoración's sugar candy!

Fernandita comes in.

FERNANDITA.   Holy Mother!

DON PASCUAL.   Well . . . did she give you her good-night kiss?

FERNANDITA. She did . . . and twenty of them! And I'm in no mood to be cuddled. I'm afraid I was almost rude to her.

DON PASCUAL. What's wrong?

FERNANDITA. You know perfectly well. I'm worried to death about Blanca.

DON PASCUAL. Yes . . I heard them at it . . . from my study. I was strongly tempted to come and kick him down the stairs.

FERNANDITA. My dear . . . for heaven's sake don't start doing that!

DON PASCUAL. Fernandita, I am a patient man . . . but I cannot stand the Porcupine.

FERNANDITA. Don't call him the Porcupine, Pascual. It'll make such trouble if he hears that you call him the Porcupine.

DON PASCUAL. I have it from his affianced wife that at school he was known as the Porcupine. When more than usually exasperated by the brute she herself refers to him as the Porcupine. And the name fits him admirably.

FERNANDITA. Oh . . . when once you turn against anybody!

DON PASCUAL. My dear . . . isn't it pretty plain that we cannot put up with the young boor's behaviour any longer . . . and to a girl staying in our house!

FERNANDITA. Such a voice as he has!

DON PASCUAL. In our house . . . where an angry word is never spoken! What on earth did she see in the fellow?

FERNANDITA. Nothing. Nothing to fall in love with, anyhow. What Blanca saw in any sort of a husband was a way of escape from a home where her life was a purgatory. But why she should have had the bad luck to stumble on just such another brute as her stepfather! Such a sweet girl as she is! Pretty and gentle and unselfish . . . and as good as gold.

DON PASCUAL. In fact . . . she comes from Alfaqueque.

FERNANDITA. Don't make fun of me now. I'm very, very troubled about her. I wish I were her mother.

DON PASCUAL. Don't wish that, Fernandita. You've taken quite enough responsibility on yourself already. Too much.

You really will have to learn to stop interfering with other people's affairs. Our work 's cut out to see our own go right. Be as sorry for the girl as you like. And pray God . . . or the Virgin of the Medals in Alfaqueque if you prefer . . . that she may realise what 's ahead of her before it 's too late. And as for the young man . . . we 'll make it quite clear to him that this house is not a bear-garden.

FERNANDITA. Oh dear . . . it 's all very difficult!

Alberta appears. She looks bewildered.

ALBERTA. Señora!

FERNANDITA. What 's the matter?

ALBERTA. There 's a young gentleman at the door . . . says he must see you.

FERNANDITA. At this time of night! Who is he? Has he ever been here before?

DON PASCUAL. Never mind who he is. Tell him the Señora sees nobody at this hour.

ALBERTA. That 's what I told him, Señor. But he made me bring the message. He said he would n't go away without seeing her.

DON PASCUAL. The impertinence!

ALBERTA. But I think he 's ill. He was shaking all over . . . and as white as a sheet.

FERNANDITA. Well . . . you 'd better find out his name.

ALBERTA. Very good, Señora.

She goes out.

DON PASCUAL. I will not have you worried like this just as you are going to bed. Let him come back to-morrow . . . whoever he is.

FERNANDITA. But, my dear . . . suppose . . .! I was so startled. If he 's ill . . .!

DON PASCUAL. If he 's ill he can go to the hospital.

FERNANDITA. Yes . . . of course . . . he could do that.

With dramatic suddenness Felipe Rivas appears, followed by Alberta, whose description of him he fully justifies as he stands there pale and shaken. He is young and handsome and roman-

*tic looking. He wears a capa. He is evidently in great
distress. No sooner does he see Fernandita than he rushes
towards her, flings himself on his knees and kisses her hand —
to her evident and considerable alarm.*

FELIPE. Señora!

FERNANDITA. What is it . . . what is it?

DON PASCUAL. Who on earth . . .?

Felipe rises.

FELIPE. Señora . . . look at me. Look at me well.

Fernandita looks at him in some doubt.

FERNANDITA. You 're not . . . Felipe?

FELIPE. I am . . . Fernanda . . . I am indeed.

FERNANDITA. God bless me . . . I 'd never have known you!
Who 'd ever have thought . . .! I had a letter from your mother
only this morning. What has brought you here? Holy Mother
. . . what 's the meaning of it?

FELIPE. You shall hear.

FERNANDITA. You can go, Alberta.

Alberta obeys.

FERNANDITA. Pascual. . . .

FELIPE. Oh . . . Señor.

FERNANDITA. This is my husband. This is Felipe Rivas.

DON PASCUAL [*ironically bland*]. From Alfaqueque?

FERNANDITA. Yes . . . of course . . . from Alfaqueque. He 's
Carlota Portillo's boy. You know . . . we always write to each
other. And in the letter I had to-day she said she was very
worried . . . she did n't know what had become of you . . .

FELIPE. Señora . . . I hope to God she never may.

DON PASCUAL. Good heavens!

FERNANDITA. Now what have you been doing? Something
outrageous, I 'll be bound. You always were a scapegrace.
What is it, Felipe? Tell us.

FELIPE. First . . . forgive me.

DON PASCUAL. What for?

FELIPE. For breaking in on you in this fashion. If you forgive
me I 've but one thing more to ask: Let me pass the night here.

FERNANDITA. Here?

DON PASCUAL. The night?

FELIPE. Yes . . . in a chair . . . on a sofa! I 'll lie in the passage!

DON PASCUAL. No, no, no!

FERNANDITA. No, of course not . . . we 'll make up a bed for you.

DON PASCUAL. My dear . . . are you out of your senses? Here 's a man who comes running for shelter . . . goodness knows what he has done or what trouble he may n't get us into!

FELIPE. Señor, I give you my word of honour . . .

DON PASCUAL. I don't want your word of honour.

FERNANDITA. What have you been up to . . . why are you running away?

FELIPE. I cannot tell you that.

FERNANDITA. Well . . . where are you running from?

FELIPE. I must not say.

DON PASCUAL. Very well then . . . you can't be surprised if I refuse absolutely. . . .

FELIPE. Fernandita . . . intercede for me! For my mother's sake. . . .

FERNANDITA. Oh . . . your poor mother!

DON PASCUAL. Confound your mother! No . . . I will not have it.

FELIPE. For my children's sake.

FERNANDITA [dumfounded; for he looks about twenty]. Your children! !

FELIPE. In the name of the Virgin of the Medals . . . protectress of Alfaqueque!

FERNANDITA. Pascual . . . dear Pascual . . . don't you hear?

DON PASCUAL. I hear perfectly well . . . and it makes no difference whatever. He may invoke all the saints in the Calendar. Let him tell me what he 's running from and why he wants to hide . . . and I 'll see what can be done for him . . . if anything.

FELIPE. Ah! Then my last hope has gone.

He covers his face with his hands; and, after a moment, he begins to sway to and fro.

FERNANDITA. What's the matter, Felipe?

FELIPE. Nothing. A little giddiness . . . it will pass. All these hours of suspense . . . the strain . . .!

FERNANDITA. Felipe!

FELIPE. It's nothing, I assure you. Don't trouble about me. . . .

Nevertheless he faints in the nearest arm-chair.

FERNANDITA. Oh . . . he's ill!

DON PASCUAL. Not dangerously, I think.

FERNANDITA. How can you! Felipe! Felipe! He has fainted. Pascual, he has fainted.

DON PASCUAL. I daresay, my dear. But you won't improve matters by fainting, too. It's nothing serious. Alberta! Rosita!

He opens the door and calls.

FERNANDITA. Mother of God! What is the matter with him?

DON PASCUAL. My dear . . . don't fret yourself.

Alberta appears at the door.

DON PASCUAL. Go and get a glass of water.

Alberta disappears.

DON PASCUAL. We'll sprinkle a little water on him. Yes . . . undo his collar . . . then he can breathe better. And you might fan him perhaps.

FERNANDITA. Poor boy . . . poor boy! How lucky that it happened here!

DON PASCUAL. Lucky . . you think?

Rosita now arrives on the scene.

ROSITA. Did I hear some one call? Oh . . . have you caught a burglar? Fancy!

FERNANDITA. Hold your tongue.

Alberta returns with a glass of water.

ALBERTA. Here's the water, Señor.

FERNANDITA. Give it to me.

DON PASCUAL. He 'll come round.

They bedew the patient's countenance.

ROSITA. Could I do anything? There 's the water jug in my room.

DON PASCUAL. No need.

FERNANDITA. He 's coming to.

DON PASCUAL. A very mild attack!

Blanca now joins them.

BLANCA. What has happened? Who 's this?

FERNANDITA. A friend. I 'll tell you in a minute.

BLANCA. He 's very white. He 's not dead?

DON PASCUAL. No, he 's not dead. There 's nothing the matter with him.

FERNANDITA. Pascual . . . listen, please! This is the son . . . the only son . . . of a woman who has been like a sister to me. Whatever he has done or not done we must give him shelter for to-night . . . just for to-night. So that she may never be able to say to me that when her boy came asking for help I turned him away.

Poor Don Pascual resigns himself.

DON PASCUAL. Well, if it 's the will of Heaven . . . and of the Virgin of the Medals . . .!

FERNANDITA. Oh, Pascual . . . you are good!

DON PASCUAL. I am. I can't help myself.

BLANCA. He 's better.

ROSITA. He 's coming to.

FERNANDITA. Felipe!

The afflicted Felipe opens his eyes at last. They rest first upon Alberta, buxom and fresh, quite pleasant to look upon; then upon the pretty and ever-smiling Rosita; next upon Blanca's charming face, in itself a sight worth the opening of any young man's eyes. What is the question that he naturally asks?

FELIPE. Where am I?

FERNANDITA. Safe with me! Safe with us!

DON PASCUAL. Yes, Señor . . . your foot is upon the soil of Alfaqueque.

But Felipe conveniently ignores the irony. He looks instead from those three charming faces to Fernandita's, its unquestioned beauty made more beautiful by its goodness.

ACT II

We are in the same room, but three weeks have passed. It is morning and the doors of the enclosed balcony are open, so that we can see the flowers which fill it. There is just one change in the room. Upon the walls hangs a very showy picture, and its subject — wonderful to relate — has no connection with Alfaqueque.

Noblejas, in his Sunday best, accompanied by his daughter Paloma in hers, is waiting to see the mistress of the house. Paloma is a typical Madrileña and about twenty-five. She is very pretty, with her soft dark eyes. But she speaks affectedly, and always prefers long words to short.

Alberta comes from the left, saying as she crosses the room . . .

ALBERTA. The Señora will be here directly.

And she leaves them to wait.

NOBLEJAS. Thank you.

There is a little silence.

NOBLEJAS. See the balcony, Paloma! Pretty, is n't it?

PALOMA. Enchanting! And this orange tree! Orange trees require some cultivating in Madrid.

NOBLEJAS. I believe anything would grow for her. Here she is!

PALOMA. Now remember, Father . . . you must tell her. It would be most unsuitable for me to do so.

Fernandita comes in, her mantilla on. She is dressed for Mass.

FERNANDITA. Well . . . and how are you, Paloma?

PALOMA. How do you do, Señora? I trust you are very well.

FERNANDITA. Quite well, thank you.

PALOMA. And Señor Don Pascual?

FERNANDITA. He's keeping his end up . . . as he always says.

He 'll be here in a minute. We 're going to Mass. Anything you want, Noblejas?

NOBLEJAS. I want first to say, Señora, how very glad I am to find you well . . . also to find that the respected head of this household is . . . keeping his end up. Further . . .

FERNANDITA. Thank you . . . thank you! Paloma, my dear . . . what about the altar cloth?

NOBLEJAS. The altar . . . ?

PALOMA. I 'll have it finished by Saturday. It can go off to Alfaqueque by express. It should reach its destination in ample time. My fingers may be faulty now and then, Señora . . . but my word is my bond.

FERNANDITA. That 's right. I knew you would n't fail me. But what have you come about, both of you? Sit down.

NOBLEJAS. But you 're just off to Mass.

FERNANDITA. My husband 's not ready. We can talk till he comes. What is it? Something to do with this ugly duckling?

Father and daughter exchange an embarrassed glance.

PALOMA. You speak, Father dear.

NOBLEJAS. Then . . . if our kind friend will allow me to put it very abruptly . . . very abruptly. . . .

FERNANDITA. Why, of course!

NOBLEJAS. Does any one happen to be occupying your second spare room?

Paloma, as her habit is, takes the words out of his mouth.

PALOMA. Now, Father . . . what 's the use of asking that . . . when we know perfectly well that there does? There is some one in Don Pascual's dressing-room . . . the room that looks out on the court. Who is it? That 's what you want to know.

NOBLEJAS. I was about to. . . .

PALOMA. And you want to know his name and all about him. And you 're not to be put off with any subterfuges, Father dear.

NOBLEJAS. And you are not, if you please, to put upon me any such phrases as that.

Fernandita, at all this, is both vexed and astonished.

FERNANDITA. But you know, then . . . you 've found out?

PALOMA. Is it such a secret, Señora?

FERNANDITA. Yes, it is.

NOBLEJAS. Do we embarrass you by asking, Señora?

FERNANDITA. Yes, you do.

NOBLEJAS. Then perhaps, Paloma, we had better. . . .

PALOMA. No, Father, . . . be firm.

NOBLEJAS. The fact is, Doña Fernandita, that the young gentleman, who has been for this little while past the occupant of your spare room, has also been . . . if I may so express myself . . . casting glances. . . .

PALOMA. Really, Father! He has done a little more than cast glances, I think.

FERNANDITA. What . . . what has he done?

PALOMA. He has written to me. Three letters. Three consecutive letters.

FERNANDITA. Three letters?

PALOMA [*rejoicing in the word*]. Consecutively.

NOBLEJAS. Which he sent her . . .

PALOMA. By the clothes line . . . across the roof. Also some poems . . . beautiful poems . . . in the same way. I have memorized them. I could recite them to you. Also some flowers. And he has gesticulated . . . most significantly. So I'm sure you will agree, Señora, that "casting glances" is hardly the word for it.

FERNANDITA. Well . . . and what have you done?

PALOMA. I. . . .

NOBLEJAS. She. . . .

PALOMA. You speak, Father.

NOBLEJAS. Naturally she did not wish. . . .

PALOMA. Naturally I did not wish things to go any further without your knowledge, Señora.

FERNANDITA. Quite right!

NOBLEJAS. For you can tell her. . . .

PALOMA. For you can tell me . . .! Even Father had no idea that you'd any one staying here. . . .

FERNANDITA. I daresay not. It happened very suddenly. It was all a little rash . . .! Well . . .! He is in hiding here.

So much I may tell you.   The victim of a vile persecution.   In due time all will be made clear.   But, till it can be, I do beg you both to keep the secret.   I 've told the servants they may find themselves in gaol if they let it out.

Noblejas and Paloma are both much impressed.

NOBLEJAS.   You may rely on me, Señora.

PALOMA.   You may rely on me.

NOBLEJAS.   It 's your mother I 'm thinking about.

FERNANDITA.   You must make her hold her tongue.

NOBLEJAS.   We might cut it out, Señora, and she 'd manage to talk still.

PALOMA.   I 'll look after Mother!   But you said he was. . . .

FERNANDITA.   A gentleman . . . and a most distinguished one too.   And he has to hide himself away as if he were a criminal!

PALOMA.   Fancy that!

FERNANDITA.   And even we do not know why . . . as yet. He is under a pledge not to tell us.   It 's a point of honour.   But I know all about him otherwise.   He 's of a very good family. Oh . . . a most remarkable young man!   He 's a poet.   Not just an ordinary poet either.   He never speaks of his poems.   He calls them his children.   I did n't understand that at first.   And he comes from Alfaqueque.   There 'll be a street there called after him some day.

PALOMA.   A street!

FERNANDITA.   And a tablet on the house where he was born.

PALOMA.   Really!

FERNANDITA.   A statue of him perhaps.

NOBLEJAS.   D' you really think so?

FERNANDITA.   Yes, I do.   But don't mention all this to my husband . . . for we don't quite see eye to eye about it.

NOBLEJAS.   Dear me!

FERNANDITA.   No . . . we don't . . . I 'm sorry to say.

Paloma, however, remains much impressed, as she does her best to show.

PALOMA.   I trust you understood, Señora, that when I asked for enlightenment. . . .

FERNANDITA. Yes, yes . . . quite!

PALOMA. We may be poor. And I work for my living. But my self-respect is most precious to me. I do trust, Señora, that you understand.

FERNANDITA. Quite, my dear!

PALOMA. For a young lady's reputation is not . . . if I may make the comparison . . . like one of Father's collars . . . which a little soap and water will clean. No . . . the very slightest stain upon a young lady's reputation. . . .

FERNANDITA. Yes, yes! But I don't want my husband to hear about this for the moment. So shall we say you came about the altar-cloth? Or, better still, won't you both go away at once?

NOBLEJAS. Señora . . . you have only to ask.

PALOMA. By all means, Señora. Come, Father.

FERNANDITA. Thank you very much.

PALOMA. Father . . . where's your hat?

Noblejas looks a trifle embarrassed.

NOBLEJAS. I . . . I left it on the hat-stand.

FERNANDITA. Good-bye, then . . . good-bye. I'll see you again soon.

PALOMA. And thank you for confiding in me. And when there's more you want to tell me. . . .

NOBLEJAS. Señora!

He bows himself out. And the last we hear is Paloma saying. . . .

PALOMA. Father . . . how wonderful! A poet . . . a tablet . . . a statue!

But Fernandita is left very uneasy.

FERNANDITA. Holy Mother . . . what silly pranks has the boy been playing! Oh, of course . . . Paloma looked so pretty sitting sewing at her window! Wait till he hears her silly tongue clacking!

Rosita's arrival interrupts her; though the young woman does n't see her mistress for the moment, as she is absorbed in the contemplation of her own finger-nails, which, apparently, she has just been polishing.

ROSITA. They do shine! And with a ring or two . . .! Oh! Not gone yet, Señora? You 'll be late for Mass.

FERNANDITA. What has happened to the Señor? I shall go to the eight o'clock next Sunday with Señorita Blanca.

ROSITA. I prefer the late one myself at San José.

FERNANDITA. Ah! That 's the one the King and Queen go to, is n't it? Has Realito turned up yet for his cup of chocolate?

ROSITA. No. He 'll be on his way.

Don Pascual arrives at last, dressed for Mass.

DON PASCUAL. Ready?

FERNANDITA. And waiting. Who 's always scolding us for being late?

ROSITA [*pleasantly*]. Ah . . . who?

DON PASCUAL. There are mornings when tying my tie is harder than solving quadratic equations.

ROSITA. Goodness! What are quadratic equations?

FERNANDITA. They are no concern of yours. Come . . . let 's start.

DON PASCUAL. Right! What did Noblejas and Paloma come about?

FERNANDITA. [*Who can no more tell lies than she can fly.*] Oh . . . about the altar-cloth . . . to tell me it would be ready next Sunday.

DON PASCUAL. Really!

FERNANDITA. Don't you believe me?

DON PASCUAL. No . . . frankly, my dear . . . I don't.

Into the short and slightly uncomfortable pause that follows Rosita intrudes.

ROSITA. I don't know if it has occurred to you, Señor . . . that this poor young gentleman you keep shut up here is risking his immortal soul. He has not been to Mass these three weeks.

DON PASCUAL. Well . . . if the Powers above will only let him talk for ten minutes I 've no doubt he 'll get round them.

FERNANDITA. Why can't you be fair to the poor boy!

DON PASCUAL. Mark my words . . . you 'll be sorry you ever saw him.

FERNANDITA. Come along. We shall be late.

They depart, Rosita watching them and ready to turn her attention elsewhere the moment they are really gone. She is indeed just off in the opposite direction, when the sound of Realito's voice in the hall stops her — very much to her annoyance.

REALITO'S VOICE. Good morning. May I? Oh, thank you.

ROSITA. Realito! And I thought I 'd have a chance to. . . .
Realito comes in.

REALITO. Hola, my pretty!

ROSITA [*stiffly*]. Good morning.

REALITO. I 'm all of a sweat. What weather! Call this Madrid in October!

ROSITA. October is often a fine month in Madrid. April and May can be pleasant too. So can February sometimes. Have you been to Mass?

REALITO. I 've been to four. Is n't that enough for you? I 've been dodging in and out of churches all the morning. I 'm just about done in.

ROSITA. Well . . . it 's the way to heaven.

REALITO. Is it? It 's the way to get a good look at all the pretty girls. You 're very smart this morning. Let 's have a look at you. A bit closer!

ROSITA. Impudence! D' you want your cup of chocolate?

REALITO. Yes, I do . . . when I 've cooled off a bit.

ROSITA. I thought you were going back home.

REALITO. I am. I 've got to. I can't wear out much more shoe-leather looking for a job here. So Doña Fernandita 's going to buy me a third-class ticket home. Farewell, Madrid! And it 'll never know what it has missed. I 'll have to try crowing on my own dunghill.

ROSITA. I 'll dig up stones with my teeth before I 'll go back home.

REALITO. Lucky stones! But what 's the matter with home?

ROSITA. What 's the matter with it! Nice prospects for me there, are n't they! I 'd have to marry some fool like you . . .

and have a dozen children . . . and scrub and wash and iron for the rest of my days. No thank you! Not now I 've seen life. Oh, you may laugh! But I 've prospects here . . . if I know anything.

REALITO. Anybody particular in your eye?

ROSITA. Never you mind! I don't say there is n't. Somebody most particular. One thing 's as clear as daylight. God did n't give me my good looks and mean me to waste them, did he? But mum 's the word . . . or there 'll be trouble. Talk about romance, though! These novelists . . . what do they know about it? But mum 's the word. Still, if you find yourself in Alfaqueque, drop in on my mother and say I 'm getting on quite nicely, thank you . . . though mum 's the word for a bit.

REALITO. Mum as you like! This is all Greek to me. But, talking of romances . . . who 's this young man that 's hiding here? So Paloma's mother says!

Rosita just manages not to jump.

ROSITA. Nonsense!

REALITO. But she says there is. She has seen him at the window. And he has been making love to Paloma.

This time Rosita does jump, as if an adder had bitten her.

ROSITA. What!

REALITO. And he has written her three letters . . . consecutively.

ROSITA. What!

REALITO. And sent her flowers . . . and made up some poems to her.

ROSITA. You don't know what you 're talking about.

REALITO. That 's what she told me. What 's wrong?

For Rosita might be on the verge of hysterics.

ROSITA. Nothing. You 're talking nonsense, that 's all. Simple nonsense. But mum 's the word! I don't believe it. I won't believe it. I 'm good enough for any one. My father 's . . . the best jeweller . . . in Alfaqueque! Oh . . . oh . . . mum 's the word . . . oh dear me!

REALITO. You 're off your head, I think.

She evidently does not know what she is saying. At this moment Blanca comes in.

BLANCA. Good morning, Realito.

REALITO. Good morning.

BLANCA. Alberta 's asking for you, Rosita.

ROSITA. She 's always asking for me. Come on, Realito, and have your chocolate. I want to talk to you.

BLANCA. Oh?

ROSITA. Yes, I do!

REALITO. Will you excuse me while I go and have my chocolate?

BLANCA. Certainly. Good appetite!

ROSITA. We 'll see if Madrid can get the better of Alfaqueque! *With which cryptic remark she departs, taking Realito with her.*

BLANCA. Whatever is the matter with the girl?

And now — but very cautiously — Felipe appears.

FELIPE. Blanca.

BLANCA. Hush . . . wait a minute!

FELIPE. Have n't they gone to Mass?

BLANCA. Yes. But Realito 's here . . . in the dining-room.

FELIPE. Oh, they 'll keep him chattering for hours! What about the letter?

BLANCA. Here.

FELIPE. What have you said?

BLANCA. I copied it as you wrote it . . . word for word. It 's not much like one of mine. Where shall I leave it?

FELIPE. On the table. She 'll see it as soon as she comes in.

So Blanca props up the letter conspicuously on a table.

BLANCA. Oh dear . . . oh dear!

FELIPE. Are you sorry?

BLANCA. It 's all very upsetting.

FELIPE. Come . . . come!

BLANCA. Sh!

FELIPE. Somebody coming?

BLANCA. I thought I heard . . . no! But of course it 's upsetting! And when I 'm by myself I feel I 'm doing wrong. Then

been in helping me get free from this wretched marriage . . . and how you 've let me talk to you and been so patient and understanding. And when I think of that. . . . There 's some one in the hall!

FELIPE. Yes.

BLANCA. I 'll see who it is.

FELIPE. Never mind. I 'll go back to my room.

BLANCA. No . . . don't. . . .

She goes out. Felipe, left alone, walks up and down and turns things over in his mind.

FELIPE. It 's about time I got out of this . . . though I 'll hate to go. After all . . . what harm have I done? Said a few pleasant things to one of them. Flattered the other a little. And . . .! And they like it. It makes them happy. But Blanca . . .! I wish . . .! She 's different.

Blanca comes back.

BLANCA. It 's that woman who makes the sweets. You know . . . she 's always about. I 'm afraid she may come in here.

FELIPE. Then I 'll bolt back to prison. Well . . . good-bye.

BLANCA. And I 'm to leave the letter there?

FELIPE. Yes, yes. Don't let us have any going back on that. And lie low. Keep out of everybody's way.

BLANCA. Indeed I will.

FELIPE. But there 's nothing to be afraid of. Fernandita will take it quite well . . . I promise you. Good luck!

BLANCA. Good luck!

They stand for a moment looking at each other. Then they vanish, he by one door, she by another. The room stays empty a moment. Then Adoración appears.

ADORACIÓN. Where was that girl off to in such a hurry? Not to meet that young man of hers, I 'll be bound! I 'd run a mile . . . if I could! . . . to get away from him. But something was up. Dashing past me . . . and downstairs . . . without a word. Poor child! She has a hard time of it. Ah! [*It is a happy sigh.*] It 's blessed to be back here again! A whole fortnight since I saw Fernandita! Heaven knows, though, I 'd have come if I could have crawled. My legs are n't what they might be yet. [*A pause while she settles down.*] I 'll wait a bit. To give her just one kiss. It is warm. [*She fans herself vigorously.*] I do just hate to see that young man Realito at his breakfast. Gobble . . . gobble . . . gobble! I never saw anything like it. He butters an entire roll . . . and it vanishes! More like a conjurer than a Christian! How they all sponge on her . . . the dear woman! Oh . . . a new picture! A present! A little thank-offering, let 's hope. [*She has risen to examine it and from it she turns to the balcony.*] What a vision! What an aroma! It 's a perfect paradise. Jasmine. Camellias. And the orange tree. Ah, if it could speak . . . of our dear sun-kissed Alfaqueque! [*By this time she has reached the letter propped up so conspicuously on its table.*] And what 's this? Blanca's writing. For Fernandita. "Urgent." What has happened? Oh . . . this is why she was dashing downstairs! Saints in glory . . . what is it all about? I declare I could steam it open. I believe I could read it through the envelope!

> *Whether she could — and would — or no we shall never be able to tell; for at this moment Fernandita appears.*

FERNANDITA. Why . . . Adoración! How are you?

ADORACIÓN. My dear . . . my dear! I thought you were never coming. Such ages since I 've seen you. Such ages!

> *Fernandita is just a little restless under the ecstatic onslaught.*

FERNANDITA. There . . . there . . . there!

ADORACIÓN. And thank you a thousand times for the sherry. You don't know the good it did me. And for the cream! But I 've been longing to see you. As greedy for a sight of you as Realito is for his breakfast.

FERNANDITA. And you 're quite all right again?

ADORACIÓN. Now I am . . . now that I 've seen you . . . it only needed that. But . . . oh dear me . . . I was forgetting. Something has happened. Listen. As I came in I met Blanca. She did n't speak. She rushed downstairs. And here 's this letter for you. Whatever can it mean?

FERNANDITA. From Blanca? Well . . . give it me. Rushed

downstairs? Good Heavens! [*She has torn the letter open and begins to read.*] "Fernandita, dearest friend, my second mother, don't be alarmed when you read this. I am not going to kill myself, though it might. . . ."

ADORACIÓN. Saints of God! She has taken poison!

FERNANDITA. No, no! Can't you hear? "I am not going to kill myself, though it might be better if I did. And I'm not eloping with Nicolás. I'm going home." Going home? The child's off her head. "And I'm going without warning you so that you may n't try to stop me. I've brought trouble enough on you . . . and such discord into your home where there never was discord. . . ." I shall fetch her back at once.

ADORACIÓN. But finish the letter . . . finish the letter. It's simply heart-breaking. Do finish it.

FERNANDITA. "It's Nicolás that's to blame. From the time I said I'd marry him. . . ."

> *At which very moment Nicolás himself comes in. And, by the oddest irony of fate, he is, for once, in a good humour. Fernandita and Adoración are flabbergasted at the sight of him.*

NICOLÁS. Señoras . . . your most obedient.

FERNANDITA. Nicolás!

ADORACIÓN. Nicolás!

NICOLÁS. I heard you'd been ill.

ADORACIÓN. Yes. But I'm well again . . . thanks be to God!

NICOLÁS. That's right. Life's too short to waste in bed. Well . . . the world looks a pretty rosy place to me to-day.

FERNANDITA [*all but deploring it*]. Rosy! Does it?

NICOLÁS. Yes . . . it all depends how I start the morning. Some days I get out of bed feeling like the devil . . . and then everything goes wrong!

FERNANDITA. Of course!

NICOLÁS. But if I only make a good start . . . you can't upset me.

FERNANDITA. Really!

NICOLÁS. I met Don Pascual on my way here . . . swaggering along the Castellana as if he were one and twenty. Where's

Blanca? He said a very good thing . . . most amusing . . . while he was paying for his chair. I 'll tell you when Blanca comes. No use repeating it twice. Where is Blanca?

FERNANDITA. Well . . . the fact is, my dear Nicolás, Blanca has run away from us. She has gone home.

NICOLÁS. What?

FERNANDITA. I was reading her letter when you came in.

NICOLÁS. Rubbish!

FERNANDITA. No. I 'm afraid it 's true.

NICOLÁS. Rubbish, I tell you. Is the girl a born fool? You rescue her from her bully of a stepfather. And she goes back there !

FERNANDITA. That 's what her letter says.

NICOLÁS. I 'd like to hear it, please.

FERNANDITA. Certainly. . . . "I 'm going home. And I 'm going without warning you so that you may n't try to stop me. I 've brought trouble enough on you . . . and such discord into your home where there never was discord . . ."

NICOLÁS. She never wrote that.

FERNANDITA. "It 's Nicolás that 's to blame. From the time I said I 'd marry him . . ."

NICOLÁS. Well . . . of all the nonsense!

FERNANDITA. " . . . he has done nothing but ill-treat me."

NICOLÁS. Why . . . you 'd think I 'd been kicking her! Let 's hear the rest. Then I 'll have something to say.

FERNANDITA. "Forgive me. I know Don Pascual will forgive me. He 'll be glad. He has told me so often to send Nicolás about his business. . . ."

NICOLÁS. Has he!

FERNANDITA. " . . . and that I can never make a silk purse out of a sow's ear."

NICOLÁS. Is that supposed to be funny?

FERNANDITA. "So good-bye, dear, dear friend. I shall always pray for you and be grateful to you . . . Blanca. P.S. Tear this up at once please. I don't want the Porcupine himself to read it."

At the postscript, which she quite unwittingly reads out, Fernandita pales with horror, while Nicolás purples with wrath.

NICOLÁS. What's that! Porcupine! Oh . . . she can laugh at me, can she! That shows how unhappy she is . . . does n't it! Does n't it? What?

FERNANDITA. Now . . . do be calm!

NICOLÁS. I won't be calm. A heartless little baggage . . . that's what she is! And I always knew it. A lot she ever cared . . . for me or for you or her mother. Dirt under her feet . . . that's what we are. And I'm a Porcupine . . . am I? Very well! I'll show her. Don't let her think she's going to bring this off. She's going home, is she? Well . . . I'm going after her. And there's going to be a most almighty row.

FERNANDITA. For heaven's sake, Nicolás . . . don't! You'd far better try and forget all about it.

NICOLÁS. Had I? Thank you. Yes . . . you're very calm. You put her up to this, perhaps.

FERNANDITA. How dare you say such a thing! Well . . . what more can I expect from such a . . . a Porcupine!

ADORACIÓN. What more can we expect if we get engaged to a . . . to an ill-conditioned steam-roller?

FERNANDITA. You've made all our lives here a perfect nightmare. The times that I've seen that poor child sitting there crying and wishing she was dead!

ADORACIÓN. And so have I!

Nicolás rounds like an angry bull upon the gallant Adoración.

NICOLÁS. And will you be kind enough to go and bake your toffee and mind your own business?

ADORACIÓN. Señor . . . I make this my business.

FERNANDITA. No, Adoración . . . don't answer him. We'll say nothing more at all. Silence is best.

NICOLÁS. Is it? No doubt! You'll see how silent I'll be. I'm not to be made a fool of. I'll stir up such a scandal! I'll have the whole thing in the papers. You wait! You'll see! And where are you coming to?

For in turning to the door he has run bang against Don Pascual.

DON PASCUAL. Into my own drawing-room . . . by your kind permission.

NICOLÁS. Are you? Well, let me warn you, Señor, that I am not to be called names with impunity.

With which he vanishes.

DON PASCUAL. Dear me! What have you been doing to the Porcupine?

FERNANDITA. Oh Pascual . . . I 'm in such trouble! A letter from Blanca! She has gone back home because she just can't stand Nicolás any longer.

DON PASCUAL. Trouble! It 's the best news I 've heard for a long time. I congratulate you . . . both! Blanca should have a medal.

ADORACIÓN. So she should!

DON PASCUAL. I tell you . . . things had come to such a pass for me with that young man . . . I 'd settled to move to a hotel until the wedding was over.

FERNANDITA. Don't joke. He has been shouting . . . and threatening! Holy Mother!

DON PASCUAL. Now, now . . . there 's no need to distress yourself.

ADORACIÓN. My angel . . . don't distress yourself.

FERNANDITA. I must go after the child this very minute.

DON PASCUAL. You 'll do nothing of the sort.

FERNANDITA. But I can't sit here on thorns, Pascual . . . and not know what has happened to her.

DON PASCUAL. Very well . . . I 'll go and find out.

ADORACIÓN. I 'll go. But you 're not to distress yourself . . . you 're not to distress yourself.

DON PASCUAL. And do let this be a lesson to you.

ADORACIÓN. Yes . . . let it be a lesson to you. Now this is what I say, Don Pascual. Let her help every one she wants to. You 'll never stop her. It 's her nature . . . whether they 're from Alfaqueque or from Timbuctoo. But let them keep their distance. And on no account have them to stay here.

DON PASCUAL. I agree.

ADORACIÓN. Or have them dropping in to breakfast.

DON PASCUAL. I quite agree.

ADORACIÓN. That 's my opinion.

FERNANDITA. I 'm sure no one could find fault with Blanca. The dearest girl! Quiet . . . tactful . . . she could n't do enough for me.

DON PASCUAL. But her Nicolás, unluckily, did not resemble her.

ADORACIÓN. No indeed! Believe me . . . once you let people into your house something always goes wrong. You know . . . before my husband had his troubles I was a bit of a Lady Bountiful too . . . in a small way. And shall I tell you what once happened to me? Oh, it sounds funny now . . . but it was no joke at the time. One night, just as we were going to bed, the maid came in . . . in a great state . . . and said there was a mysterious young gentleman at the front door insisting on seeing me.

Don Pascual and Fernandita begin to listen more attentively. And while we were wondering what to do . . . in he burst . . . without with your leave or by your leave . . . pale and haggard . . . with his cloak all dragging behind him . . . flung himself on his knees and kissed my hand. . . .

FERNANDITA. What?

DON PASCUAL. What?

ADORACIÓN. And begged me for his mother's sake and his children's sake and in the name of all the saints to let him hide there for just one night. And d 'you know who it was? You 'll know his name. A crazy young good for nothing who lives by his wits. Carlota Portillo's boy. Felipe Rivas. Yes . . . he comes from Alfaqueque.

FERNANDITA [*stabbed to the heart*]. Felipe Rivas!

ADORACIÓN. Do you know him?

FERNANDITA. Yes . . . a little.

DON PASCUAL. A very little! But she knows him. We should like, I think, to hear the rest of the story.

Fernandita, distressed and distracted, gets up and begins to wander round the room. She stops before the calendar and

without knowing what she is doing tears a leaf from it; then
wanders on. But Don Pascual sits at his ease, taking, one
fears, a mischievous delight in these revelations.

ADORACIÓN. Well . . . you 'll never believe it.

FERNANDITA. Shan't I?

DON PASCUAL. And did you hide him . . . just for the night?

ADORACIÓN. Yes. What else could we do? Though my husband . . . though poor Carreño did n't want me to.

DON PASCUAL. Really? Do you hear that, Fernandita? Poor Carreño did n't want her to.

FERNANDITA. I hear. Carreño did n't want her to.

DON PASCUAL. Well, Carreño did n't want you to. . . .

ADORACIÓN. No. But all of a sudden he fainted.

DON PASCUAL. Carreño?

ADORACIÓN. No . . . Felipe. And then, of course, we had to keep him.

DON PASCUAL. Just fancy! He fainted. He fainted and all. Do you hear that, Fernandita?

FERNANDITA. I hear. I 'm not deaf.

ADORACIÓN. And you can't think what it all led to . . . all through my being such a goose.

DON PASCUAL. All through her being such a goose, my dear!

ADORACIÓN. We had that young gentleman on our hands for an entire month.

DON PASCUAL. Ah! We 're still ten days short of that.

ADORACIÓN. What did you say?

DON PASCUAL. Nothing! Could n't you find any way of getting rid of him?

ADORACIÓN. No, we could n't. Each day he told us some new tale. And as he 'd told us to start with . . . and we believed it! . . . that he 'd be ruined and disgraced if they found him . . . why, we were his accomplices in a sense. When any one came to the house he 'd bolt to his room like a rabbit. And we had to lie and prevaricate. We might have been criminals ourselves. And things went on like that for a month.

Again, without knowing in the least what she is doing, Fernandita has taken up a little hand-bell from the table and is ringing it spasmodically.

DON PASCUAL. What are you ringing for?

FERNANDITA. Nothing . . . I was n't ringing. I mean I . . .

Alberta presents herself.

FERNANDITA. Thank you, Alberta . . . I did n't ring. I mean . . . never mind, thank you!

Alberta vanishes.

DON PASCUAL. And so the young man was a fraud?

ADORACIÓN. You 'll think I 'm exaggerating.

DON PASCUAL. No, no! No, no, no!

ADORACIÓN. I told you he begged us to save him for the sake of his children. He had n't any children. He wrote poems. He called them his children.

DON PASCUAL. That was a pleasing fancy.

Fernandita tears another leaf from the calendar.

ADORACIÓN. Yes, he was a poet. And so, of course, he 'd no more morals than a tom-cat. Flirt! He 'd flirt with any woman he set eyes on.

DON PASCUAL. Really.

ADORACIÓN. He made love to my daughter, Salud . . . and to a girl that lives above us on the second floor . . . and to one on the third floor . . . and to the housemaid. No . . . not so much morals as a tom-cat!

DON PASCUAL. Dear me . . . dear me!

Fernandita is wandering round again in her distraction; and she begins to move all the chairs from their places, evidently under the impression that she is putting them straight.

ADORACIÓN. And another thing! He used to disguise himself and go out after dark and come back with some little present for us . . . to show his gratitude, so he said. We were quite taken in by it.

DON PASCUAL. Was Carreño taken in by it?

ADORACIÓN. Quite.

DON PASCUAL. Ah . . . men are not all alike!

ADORACIÓN. Sweets or flowers or a book. Once it was a bird in a cage. And once he brought us back a picture . . . a big oil-painting!

Don Pascual and Fernandita turn instinctively towards their own new picture.

ADORACIÓN. But after he 'd gone . . . why, then the bills came in! For the flowers and the sweets and the books and the little bird. And for the picture! He 'd had them all charged to Carreño. We were nearly bankrupt.

FERNANDITA. Saints in heaven!

She begins to tear leaves off the calendar as if she meant to strip it bare.

DON PASCUAL. I fear you won't make the month go quicker by doing that.

FERNANDITA. What? Oh . . . I did n't know! My mind was . . .! I was thinking of dear Blanca.

DON PASCUAL. Now tell me, Adoración . . . did you ever see or hear of that young scoundrel again?

ADORACIÓN. He 's in America. I think so . . . I 'm not sure. But I know that he played the same trick on four or five other people before he went. Did you ever hear of such conduct? He did it whenever he wanted a little holiday.

Don Pascual breaks out into a roar of laughter. Fernandita is almost in tears.

FERNANDITA. Well . . . dear Adoración . . . thank you for the warning. I 'll take care, of course, that such a thing . . . never happens to me. But now it would be very kind of you if you 'd find Blanca somehow . . . and let me know just what has become of her.

ADORACIÓN. Why, of course I will! I love doing things for you. I 'll go at once. You 're not to worry. Shall I make you a cup of camomile before I go?

FERNANDITA. No . . . no, thank you . . . I 'm quite all right.

ADORACIÓN. There 's nothing I would n't do for you! I 'd shed my heart's blood for you. I 'll be back in a twinkling.

At each apostrophe the ardent lady kisses her ecstatically.

FERNANDITA. Thank you . . . thank you! Yes . . . as soon as possible.

ADORACIÓN. But after this . . . let them all keep their distance! That's what I say.

Adoración hurries off. A silence. Don Pascual looks at his wife, a little smile twitching irrepressibly at the corner of his mouth.

DON PASCUAL. Well, Fernandita . . . you see!

FERNANDITA. I'd rather you did n't talk to me for a moment, please. Are you laughing at me?

DON PASCUAL. Yes . . . of course I am! It's very funny.

FERNANDITA. Funny! I could cry my heart out. Funny . . . to be tricked like that . . . and lied to! How could he? How could he? Yes . . . laugh at me! I deserve it . . . for being a fool. That's the truth . . . I'm just a fool. Dear Pascual . . . say I'm a fool.

DON PASCUAL. Well, my dear . . . if you insist . . .!

FERNANDITA. But who'd ever have suspected it? Carlota's boy. So clever . . . so charming! And he talks so well. And he comes from Alfaqueque. I never was so glad to do anything as I was to give him shelter that night. And now! No . . . I'm just a fool. And I suppose . . . at my age . . . I shall never be anything else. A perfect idiot! The idiot from Alfaqueque.

She cries a little, quite quietly, and goes out.

DON PASCUAL. Poor darling! I fear she won't get over this in a hurry. But I'm very much obliged to Adoración all the same.

Rosita shows in Noblejas. He is as dignified and courteous as ever. But she — for the first time since we had the pleasure of making her acquaintance — looks crushed.

NOBLEJAS. Señor don Pascual.

DON PASCUAL. How are you, Noblejas?

NOBLEJAS. I am delighted to see you . . . and to see you looking so well.

Rosita now speaks; that is, she appears to be speaking, but her voice is as the voice of a dying linnet.

ROSITA. Señor.

DON PASCUAL. Eh?

ROSITA. Señor.

DON PASCUAL. Are you speaking to me? What is it?

ROSITA. Where shall I find the Señora?

DON PASCUAL. What?

ROSITA. The Señora.

DON PASCUAL. I can't hear you, my girl. Speak up!

ROSITA. Voice gone!

NOBLEJAS. She says, Don Pascual, that her voice has gone.

DON PASCUAL. What made it go?

ROSITA. The shock. Most dreadful shock! Cruel! Never in all my life . . .!

DON PASCUAL. I don't know what you 're talking about.

ROSITA. Must tell the Señora . . .!

DON PASCUAL. Well . . . you 'll find her in her dressing-room.

ROSITA. Outrage . . .! Infamous man . . .! Never recover . . .! Whole life wrecked . . .!

She departs moaning incoherently.

DON PASCUAL. D 'you know what that 's all about?

NOBLEJAS. Señor Don Pascual . . . my position is a delicate one. I may know . . . and be under some obligation not to impart my knowledge to you. But whether a slight hint might be allowable . . .

DON PASCUAL. I think it might!

NOBLEJAS. Well . . . she has been having a little talk with my daughter Paloma.

DON PASCUAL. I see! About the young man in our spare room.

Noblejas gapes with astonishment.

Oh, I know all about it. My wife warned you, did she, on no account to tell me? But she told me herself on the way to Mass.

NOBLEJAS. Dear me! Did she indeed? Well, that 's a great relief to me!

DON PASCUAL. So now we can account, I think, for that vanished voice. He has been saying pretty things to Rosita too?

NOBLEJAS. Yes, he has.

DON PASCUAL.   My friend . . . you tell Paloma from me to
send back those three letters and those poems and to give neither
another look at him nor another thought to him . . . for he 's
a shameless impostor.

NOBLEJAS.   I 'm afraid my voice will vanish when I start to tell
her that.

DON PASCUAL.   Then try talking on your fingers.   Off you go!

NOBLEJAS.   I will.   She 's to give neither another look nor a
thought to him because he 's a . . . might I call him a damned
scoundrel?

DON PASCUAL.   Yes, I think you might.

NOBLEJAS.   The poor girl will be struck all of a heap . . . if
I may so express myself.

DON PASCUAL.   Better she should be.   I 'll go and see if something can't be done for Rosita's vocal chords.

Don Pascual departs.   Noblejas lingers a moment medi-
tating upon the uncertainties of human life.

NOBLEJAS.   Poor little Paloma!   So it 's all a dream.   Honour
and glory . . . and a tablet on his birthplace . . . and a statue.
All a dream!

As he also departs, grieving for his Paloma, Blanca comes in.

BLANCA.   How do you do, Señor don Salustiano?

NOBLEJAS.   Your servant, Señorita Blanca.

The two meet and pass each other.

BLANCA.   Nicolás looked pleasant, I must say!   What did
happen?   I can guess.   Am I really free of him.   But what will
Fernandita say?

At this moment, Fernandita comes in and is amazed at the sight
of Blanca.

FERNANDITA.   Blanca!

BLANCA.   Yes.

FERNANDITA.   But . . . have you been home?

BLANCA.   No.

FERNANDITA.   But you said you were going home.

BLANCA.   Yes.   That was so you should n't think I was doing
anything wrong.   And I knew Nicolás would n't go there after me.